Physical Education

Carl Atherton   Symond Burrows   Sue Young

Philip Allan Updates, an imprint of Hodder Education, an Hachette UK company, Market Place, Deddington, Oxfordshire OX15 0SE

Orders
Bookpoint Ltd, 130 Milton Park, Abingdon, Oxfordshire OX14 4SB
tel: 01235 827720
fax: 01235 400454
e-mail: uk.orders@bookpoint.co.uk

Lines are open 9.00 a.m.–5.00 p.m., Monday to Saturday, with a 24-hour message answering service. You can also order through the Philip Allan Updates website: www.philipallan.co.uk

© Philip Allan Updates 2009

ISBN 978-1-84489-642-4

Impression number   5 4 3 2 1
Year   2013   2012   2011   2010   2009

Printed in Italy.

Hachette UK's policy is to use papers that are natural, renewable and recyclable products and made from wood grown in sustainable forests. The logging and manufacturing processes are expected to conform to the environmental regulations of the country of origin.

P01355

Contents

HAYBRIDGE HIGH SCHOOL
HAGLEY.

Unit G454 The improvement of effective performance and the critical evaluation of practical activities in physical education

Answers

Index

Introduction

About this book

This textbook has been written specifically to meet the needs of students following the OCR specification for A2 Physical Education from September 2009. The book is divided according to the OCR specification. The first unit (G453) comprises two sections: the sociocultural section looks at historical and comparative studies; the scientific section looks at exercise and sport physiology, sports psychology and biomechanics. The second unit (G454) is covered by the final part of this book, which gives advice on the practical and coursework sections of the OCR course.

It is common for the A2 Physical Education course to be taught in accordance with the way this book is structured. Students tend to follow lessons on physiology, sports psychology and/or biomechanics and then sociocultural issues as separate entities and indeed the exam at the end of the course asks questions that are related to these topics. The way to use the book, therefore, is to link the appropriate section of the book to the lessons you are currently undertaking. Each section is set out to form a logical progression so that knowledge gained in earlier chapters can be used as a basis for some of the concepts detailed in later chapters.

Special features

This book contains several special features designed to aid your understanding of the requirements of the OCR A2 Physical Education course.

Key terms

These are concise definitions of the main terms needed throughout the course. You are often required to define such key terms in the early part of exam questions. The answers to most exam questions will be based on a clear recollection of such definitions and the examiner will very often have these key terms listed in the examiners' marks scheme. If you can remember them and explain them, you are almost guaranteed to score a mark.

Top tips

This feature offers advice on what you should do and, equally importantly, what you should not do, in order to ensure exam success. The authors use their examination experience to give students valuable advice on how to answer exam questions, using typical examples and relevant knowledge.

Tasks to tackle

The authors have included some activities throughout each chapter that are designed to improve and reinforce your understanding of the main concepts covered in each chapter. As you do the activities, you should look back over the chapter to help you complete each task. Tasks can be carried out individually or in groups, so you may be able to do them as part of your lesson or with your fellow students as part of the revision process. Where appropriate, answers to tasks are given at the back of the book.

Practice makes perfect

At the end of each chapter there is a set of questions appropriate to that particular section of work. The questions are based on examiner knowledge of the main topics and are often divided so that early questions may ask for definitions and lists, while later questions may require more of an explanation. The answers to these questions are offered at the end of the book and it is strongly recommended that you use this feature to help gauge your understanding of the relevant topics. Having read the chapter and perhaps covered that same topic as part of your course, you should attempt the questions without looking at the answers. Once you have completed the questions and checked them, it may then be possible to look back over the chapter to see if you can uncover any answers that you may have missed. Repeat this process so that you know the answers to some of the questions you might face during the exam. This is a great way to do your revision and ensure exam success.

Scheme of Assessment

Unit G453 Principles and concepts across different areas of physical education

This unit is assessed by a $2\frac{1}{2}$-hour written exam. The paper has two sections: Section A has questions on sociocultural aspects and Section B has questions on scientific options. In Section A the questions can be chosen from two options: option A1 is a question on historical studies in PE, while option A2 is a question on comparative studies in PE. Both these options relate directly to the chapters of this book. In Section B there are three options: option B1 contains a question on sports psychology, option B2 is a question on biomechanics and option B3 is a question on exercise and sport physiology.

Candidates for the exam usually study three of the above options. One of the options of study must be from Section A. In the exam, candidates must answer three questions, one of which must be from Section A. In other words, you could answer questions on both comparative and historical studies and then one other from psychology, biomechanics or physiology. Another route would be to answer a question on either historical or comparative studies and then two questions from Section B on psychology, biomechanics or physiology.

All the questions in the exam follow a similar format. The questions are stepped and often example based. Each question is split into parts (a), (b), (c) and (d). Parts (a)–(c) are shorter, paragraph-style questions that together are worth 15 marks from a total of 35 for the whole question. Question (d) is a longer and more demanding question that requires careful consideration. In this longer question, marks are awarded not only for correct answers and valid points but also for the quality of written communication. You should make sure that spelling, punctuation and grammar are clear and accurate. You will often be required to discuss, evaluate and analyse a topic, so the ability to present a balanced and carefully constructed answer is important. In all parts of the question you should use specific vocabulary — often such key words are highlighted in this book. All answers should be organised in a coherent manner and you should follow the advice on exam technique given below.

While you should treat all questions with care, the longer question (d) should obviously be given special attention as it is worth 20 marks. It is a good idea to plan your answer to this question before you start writing. Such planning will ensure that your answer is organised, that you do not forget a relevant point and if you jot down a brief plan on your exam paper you might even get some credit for it.

Unit G454 The improvement of effective performance and the critical evaluation of practical activities in physical education

The practical element of the course is externally set, internally marked and externally moderated by the exam board. You will be assessed in one role, similar to those chosen at AS and you can choose from performing, officiating or coaching/leading in one activity that must be one of the activities offered for assessment at AS. The activity profiles from which you can choose are listed below:

- athletic activities
- combat activities
- dance activities
- invasion game activities
- net/wall game activities
- striking/fielding games
- target games
- gymnastic activities
- outdoor and adventurous activities
- swimming activities
- safe and effective exercise activities

In all the roles, you need to be precise and consistent in demanding sporting situations and should be able to explain the factors that contribute to an efficient performance, coaching session or officiating event.

You are expected to develop an understanding and appreciation of the various pathways to success. (The concept of success underpins this unit.) OCR identifies a variety of pathways to success, including:

- outwitting opponents
- accurately replicating skills/movements
- exploring and communicating ideas, concepts and emotions
- performing to your 'maximum' level
- identifying and solving problems
- exercising safely and effectively

Any activity may include a variety of pathways to success.

OCR recommends that you should have the opportunity to experience a variety of roles:

- performing, for example different playing positions in invasion games, or singles and doubles in racket games
- coaching/teaching, for example teaching skills/application of tactics to a fellow student
- officiating, for example judging/refereeing to appropriate rules, regulations and codes of conduct

You need to be aware of the short- and long-term health and fitness benefits of the activity and of the opportunities for participation and progression, both locally and nationally. You also need to be able to explain the factors that contribute to an effective performance through development of your knowledge and understanding of the relationship between skill, strategy and fitness.

Studying for the exam

Read each chapter thoroughly

On completion of each topic, make sure that you have read each page of the relevant chapter and use the Tasks to Tackle to test yourself. If you adopt this approach for every chapter of the book, then your revision will be just that, i.e. *revising* what you have already learned rather than learning material for the first time.

Complete the Practice Makes Perfect exercises

If you tackle these specific exam-style questions at the end of each chapter, you will have checked that you have understood the key concepts. You will also gain useful examination practice and perhaps build some confidence based on a realisation of what you can achieve in the exam. You will also develop good exam technique, especially if, as you answer the questions, you adopt the strategies listed below.

Develop your practical skills

Up to 30% of the marks for the A2 course are gained from your practical coursework (Unit G454). Follow the advice given in Chapter 20 of this book and the specification to help you perfect your practical skills.

Read the Chief Examiner's Report

This report will alert you to the strengths and weaknesses shown by previous students and will help you to refine your approach. Along with previous examination papers and mark schemes, these reports are available in pdf format from the OCR website (www.ocr.org.uk).

Make your own notes

As you progress through this book, build up your own index of terms or small explanations of key topics and write them down in a format that you find easy to relate to. When it comes to revision, you can then use these notes to help you and much of your revision will seem to have been done for you.

Keep up to date

This book contains many topical examples and these are a vital part of any examination answer. However, the world of sport is constantly changing and if you read newspapers and magazines or simply refer to sport programmes on television, you might be able to find even more up-to-date examples to use in the exam. You will also find that by researching these examples yourself you are more likely to remember them.

Advice on exam technique

Success in the exam is not just based on subject knowledge. A successful student needs to marry subject knowledge to the question set. In order to succeed in the exam there are four main pieces of advice that the successful student may need.

Key words

Most exam questions require the definition, explanation, evaluation or application of key phrases and terms, which are featured throughout this book. You should identify such key definitions, which are often asked for directly in the question, and be able to write about them thoroughly. The examiner will have a list of these key terms in the mark scheme and if you mention them you are almost certain to be awarded marks.

Read the question

It is no use knowing all your key terms if you write about the wrong one, or one that is not asked for in the question, so make sure you take some time before you start to write any answers to read the whole question carefully. When you have read the question, it might be a good idea to use a highlighter pen to identify the key phrases mentioned above and you may even jot down some key answers to these phrases before you begin to answer a question properly. Take a few minutes to plan each answer before you begin.

More answers than marks

Each question identifies the maximum number of marks that are available for each part. If the question part is worth 3 marks, then it would be unwise to give only two answers! Successful students will often write more answers than there are marks available to act as an insurance policy for success. Examiners award credit for correct answers, and do not deduct marks for any incorrect answers, so the more you write, the more chance you have of success. It is also worth using examples to back up each point you make, mainly because many questions ask you to do exactly this and they will often start with the phrase 'using examples from sport...'. In any case, the example you give may indicate a thorough understanding of what the question is asking and the examiner may give you credit for showing your knowledge in this way.

Unit G453

Principles and concepts across different areas of physical education

Section A
- Historical studies
- Comparative studies

Section B
- Sports psychology
- Biomechanics
- Exercise and sport physiology

What you need to know

By the end of this chapter you should be able to:

- identify key phases in the development of sports history
- describe key characteristics of popular recreation
- explain the social and cultural factors that influenced the nature and development of popular recreation activities in pre-industrial Britain and their impact on sports participation today
- describe the varying opportunities for participation between the peasants and gentry in a two-tier society
- analyse case study activities as popular recreation — bathing and swimming, athletics, football, cricket, tennis

Key phases in the development of sports history

To understand the contemporary sporting situation in Britain, it is essential to consider the various stages of sports history. This historical development can be divided into four main parts:

1. Popular recreation relates to pre-industrial sports and pastimes (i.e. up to around 1800) and will be our consideration in this chapter.
2. Chapter 2 examines how sport became more rationalised in an urban industrialised society after 1800, and particularly towards the end of the nineteenth century.
3. Developments in nineteenth-century public schools illustrate how sport played a key role in reforming these institutions as well as society in general. We will look at this in Chapter 3.
4. The development of state school PE in an urban industrialised society must also be considered. Chapter 4 looks at the progression from initial military drills (preparing the working classes for their 'role in society') to PT and through to present-day National Curriculum PE.

> **Top tip**
>
> Knowledge of key time periods in the history of sport is important. Exam questions will often ask you to relate your knowledge to either a particular century (for example 'the nineteenth century') or dates (for example 'the 1800s').

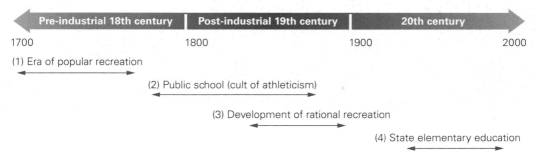

Figure 1.1 Key aspects of sports history

Tasks to tackle 1.1

It is important that you get your dates right when answering questions from specified time periods. You must relate your knowledge to the appropriate era or you will lose marks.

Copy and complete the following table.

1700s	.... century	(Pre-industrial era)
1800s	.... century	(Industrialisation process)
....	Twentieth century	(Post-industrial era)

Overview of sport pre-1800s

In this pre-industrial era, the population of the UK was almost totally rural and was split into two main tiers or groups: the gentry and the peasants.

The gentry had lots of free time available, as well as economic and social advantage with which to pursue activities of their choice. Those choices reflected their superior position in society. Real tennis, for example, has sophisticated courts and equipment that would have been unavailable to the peasantry.

The peasants only had time to play sport on holy days/'holidays'. They also had less access to resources and travelling was difficult, so their activities had to be local and had to use ready-to-hand materials.

Classifying popular recreation activities

Popular recreation activities can be placed into different categories, as shown in Table 1.1. There was a range of individual activities, including country pursuits (such as hunting), festival games (such as whistling matches), animal/blood sports (such as cock fighting) and combats (such as boxing). Game activities included invasion games such as mob football for the working classes, and court games such as real tennis for the

Table 1.1 A classification of popular recreation activities

Individual activities	Country pursuits (hunting)	
	Festival games (whistling matches)	
	Blood sports (cock fighting)	
	Combats (boxing, bare-knuckle fighting)	
Game activities	Mob games (mob football)	
	Target games (skittles, quoits)	
	Court games (real tennis)	
Pedestrianism	Competitive walking by footmen chosen from the lower classes, with wagers on outcomes placed by noblemen	

gentry. Pedestrianism (i.e. competitive walking) developed in the late sixteenth century, with noblemen wagering on lower-class participants.

Key characteristics of popular recreation

Popular recreation covers those activities and pastimes undertaken by the majority of the population before physical activity became 'rationalised' and developed into the sports we know today. As shown in Figure 1.2, popular recreation activities were occasional and often linked to festivals. The activities tended to be locally based and locally **codified**. Rules were therefore simple and often unwritten. Sports were social occasions and reflected the rural and often isolated nature of the communities taking part. Violence, cruelty and damage to property often occurred, with unlimited numbers taking part and consuming lots of alcohol as part of the occasion.

Key term

Codification: the creation and maintenance of rules.

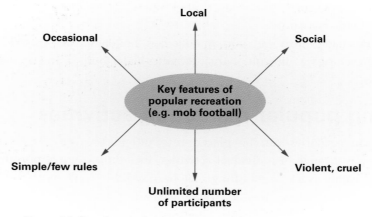

Figure 1.2 Key characteristics of popular recreation

Social and cultural determinants of popular recreation

Popular recreation activities and pastimes were influenced by a number of sociocultural factors. As shown in Figure 1.3, each of the key characteristics listed above was shaped by the life of the peasant class. Rules were simple and unwritten largely due to the fact that most people were illiterate. The 'seasonal festival day' characteristic reflected the peasants' lack of leisure time. The existence of localised versions of activities reflected limited travel opportunities and poor communications.

> **Top tip**
>
> Popular recreation activities reflected the society of the time in a variety of different ways. Clear class differences were very much evident — for example, mob football for the working classes versus real tennis for the ruling classes.

> **Top tip**
>
> It is important to note that the gentry in this popular recreation era pursued activities of a totally different nature as they were literate, and had lots of free time and economic advantage, all of which enabled activities to be played with rules, facilities and equipment.

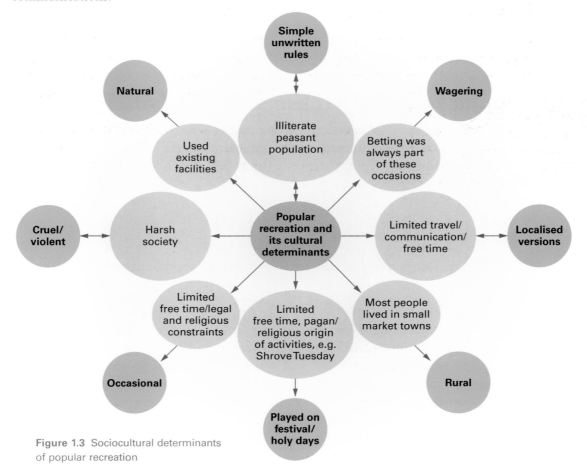

Figure 1.3 Sociocultural determinants of popular recreation

Tasks to tackle 1.2

Copy and complete the following table, which contains a number of social and cultural factors that influenced the playing of mob games in the era of popular recreation for the peasant population.

Social/cultural factors	Explanation
1 Local	1
2 Rural	2
3	3 Low literacy levels; no National Governing Bodies of sport
4	4 Limited free time; legal and religious constraints
5 Violent and cruel	5
6	6 Held on religious days; games had festival origins
7 Wagering	7
8 Natural and simple	8

Popular recreation: case study activities

You need to understand the following five case studies in relation to their initial, popular development and the participation of various sections of society:

- bathing and swimming
- athletics
- football
- cricket
- tennis

Each will be considered in turn in relation to how it reflected various characteristics of popular recreation.

Bathing and swimming

Bathing and swimming can be seen to have experienced several developmental phases.

Recreational bathing used natural rivers and water meadows. This was largely a lower-class activity and was, understandably, seasonal — being practised usually in hot weather. The aim of recreational swimming was largely functional: swimming was a survival skill (particularly for those living and working along waterfronts), it was a preparatory skill for the military, and it promoted good health and cleanliness. In addition, it was an enjoyable activity. Bathing stations were established in pools and rivers with different levels of difficulty. The first open air swimming bath in London was opened in 1734.

The upper classes had their own fashionable form of bathing, known as the **spa water cure**. This socially exclusive pastime took place in indoor facilities at inland spa towns such as Harrogate, Malvern and Bath. 'Taking the waters' meant either drinking or immersing oneself in the local water — the theory being that the minerals were good for health. Some spa facilities included a plunge bath for swimming.

Seaside bathing, also known as the **cold water cure**, focused on health benefits to be achieved by swimming in the sea (salt water or brine). Beaches were single sex and socially exclusive so that the classes did not mix. Seaside holiday towns developed and, along with the development of the railways, maintained this social divide. Beaches within a day's journey of towns attracted the working classes; those who could afford a week's holiday went to middle class resorts; the upper classes could visit the Riviera and other foreign seaside destinations.

The rationalisation of swimming began with the arrival of **public baths**. You will learn more about this in Chapter 2.

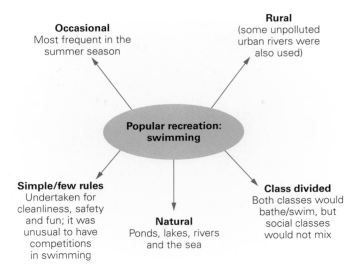

Occasional
Most frequent in the summer season

Rural
(some unpolluted urban rivers were also used)

Popular recreation: swimming

Simple/few rules
Undertaken for cleanliness, safety and fun; it was unusual to have competitions in swimming

Natural
Ponds, lakes, rivers and the sea

Class divided
Both classes would bathe/swim, but social classes would not mix

Figure 1.4 The popular recreation characteristics of swimming

TopFoto

Pensarn Beach, near Colwyn Bay in northwest Wales, circa 1880. To preserve modesty, swimmers entered the sea from booths on wheels, seen in the background.

Competitive, long-distance foot races were hugely popular

Athletics: pedestrianism

Up until the eighteenth century, roads and communications were poor and men of nobility employed 'running footmen' to carry messages or race ahead to an inn to announce their arrival. Some became very gifted runners and their employers placed wagers on them against the footmen of rivals.

With better roads and coach services, running footmen became redundant and in order to continue in the sport, they began to arrange their own matches and wagers. They then became known as 'pedestrians'. You will see how this popular recreational activity became modern-day athletics in Chapter 2.

The first and possibly greatest pedestrian was Captain Barclay. In 1809, Captain Barclay walked 1000 miles — 1 mile in each of 1000 consecutive hours — for a 1000 guinea wager (1 guinea was £1.05). Many people bet against him because they doubted he could endure 42 days without a night's sleep. When he succeeded, he became a very rich man — apart from the 1000 guineas, he made a lot of money from side bets.

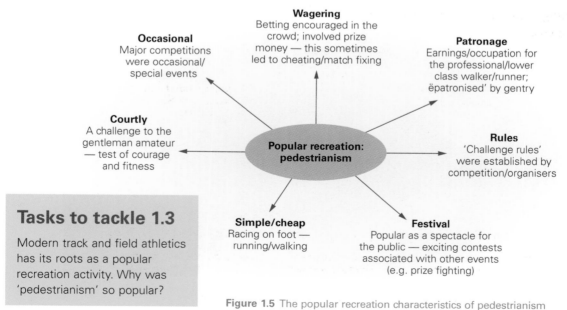

Wagering
Betting encouraged in the crowd; involved prize money — this sometimes led to cheating/match fixing

Occasional
Major competitions were occasional/special events

Patronage
Earnings/occupation for the professional/lower class walker/runner; 'patronised' by gentry

Courtly
A challenge to the gentleman amateur — test of courage and fitness

Popular recreation: pedestrianism

Rules
'Challenge rules' were established by competition/organisers

Simple/cheap
Racing on foot — running/walking

Festival
Popular as a spectacle for the public — exciting contests associated with other events (e.g. prize fighting)

Figure 1.5 The popular recreation characteristics of pedestrianism

Tasks to tackle 1.3

Modern track and field athletics has its roots as a popular recreation activity. Why was 'pedestrianism' so popular?

Mob football

As already stated, mob football was an example of a popular recreation 'mob game'. Key characteristics of mob football included the fact that matches occurred on an occasional/holy day basis. It had few rules and a limited structure, which meant large numbers participated in what was a violent pastime with limited equipment and facilities. There were many localised variations of mob football, which was played in the main by lower-class males. Mob football games were basically massive brawls with the aim of moving a ball (as in the Ashbourne game) or leather 'hood' (as in the Haxey Hood Game) between villages. The contests arose from maintaining rights of way between villages or towns.

Shrovetide football (the Ashbourne game) is a version of mob football still played in Ashbourne in Derbyshire

> **Top tip**
>
> It is important to be able to relate the key characteristics of mob football to the features of pre-industrial society (see earlier notes). While laws were passed banning street football, many of these games still exist today as a way of maintaining traditions of the past (such as the Ashbourne mob game).

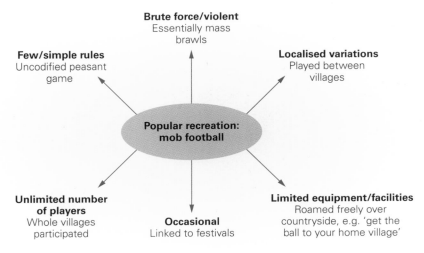

Brute force/violent
Essentially mass brawls

Few/simple rules
Uncodified peasant game

Localised variations
Played between villages

Popular recreation: mob football

Unlimited number of players
Whole villages participated

Occasional
Linked to festivals

Limited equipment/facilities
Roamed freely over countryside, e.g. 'get the ball to your home village'

Figure 1.6 The popular recreation characteristics of mob football

Cricket

Cricket was played in rural areas and villages from the early eighteenth century, especially in Kent, Sussex and Hampshire. It was, from the outset, a game played by all social classes together, reflecting the feudal/class structure of the village. Gardeners, gamekeepers, etc. were employed by patrons from the gentry specifically for their cricketing talents. Some freelance professionals played in a servant role to their employer. The game was limited in terms of its

A cricket match at the Artillery Ground in London, 1743. The bat was longer, heavier and club-shaped, and a two-stump wicket was used.

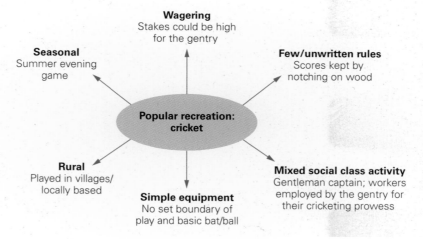

Figure 1.7 The popular recreation characteristics of cricket

technical development — for example, a club-shaped bat was used, bowling was underarm, and two stumps, not three, were used. No special kit was involved, and no distinct boundaries were used, so the game had limited organisation. Indeed, scores were kept by marking notches on wood.

Real tennis

Real tennis originated in France and became a game of the aristocracy in eighteenth-century Britain. It was played in the courtyards or quadrangles of castles and great houses belonging to kings, nobles and merchants. Courts were built and were expensive to hire, making the game **exclusive** to the rich. For example, the real tennis court at Hampton Court Palace, in London, is still in use today. The rules were complex (involving specialist language) and written down, necessitating literacy in order to compete, and were based on courtly politeness or etiquette. There was also a strict dress code. The game required a lot of time to master which, of course, the upper classes had. Spectators were separated from the players.

As social inferiors, and not being eligible to play, the mass populace copied the game. They adapted it to use church and pub walls, and developed the games of fives and racquets.

Top tip

Interest and patronage from the gentry led to the early establishment of some rules, but these tended to be adapted locally.

Key term

Exclusive: describes certain sports that only 'privileged classes' could play.

TopFoto

Real tennis being played at Hampton Court

The characteristics of real tennis, as shown in Figure 1.8, are the exact opposite to more traditional popular recreation activities. They are actually the epitome of rational sport, 100 years before the rational movement evolved in the mid-nineteenth century.

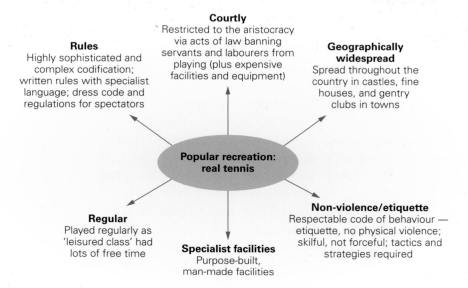

Courtly
Restricted to the aristocracy via acts of law banning servants and labourers from playing (plus expensive facilities and equipment)

Rules
Highly sophisticated and complex codification; written rules with specialist language; dress code and regulations for spectators

Geographically widespread
Spread throughout the country in castles, fine houses, and gentry clubs in towns

Popular recreation: real tennis

Regular
Played regularly as 'leisured class' had lots of free time

Specialist facilities
Purpose-built, man-made facilities

Non-violence/etiquette
Respectable code of behaviour — etiquette, no physical violence; skilful, not forceful; tactics and strategies required

Figure 1.8 The characteristics of real tennis

Tasks to tackle 1.4

Compare real tennis with mob football as eighteenth-century 'games'.

Top tip

Real tennis is a good example of a 'popular recreation' activity to compare and contrast with mob football.

Practice makes perfect

1 The sporting gentry wagered on almost any chance event, but also used pedestrians as opposition to test themselves. Describe the early development of pedestrianism. *(3 marks)*

2 Popular recreation activities reflected the society of the time. List three key features of mob football as a popular recreation activity. *(3 marks)*

3 Why was bathing important as a popular recreation activity of the 'masses'? *(2 marks)*

4 Give reasons to account for the exclusivity of real tennis. *(3 marks)*

Chapter 2

Rational recreation in post-industrial Britain

What you need to know

By the end of this chapter you should be able to:

- describe the key characteristics of rational recreation, and contrast these with the key characteristics of popular recreation
- explain how a range of social and cultural factors influenced the nature and development of rationalised sports
- explain how case study activities became rationalised — swimming, athletics, football, cricket, tennis

The main purpose of this section of historical study is to help you understand how and why sport changed, becoming more **rational** in the post-industrial era. This will help you in comparing such developments with what had gone before, as popular recreation in the pre-industrial time period.

Characteristics of rational recreation

As society developed as a result of **urbanisation** and the **Industrial Revolution**, sport became more 'rational'. It was played regularly, to set rules, in purpose-built facilities. There was an ethos of fair play, in an atmosphere of respectability, with gambling controlled. Elements of both amateurism and professionalism were evident as sport became rationalised.

> **Key terms**
>
> **Urbanisation:** a massive expansion in the number of people living in towns and cities as a result of industrialisation.
>
> **Industrial Revolution:** deemed to cover the century 1750–1850, this period marked a change in Britain from a feudal, rural society into an industrialised, capitalist society controlled by a powerful urban middle class.
>
> **Agrarian Revolution:** a major change in agricultural methods (such as harvesting) in mid-eighteenth-century Britain, prior to the Industrial Revolution. It involved the use of 'minor machinery' to help improve efficiency of agricultural production.
>
> **Rational recreation:** post-industrial development of sport which was characterised by respectability, regularity, stringent administration and codification.

> **Top tip**
>
> Some of the characteristics of rational recreation can be remembered using the letter 'R' (rule based, regular, respectable, regional).

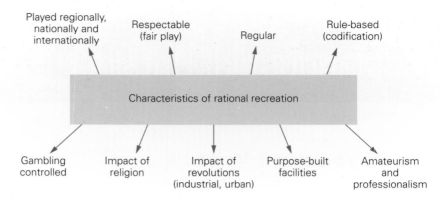

Figure 2.1 Summary of the characteristics of rational recreation

A comparison of rational recreation characteristics with those of popular recreation

The differences between popular recreation and rational recreation were largely the result of cultural changes as society became more industrialised and organised. Rational recreation was played in urban areas to codified rules, whereas rurally played popular recreation only had simple, unwritten rules. While rational recreation was respectable, with gambling controlled, popular recreation often involved cruelty, violence and wagering. Regular regional, national and international competitions in rational recreation took the place of irregular, local events during the popular recreation era.

The purpose-built facilities for rational recreation, such as football stadia, replaced the natural resources used during popular recreation. While strength (and often brute force) was important for popular recreation activities, like mob football, association football as its rational counterpart required the use of physical skills and tactical awareness.

Table 2.1 A comparison of rational recreation characteristics with those of popular recreation

Rational recreation	Popular recreation		
Regular competitions held regionally, nationally and internationally	Occasional competitions held locally		
Strict codification	Simple, unwritten rules		
Respectable, fair play, non-violent	Violent, unruly, cruel		
Control of gambling	Wagering		
Purpose-built facilities	Natural/simple environment		
Urban	Rural		
Skill based, tactical	Strength based, few tactics		

Tasks to tackle 2.2

Copy and complete the following table, which summarises key differences between popular recreation in pre-industrial Britain and rational recreation in post-industrial Britain.

Popular recreation	Rational recreation
1 Local	1
2	2 Codified
3	3 Respectable
4 Occasional	4
5 Rurally based	5
6 Natural resources	6

Social and cultural determinants of rational recreation

Rational recreation differed from popular recreation in relation to who was playing, and where, when and how it was being played. Such changes reflected societal and cultural change. By the mid-nineteenth century, Britain was an urbanised society and fully industrialised.

> **Top tip**
>
> The characteristics of rational recreation compared with popular recreation changed due to cultural changes as society became more industrialised and organised. In exam questions, it is important that you can compare the characteristics of rational recreation with popular recreation *and* explain the sociocultural factors that determined such changes.

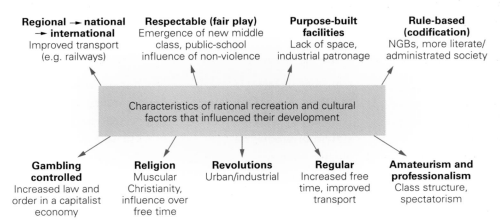

Figure 2.2 Social and cultural influences on the characteristics of rational recreation

The early 1800s

The early stages of the Industrial Revolution had many negative impacts on the working classes. Urbanisation on a massive scale saw the lower classes migrating into newly formed cities, with a consequent loss of space. Overcrowding was often accompanied by poor living and working conditions, as labour shifted from the seasonal work of agriculture to the 'machine time' of factories — often 12-hour shifts. Coupled with low incomes, workers' health was often poor and there was little energy or time left to play sports. Furthermore, the workers' traditional sports — so called mob games and blood sports such as cock fighting and bare-knuckle boxing — were criminalised, leading to the loss of the right to play.

The later 1800s

In the second half of the nineteenth century, conditions improved and played a key role in developing sport in a more rational manner. Hygiene was improved in the workplace and at home, with a subsequent improvement in workers' health. As you will see below, changes in the law gave workers slightly more free time in which to play sport, and changes in communications influenced the distances that spectators and players could travel.

In addition, these decades saw the development of a new middle class in Britain. Middle-class men were hugely influential in changing ways of playing sport — it generally became more acceptable. Those with a public school education had a strong affection for the sports ethos they had learned at school. Former public school boys grew up to gain prominence — and therefore power — in industrial and religious circles (see below), and their values of athleticism spread to the lower classes. The money and patronage that came with the middle class improved provision for recreation and sport. Factory owners set up factory teams, provided paid holidays and paid for new, purpose-built facilities.

> **Top tip**
>
> It is important to be aware that the emergence of sport for the working class masses was hard won. Initially, migration to towns was met with gloom, ill health and poverty for many. It was only in the second half of the nineteenth century that things began to improve for the working classes in society in general, as well as in a sporting context.

It was the lack of space in the urban environment that led to the reduction in size of playing areas, or pitches, for sports. Earlier versions of football, for example, moved freely over rural spaces. Less space eventually led to the provision of public parks and baths. The crowding of the urban environment was also a contributing factor in the rise of spectatorism, as there were large numbers of people looking for entertainment.

As society became urbanised and reflected a more mechanised system of production, various factors played a key role in developing sport in a more organised and rational manner.

Workers' rights and working conditions

The process of industrialisation largely relied on factories and machines. These machines had to be kept running in order to make a profit, and the result was initially long working hours for factory workers. Gradually, laws known as the Factory Acts gave workers more time off, such as half days and early closing for shops on Saturday. Holiday patterns became

Living and working conditions for many factory workers were poor in the nineteenth century

regularised, even if this only amounted to a single day or week without pay. More free time encouraged spectatorism, for example of football, a pastime made easier by the development of the railways.

Benevolent employers, also known as industrial patrons, provided paid holidays, transport and factory facilities, further encouraging participation. **Broken time payments** enabled the participation of players and spectators who could not otherwise afford to miss work. Note that such benevolence can be seen as a way of controlling absenteeism among employees. As attendance at church was also actively encouraged on Sundays, the actual free time experienced by workers remained limited.

The transport revolution

The development of the railways played a key role in increasing participation in sport and in spreading games across the UK. For the working classes, it enabled access to the seaside and other rural locations, with important implications for improving the workers' general lifestyle and health. Access to the countryside meant the possibility of engaging in field sports such as shooting, walking and climbing.

Key term

Broken time payments: money paid to some workers for time they had to take off to play sport.

Tasks to tackle 2.3

How did the 'half day' Factory Acts facilitate the development of sport at the end of the nineteenth century?

Top tip

The late nineteenth century saw sport develop rapidly in Britain. Advancements in transport played a role in enabling such developments to occur.

In a games context, both spectators and players could now theoretically travel further and faster, giving increased time in which to play and an ability to follow a team. Indeed, following a local team encouraged a sense of identity that benefited both the workers and their employers.

In reality, the costs involved were still large. Most carriages were specifically for the upper and middle classes. Workers were often reliant on the benevolence of their employers for special trips. In fact, entire trains were sometimes hired for these occasions, which could either be sport related or a trip to a seaside town.

The railways did, however, influence the establishment of national leagues. Regular fixtures grew up between towns that had stations, with matches being played on a regional and national basis. This in turn increased the need for a standardised set of rules and influenced the formation of National Governing Bodies of sport.

The Church

During the nineteenth century, football became increasingly popular in public schools. Initially there was no clear differentiation between football and rugby as the rules had not been formally established. The educational reformer Dr Thomas Arnold encouraged games at Rugby School and viewed them as a useful way of controlling the surplus energy of the scholars. His ideas were based on Christian principles, linked to the cult of athleticism, and aimed to provide the boys with a sense of discipline, moral fibre and responsibility. Such ideals went hand in hand with the development and expansion of the British Empire. (Missionaries introduced rugby to the Maoris in New Zealand and the Indian FA was established with the help of an English international soccer player who was a priest.)

The popularity of games in this era was also enhanced by the writings of the Reverend Charles Kingsley, who advocated the development of a 'healthy mind and body' and whose morality was encapsulated in I Corinthians 6:19, which states that the body should be a temple of the Lord. This was the philosophy of the Muscular Christians, who used games like football and rugby to promote Christianity among poorer sections of the community. Organised games or rational recreation were viewed as countering the vices that were reported in towns and cities. The Church could now associate itself with sport as it was far more rational and respectable than its previous 'popular recreation' counterpart.

Monarchs, aristocrats, industrialists, businessmen, professionals and in the late-Victorian era artisans, tradesmen, shopkeepers and the industrial proletariat all had an impact on the growth of games. However, the Victorian clergy, through their involvement in sport, were able to communicate with the population on a daily basis through the common denominator of a popularly held interest, and so relay their faith to the working classes in the towns and cities of nineteenth-century England.

The status of women

The place of Victorian women in nineteenth-century Britain was very much in the home. Domesticity and motherhood were considered by society at large to be sufficient for the 'emotional fulfilment' of women. Good and virtuous women of the time lived their lives centred around the domestic sphere of home and family, with little thought given to earning a living in the workplace. Educational opportunities arrived later for women than men, first within public schools for those who could afford to attend them, and then in the late nineteenth century for the working classes.

While middle- and upper-class women could afford to devote themselves to motherhood, domesticity and social engagements, working-class women often undertook badly paid work in houses and factories to gain additional income to enable families to survive.

Middle-class women of the Victorian era left their homes not just to socialise but also to visit the homes of the poor. As 'female philanthropists', they saw it as their role to educate poor working class women on cleanliness in the home (while relying on servants to keep their own homes up to the required standard). Other aims of such philanthropists included trying to improve their own education and employment opportunities as well as securing better wages and working conditions for working-class women. The right to vote was a longer-term aim so that women could have more of an influence over their own fate than they were allowed during nineteenth-century Victorian Britain.

> ## Tasks to tackle 2.4
>
> List and explain four sociocultural factors that influenced the development of rationalised sports and pastimes in late nineteenth-century Britain.

Amateurism versus professionalism
Occupation or preoccupation?

Throughout the history of sport there have been debates over the difference between an 'amateur' and a 'professional'. In recent years there has been a growth in the number of professional sportsmen and women (think of sports such as athletics and rugby union). Basically, there are two types of sportsperson at opposite ends of a continuum:

- **Amateurs** take part in sport for enjoyment and do not get paid or receive prize money.
- **Professionals** are paid for playing, coaching or managing. Initially, professionals also had another job as sport alone did not pay enough.

Eighteenth and nineteenth centuries

The gentleman amateur

The gentleman amateur was wealthy, so could take time off to play sport. He competed to prove himself as a person and to test his ability. He did not train, as that would make him a 'professional'. He was a respected member of the community with a good education.

The professional

The professional was generally from a poor background, and therefore had to make money from sport. If he could not make money then he could not afford to play. The professional was perceived to be corruptible as he was controlled by money (i.e. he might take a bribe to throw a game or contest).

Early professionals included:

- prize fighters — fighters were paid to represent the nobility. All sections of society watched and wagered.
- Boatmen — river men would race each other. Spectators would place bets on the fastest crossings.
- Footmen — the wealthy would enter their footmen (servants) into competitions and place bets on the outcome. This was the start of pedestrianism (professional running).
- Cricketers — this was one of the first truly professional games. Between 1750 and 1850 there were several professional touring teams taking part in matches in all parts of the country. Cricket coaches were employed at the large country houses to prepare wickets, coach the owners and to play for their teams. Later they worked in public schools.

The middle class

The middle class could not afford time off work to play sport, but at the same time did not want to get paid to play. They played in their free time and admired the high cultural values of the gentleman amateur.

Developments

- The modern Olympic Games began in 1896, with the intention that amateurs would compete against one another. There would be no prize money for the winners, only medals.
- As sports developed there was more scope for professionalism. To be a good player required time and money to devote to training. Teams needed money to attract the best players in order to do well in the leagues and attract supporters.
- As the class system gradually eroded, the stigmatism associated with being a professional diminished.
- The abolition of the maximum wage meant players could negotiate wages and turn from tradesmen into sporting professionals.
- In soccer, the maximum wage in England was £4 a week in 1900. George Eastham, of Newcastle United, went on strike in 1961 over the maximum wage (£10 then). A couple of years later, Johnny Haynes of Fulham became the first £100-a-week soccer player. In the twenty-first century, some Premiership footballers can earn £100000+ a week, with no maximum wage restrictions in place.

The formation of National Governing Bodies of sport

Many National Governing Bodies (NGBs) for sport in England were formed during the late 1800s. As described above, the ex-public school boys who formed them were influenced by a number of factors including the need for codification to ensure that sports were played in a more uniform manner. With more fixtures and leisure clubs being formed, teams required not only rules but also competitions and leagues to play in. In addition, the development of professionalism and commercialism in sport in the late 1800s needed regulating, as the middle classes wanted to maintain control of sport and preserve their amateur ideals.

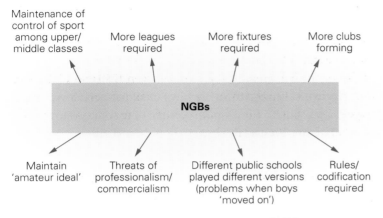

Figure 2.3 Factors affecting the formation of NGBs

Rational recreation: case study activities

Bathing/swimming

We learned in Chapter 1 about the parallel popularity of the spa movement (for the upper classes), seaside swimming (for all classes at different venues) and swimming in ponds and rivers. The appearance of swimming in its rational form was heavily influenced by several Acts of Parliament — The Wash House Acts (1846–48) — which led to money being given to towns to build public baths. The primary aim was to 'clean up' (quite literally) the working classes in order to promote exercise and combat cholera and the spread of disease (and ultimately to increase efficiency at work). Disease had become widespread, and the pollution of urban rivers meant that these could no longer be used for cleaning. Baths offered a clean and safe alternative, with facilities provided for washing both people and clothes.

The working classes paid one penny to visit the 'second-class facility' in the public baths. The middle classes used the 'first-class facility', consisting of Turkish baths and plunge pools, which facilitated competitive races and led to the development of swimming strokes. Amateur clubs and NGBs were formed as swimming became a 'respectable' activity, with the Amateur Swimming Association (ASA) emerging in 1884.

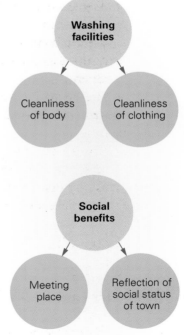

Figure 2.4 Functions of public baths in the second half of the nineteenth century

Athletics

Prior to industrialisation, rural fairs often included running and throwing competitions as demonstrations of speed and strength among the peasant population. In the eighteenth century, as we saw in Chapter 1, pedestrianism was hugely popular and involved large cash prizes and extensive gambling. Exploitation by the gentry was common, with footmen being raced against each other for the gain of their masters.

As England became increasingly urbanised, rural fairs were superseded by urban festivals, taking the sports to a wider, more organised, arena. Urban festivals took place in most large towns and cities in the early nineteenth century, attracting huge crowds (spectatorism) and widespread wagering. The lower classes took to running as a source of income. Many of the cross-country and harrier clubs that survive today are associated with these urban and working-class roots.

However, the wagering on races encouraged cheating, such as race fixing, which was frowned upon by the upper and middle classes and there was a desire to maintain separation from such negative aspects of athletics. By 1850, most major cities had purpose-built tracks, which allowed more stringent timekeeping and the beginning of record keeping — all of which meant increased organisation and rationalisation of the sport.

The Amateur Athletic Club (AAC) was formed in 1866 as an exclusive amateur club. Its organisers wanted to dissociate respectable modern athletics from the corrupt professional form and they adopted an exclusion clause — essentially banning labourers (working men) from athletics. This form of athletics was illustrated by the first Oxford–Cambridge Varsity meeting in 1864 and saw the start of sports days being embedded in the public school system. The AAC was the forerunner of the Amateur Athletic Association (AAA), which emerged in 1880. The definition employed by this body was that 'an amateur is one who has never competed for a money prize or a staked bet, or who has never taught, pursued, or assisted in the practice of athletic exercises as a means of obtaining a livelihood'.

Table 2.2 The development of athletics into its rational form

Upper/middle class	Lower/working class
Sports days — at public schools	Pedestrianism — commercial attraction
Elite athletics clubs — for gentlemen amateurs	Sports days — organised by local promoters in northern industrial towns
Urban athletic sports — as a respectable alternative to the old rural fairs	Cross-country/harrier clubs — associated with the urban working class

Tasks to tackle 2.5

Describe the emergence of 'amateur athletics' during the late nineteenth century.

Top tip

Ex-university gentleman amateurs wanted to compete against one another, but not mix with professionals. The AAA adopted an 'exclusion clause' effectively separating the middle/upper class amateurs from the 'corrupt professionals'.

Football

A rationalised game of football emerged from the popular mob games. It was organised and rule based, with NGBs forming in the second half of the nineteenth century. Ex-public school boys were responsible for the formation of the Football Association in 1863. 'Soccer' was played both as an amateur game for gentlemen as well as a professional game for the people (i.e. working class). Massive crowds and increased demand for regular matches led to professionalism being made legal in 1885 and the establishment of the Football League in 1888.

The game became more respectable as, with the involvement of the middle classes, violence became controlled by the new laws of the game. Clearly defined playing roles and official roles (such as referees) were also introduced as the rules became formalised. Spectating, too, became more controlled as stands were introduced at grounds. Soccer was played regularly on a regional and national basis. A number of key factors influenced such developments.

Improved working conditions:
- regular working hours
- decrease in the working week (for example, Saturday half day)
- workers' disposable income gradually increased and was paid to them on Saturdays, which was when matches took place
- football was cheap to watch and travel to
- football was seen as a good job to aspire to — a chance to escape urban deprivation/bad working conditions

Urban expansion:
- limited space led to a reduced/set playing area (i.e. pitch)
- working class masses in towns/cities needed entertaining — potential spectators
- potential business opportunities in running a club (for middle classes)

Improvements in transport:
- with improvements in the railways, regular fixtures could be played, leading to regional/ national leagues
- improved travel for spectators enabled people to follow a team, and develop a sense of identity

Involvement of the middle classes:
- acceptance of the rationalised, morally acceptable form of football by the middle classes/churches
- broken time payments given to workers who could not afford to miss work (i.e. compensation for loss of earnings as they played football rather than working)
- factory teams (including Arsenal and Manchester United) were set up by industrial patrons as a way of reducing absenteeism in the workforce
- churches also set up teams (e.g. Everton) and provided facilities for sports as a way of improving attendance at church and providing 'social control' of the working classes

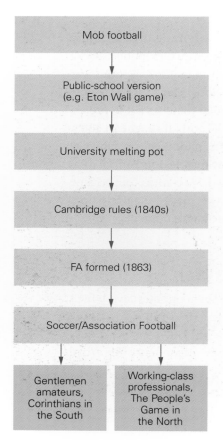

Mob football

↓

Public-school version
(e.g. Eton Wall game)

↓

University melting pot

↓

Cambridge rules (1840s)

↓

FA formed (1863)

↓

Soccer/Association Football

↓

Gentlemen amateurs, Corinthians in the South

Working-class professionals, The People's Game in the North

Figure 2.5 The emergence of Association Football from mob football

• ex-public school boys went on to universities, particularly Oxford and Cambridge, and took their various school versions of games with them. The bringing together of these 'games that were a bit like football' and the agreeing of a set of standard rules is known as the 'melting pot'.

Cricket

Cricket was a game in which all sections of society participated, with its non-contact and fair play features admired and encouraged by all classes. By the mid-nineteenth century, the upper-class patronage of cricketing was in decline and professionals began to look for employment elsewhere.

One such professional team was the William Clarke XI. This was the first 'All England XI' and was established in 1847. William Clarke himself had been a Nottingham player for 20 years; other players of note included George Parr, John Jackson and John Wisden. The team toured England for many seasons, taking on 'gentry sides' which had double the number of their own players: XI versus XXII! Many members of the team went on to coach at public schools. The impact of the William Clarke XI was extensive. By touring England, playing to revised MCC rules, the team stimulated the growth of county teams with regular fixtures.

The late nineteenth century saw the development of the County Championships (1864) and cricket grounds as a result of middle-class support. Modern rules were drawn up by the MCC in 1875. Cricket not only became national but also international when in 1877 the first 'Test' match was played in Melbourne versus Australia. Table 2.3 summarises how the development of cricket reflected social changes.

Table 2.3 Rational cricket and social change

Characteristics of cricket as a rational recreation activity	How this reflected changes in social conditions
Respectable	Influence of new middle classes
Rules/structures/codified	Literate/educated classes; NGBs formed
Regular	More leisure time available; improved transport and communications
Local/county/international fixtures	Improved transport and communications/development of 'professional game'
Fair play	Public school moral emphasis
Non-violent/gambling controlled	Increased law and order
Amateur vs. professionals	Britain as a class-based society — 'unpaid' gentleman amateurs and 'paid' working-class professionals as 'workhorses'
Skilfulness	Increased time to train; employment of specialist coaches

Tennis

Lawn tennis can claim to have been invented by the middle classes and was seen throughout the later nineteenth century as particularly suitable for this group. It was invented by Major Wingfield in 1874 as a copy of the exclusive 'real tennis' which was for the nobility and gentry only. He called it 'sphairistike' and it was played on an hour-glass-shaped court in the garden. He produced and sold kits of racquets, balls, etc.

The game still required money in order to purchase equipment. In addition, it required a garden big enough to hold a tennis court. It was generally played on the lawns of fine middle-class houses. There were also private tennis clubs, where the middle-class owners transferred their organisational experience (for example, from factory ownership) to the sporting environment.

Lawn tennis was deemed a respectable social occasion. The game could be played in a private situation — in a club or garden unseen by the general public. It could also be a mixed-sex activity — in a garden party atmosphere — and became part of the middle-class courtship scene.

Victorian ladies' clothing was cumbersome, but tennis gave women a start in sport

Spectators of both sexes watched the skilled performers, particularly as a summer activity.

This mixed gender aspect of the game led to its important place in the history of women's sport. As explained above, women's role in the early Victorian era was largely domestic. Towards the end of the nineteenth century, however, middle-class women were gaining greater freedom/emancipation. Tennis's stamp of respectability allowed an entry into the world of sport.

No special clothing was deemed necessary so the players could play in their own clothes: full length skirts and blouses. There was, though, a gradual relaxation of female dress code as time went on. The game did not involve bodily contact and so was considered refined and ladylike. Furthermore, as skill was deemed more important than physical exertion in the game, the female participants could retain decorum (no sweating or grunting!). There were even role models to aspire to, such as Lottie Dod, and the Wimbledon Championships to promote excellence. Dod won the Wimbledon Ladies' Singles title five times, the first when she was just 15 (she remains the youngest ever Singles champion).

Top tip
Tennis eventually spread to the lower classes when public parks provided courts to play on and second-hand equipment could be purchased.

Practice makes perfect

1 The Exeter College, Oxford athletics meeting in 1850 is generally recognised as the first gentleman amateur athletic sports meeting. Explain how the formation of the AAA in 1880 changed the earlier gentleman amateur code. *(3 marks)*

2 Explain the development of public baths in urban industrial towns in the second half of the nineteenth century. *(4 marks)*

3 Explain the changes in football from the 'popular' to the 'rational' form with reference to:
(a) working conditions
(b) urbanisation
(c) transport *(6 marks)*

4 Discuss 'amateurism' and 'professionalism' in:
(a) football
(b) cricket
during the second half of the nineteenth century. *(5 marks)*

Chapter 3

Sporting development in English public schools

What you need to know

By the end of this section you should be able to:

- describe the characteristics of nineteenth-century public schools
- demonstrate knowledge and understanding of the Clarendon Report, particularly with respect to its influence on sporting participation
- demonstrate knowledge and understanding of the three developmental stages of athleticism in nineteenth-century public schools:
  - Stage 1 — boy culture, bullying, brutality
  - Stage 2 — Dr Arnold and social control
  - Stage 3 — the 'cult' of athleticism
- explain the impact of nineteenth-century public schools on the case study activities — swimming, athletics, football and rugby, cricket, tennis and other striking activities/games such as fives, racquets and squash

Key characteristics of nineteenth-century public schools

> **Key term**
>
> **Public school:** a school that is controlled by trustees as opposed to private ownership (private schools).

Nineteenth-century English public schools, such as Eton and Charterhouse, were independent schools of ancient origin. They had a number of important characteristics:

- **Endowed** — an annual income, or endowment, gave the schools stability and allowed for planning, for example to build/expand sports facilities.
- **Fee paying** — fees were payable in order to attend.
- **Gentry** — as a result of the fees, these schools were for the upper classes of society. The boys' parents had money to spend on sports facilities and tended to have organisational experience.
- **Boys** — public schools were single sex, initially educating boys only. The boys tended to have lots of energy to burn, enjoyed physical activity and, as they came from the same class, had similar motivation.
- **Boarding** — as such schools were residential, the boys were together for long periods, with lots of free time to fill.

- **Controlled by trustees** — the schools' trustees influenced all aspects of policy and appointments. Their approval of sporting activities was important to the development of sport.
- **Non-local** — many boys travelled long distances to public schools. Regional variations in games were therefore introduced and adapted to create school versions.
- **Spartan** — conditions at the schools were often harsh (characterised by bullying and fagging) and this was reflected in the violent nature of the games played.
- **Rural** — the rural setting of most of the schools provided space to play 'games'.

Top tip

The characteristics listed in this section were commonplace in public schools in the first part of the nineteenth century (i.e. early 1800s) before the Clarendon Report and Arnoldian reforms (see below).

Tasks to tackle 3.1

Describe three characteristics of public schools in the early 1800s and explain how each one contributed to the development of physical activities in such schools.

The Clarendon Report

The 'big nine' public schools are shown in Figure 3.1. They were investigated by the Earl of Clarendon in 1864. The result was the **Clarendon Report**.

The Clarendon Report stated that public schools were important for building character in their pupils. It criticised many aspects of school life that did not appear to promote this aim. In terms of sports, the report placed major emphasis on moral values as opposed to skilled performance. Activities such as gymnastics and hare and hounds (see below) were criticised as being 'less animated' and of little educational value. The report included advice for the

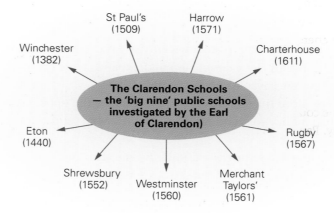

Figure 3.1 The 'big nine' public schools investigated by the Earl of Clarendon (showing dates established)

Key term

Clarendon Report: produced by the Clarendon Commission in 1864, this reported on the standards in the nine most famous public schools in England. It gave positive and influential statements on the value of team games in such schools.

Top tip

The riotous games and activities popular at these schools at the beginning of the nineteenth century were vastly different from those played a century or so later, as will be evident when studying the three developmental stages of athleticism later in this chapter.

schools on how to improve, and firmly identified team games as an instrument to achieve this. It gave an official justification for catering for physical activity in an organised form. Sport became a key reforming influence in public schools such as Rugby and Eton.

The three phases of athleticism in nineteenth-century public schools

Stage 1 (1790–1828): boy culture, bullying and brutality

During this period, schools were unruly places with a constant battle for control between staff and pupils. It was a time of bullying and brutality. Masters enforced rules in the classroom with corporal punishment. Beatings (often using a belt or a birch switch) were commonplace. Outside the classroom, the older boys bullied the younger ones using a system called fagging. Essentially, sixth formers employed younger pupils as their own servants, and could use beatings to get their own way. Overall, the result was much antagonism between the boys and the masters.

The older boys were responsible for organising games, and could use the fagging system to their advantage — using younger boys to collect balls, etc. The activities played were of a spontaneous and energetic nature. They included:

- hare and hounds — a boy (the 'hare') sets off across the school grounds leaving a trail of scraps of paper. After a certain amount of time, during which the paper trail may be blown by the wind, the rest of the players (the 'hounds') set off in pursuit. The chase often roamed freely across the countryside, straying onto private land and causing damage to crops and other property. Paper chases were later partially rationalised to create a kind of cross-country race.
- various versions of fives (see page 38)
- natural outdoor pursuits such as fishing, bathing and exploring the countryside
- mob games — often variants of football on grass and in courtyards. Some mob games, such as the Eton wall game, were school-specific and used the individual facilities of the school grounds.

Chapter 3

Sporting development in English public schools

The rules of the Eton wall game are notoriously vague and scoring is very rare!

Table 3.1 Summary of Stage 1

Key characteristics (What?)	Social developments (Why?)	Values
Institutionalised popular recreation	Boarders had the opportunity to play regularly together	Barbaric discipline. Masters 'ruled with the rod' and controlled behaviour through fear
'Melting pot' of various experiences brought into the school from all over the country and passed on if the boys moved to different schools	The boys had plenty of regular free time	
Activities tended to be:	Schools had grounds and space in which to play	Much resentment between boys and masters
• violent and riotous (e.g. mob football, bare-knuckle fighting)	Behaviour of the boys was poor	
• cruel to animals (e.g. dog fighting)	Masters had little control outside the classroom	Schooling more about 'contacts' (who you know) than 'education' (what you know)
• childlike (e.g. marbles, skipping, hoops, spinning tops)	Sports/games were organised by senior boys who controlled junior boys (fagging)	
• mischievous (e.g. poaching, gambling)	'Boy culture' of tyranny, chaos, rebellion and violence	Sport not encouraged, seen as a waste of time
• based in natural settings (e.g. fishing, bathing)		
Cricket was adopted in its original form. Other activities were adapted to suit individual school facilities (e.g. the Eton wall game)		

Boy culture: activities organised by, and for, the boys with no involvement of masters.

Key term

Tasks to tackle 3.2

Copy and complete the following table with appropriate words or sentences.

Stage 1 — boy culture, bullying and brutality	
1 Regular opportunity due to	→ →
2 Variations of activities due to	→ →
3 Violence/cruelty due to	→ →

Stage 2 (1828–42): Dr Thomas Arnold and social control

The early nineteenth century was a time of change both in society as a whole and in English public schools. Dr Arnold, Headmaster at Rugby School, and other liberal headmasters, wanted to reform the public schools so that boys behaved better without the need for the severity of punishments then imposed by masters. Their main aim was to produce Christian gentlemen and highly moral behaviour, and they believed that this could be achieved through sport. They were against bullying and violence on religious grounds. These views are summed up by the term **Muscular Christianity**: the belief in having a strong and fit body to match a robust and healthy soul. Muscular Christianity placed an emphasis on certain ethical values of team games (teamwork, loyalty, conformity to the rules, fair play rather than winning) and connected these directly to spiritual development (all performances were dedicated to God).

As public schools such as Rugby continued to reform, the house system involving sporting competitions also grew. Individual houses became the focus of boys' personal, social, recreational and sporting existence. Inter-house games, such as cricket and football, kept boys out of trouble — they used up time and

Key terms

Dr Thomas Arnold: liberal headmaster of Rugby School who had a major influence on the development of 'athleticism' in public schools.

Social control: Victorian era reforms aimed at 'taming' perceived unruly behaviour in Britain. In an educational context, social control involved taming the wild and unruly behaviour of public school boys.

Top tip

Arnold played a key role in changing attitudes to playing sport, but it is important to note that performances were for the glory of God. His main objective was delivering the Christian message, and as a by-product the status and regularity of games also increased.

Top tip

Muscular Christianity linked to ethical values. Athleticism (see Stage 3) was mainly associated with physical values.

energy — and they were more rule based than previously, encouraging respect for the laws. These improvements in the structure and organisation of sport reflected Arnold's ideas for developing a more formal overall academic curriculum for schools.

Games such as fives fell out of favour as they were not seen to provide the opportunity to develop the same levels of character building as team games. The sixth formers were given a key role in organising and controlling the playing of such 'rational games' in a more civilised manner. They were essentially considered responsible for the behaviour of the younger pupils.

In addition to team games, sports days involving other activities such as 'athletics' were promoted as a good way of showcasing a school and its facilities to governors and potential parents.

Table 3.2 Summary of Stage 2

Key characteristics (What?)	Social developments (Why?)	Values
Age of reform through liberal headmasters, such as Dr Arnold; copied by other headmasters	Queen Victoria began her reign in 1837; a more civilised society developed, striving for orderliness — 'Victorian values'	Muscular Christianity — sport played for the glory of God rather than for its own sake and to produce Christian gentlemen
Sixth form responsibility, social control through prefects	Wild escapades were deemed out of place; 'boy culture' was discouraged	Dr Arnold wanted social control via games — keen to change:
Games increased in status, regularity and organisation	Laws passed banning cruelty to animals	• behaviour of boys
Development of the house system (e.g. rise of inter-house football and cricket, decline of fives)	Transport and communications improved (e.g. Penny Post/railways)	• severity of punishment by masters
Games focus on building character		• role of the sixth form as a link between masters and boys
Sport as the focus of personal, social and recreational existence		• academic curriculum
		• level of mutual trust between masters and boys

Key terms

Athleticism: a combination of physical endeavour with moral integrity that would last throughout a person's life.
Cult: the worship of or craze for something (in this case, games).

Top tip

The 1850s are described by many historians as a key decade in the development of public school sport, as games became an integral part of the formal curriculum.

Stage 3 (1842–1914): The 'cult' of athleticism

Athleticism combined physical effort with moral integrity; or playing hard but with sportsmanship. By the late nineteenth century, athleticism had reached **cult** proportions. It had become a craze/obsession for many public schools and had the support of boys and masters alike. Sport, having been an embarrassment during Stage 1, was now the schools' pride. Pupil involvement was compulsory and staff participation increasingly expected. The wealth of the boys' parents had been harnessed to build suitable (and often very high quality) facilities on school grounds, such as swimming baths, gymnasia and extensive playing fields.

Athleticism was connected to physical values including robustness and manliness. Team sports in particular reflected athleticism, as they required participants to show a range of qualities such as endeavour — to do 'one's best' as part of a collective effort. Team sports were said to have the correct 'games ethic'. Lawn tennis, as an individual activity, was therefore seen to be less valuable than cricket as a team game. Athleticism also developed an appreciation of the discipline of physical preparation. Officials and rules were formalised in many sports, and participants were expected to respect them.

The key features of athleticism can be summarised using the following mnemonic:

- **A**ll-round, mind and body
- **T**emperament
- **H**ealth
- **L**eadership
- **E**ndeavour
- **T**eamwork
- **I**ntegrity
- **C**ohesion/competition
- **I**nstrument of education
- **S**portsmanship
- **M**uscular Christianity

Other words which tended to be associated with sports at this time include: self sacrifice, leadership, loyalty, commitment, endeavour, 'pluck', brotherhood, honour, bravery, sportsmanship, fair play and cooperation.

Schools now had a planned programme of games activities, which were played regularly as part of inter-house and inter-school fixtures to set rules. The importance of sport increased the importance of coaching, which also began to formalise:

- Specialist teacher support was provided for games. Assistant masters, for example, were academic staff who were involved in the games programme of daily, 'compulsory' activities.
- Specialist coaching support was offered at some schools. University graduates with sporting credentials (such as Oxbridge 'Blues' — those who had played for either Oxford or Cambridge) returned to their schools and coached, and even sometimes played for, school teams.
- Professional coaches also began to be used, for example in cricket.

Other social changes occurring at the time combined to make the values of athleticism spread across British society. The emergence of the middle class meant a growth in middle-class schools (such as Clifton and Uppingham), which copied the standards set by the public schools. Girls' schools (such as Cheltenham Ladies' College) also followed suit.

Top tip

Sport was important to heads and teachers in public schools in their quest to create civilised gentlemen who would become the future leaders of society.

Table 3.3 Summary of Stage 3

Key characteristics (What?)	Social developments (Why?)	Values
Games now a cult	Social control achieved; public schools now respected establishments	Cult for masters and boys
Full expression of public school athleticism and rational sport (full structure, kit, equipment, regulations)	Masters actively supporting and promoting sport in school	School sport not only a vehicle for personal development but also the essence of education itself
Specialist teacher support	1864: The Clarendon Commission; other schools and universities copied the 'big nine'	Games seen as having huge moral value (Muscular Christianity)
Specialist coaching support		
1863–88 — formation of many NGBs	Emergence of middle class led to spread of public school ways	Players encouraged to: 'win gracefully, lose with honour', 'do your best, give your life'
Magnificent facilities	Qualities gained through playing games seen to be beneficial to a career and to the country for the expansion of the British Empire	Games ethic — the value of team games for the development of character
Home and away matches against clubs and schools		
Sports days rivalled speech days for status (way of increasing recruitment via 'sporting success')		Poaching rejected as a 'barbaric' activity

Tasks to tackle 3.3

Define the term 'athleticism' and explain both the physical and social benefits boys could gain from their participation in team games such as rugby football.

After school

Ex-public school boys, the British Empire and Europe

The public schools played a key role in the development of sport, first within their own institutions and then into wider British society and beyond. In the second half of the nineteenth century, British forms of government, religion and culture were imposed by force on nations considered to be less 'advanced' or less 'civilised'. The values of courage and group loyalty, learned as part of athleticism, came into play when school graduates travelled abroad in a variety of different roles as army officers, teachers, vicars and priests.

The expansion of the British Empire had the secondary result of imposing various sports (particularly team games) on nations around the world. Ex-public school boys were dominant in such 'progressions', and also spread the value of athleticism at home as industrialists and community members and leaders.

Figure 3.2 The spread of games via ex-public school boys

Ex-public school boys and the development of rational games

The mid-nineteenth century onwards was a key time in the development of many sports. Ex-public school boys were highly influential in such developments. They were prominent in the formation of NGBs, clubs and leagues. As a result, they were largely responsible for creating the rules necessary to rationalise and develop sports.

This prominence came about primarily due to the fact that, when they finished school, many of the boys went on to universities, notably Cambridge and Oxford. This time of further study also gave the young men time and resources to pursue and refine sporting activities.

One major problem, though, was the plethora of different rules for the various games. In order to allow all to play, compromise rules were required, and this was the first step towards the rationalisation of sport. Cambridge and Oxford became known as 'melting pots' of sports. Beyond university, as we have seen, the 'old boys' took their love of sport into wider society — the church, army and workplace.

> **Top tip**
>
> Public school boys progressed through university and, on leaving these institutions, entered various professions and took the 'games ethic' with them. They spread rational sport to all sections of English society and eventually beyond, into the colonies as army officers and missionaries.

> **Tasks to tackle 3.4**
>
> Explain the spread of rational sport into wider society by public school old boys.

Why 'athleticism' was delayed in girls' public and private schools

Girls' public and private schools developed athleticism slightly after its establishment in boys' schools. A key to this was the belief at the time in the medical harm that exercise could do to girls — many believed that sporting activity would prevent girls from having children in later life. In addition, tradition saw girls as subservient to men in society and participation in sport was frowned upon. Consequently, female headmistresses were unwilling to provide equivalent sporting leadership to boys' headmasters, who actively encouraged games and athleticism. With respect to clothing, there was also concern over the wearing of 'revealing' clothes by girls when participating in games and sporting activities.

Tradition
Role of women in society (girls/women seen as subservient)

Medical
Participation seen as harmful to women/girls (i.e. affecting fertility)

Social
Sport viewed as unladylike/unfeminine (e.g. sweating)

Delay of athleticism in girls' public schools

Inferiority
Women perceived as inferior to men and unable to cope with exertion of sport

Kit
Concern over wearing of 'revealing' clothing for games

Leadership
No female equivalent to boys' headmasters, who encouraged athleticism

Figure 3.3 Factors preventing athleticism in girls' schools

Games in nineteenth-century public schools: case study activities

Swimming

Swimming in public schools linked directly to the development of the three stages of athleticism.

Stage 1: boy culture

- regular opportunities to swim in free time
- facilities were natural (ponds and rivers), as at home
- seen as a recreational activity, a release from classroom studies
- provided one of the main facilities for washing
- provided a meeting place for the boys (for example, at the river)
- seen primarily as a survival skill, but with some competition between boys

Stage 2: Arnold and social control

- promotion of discipline/control of boys by swimming
- overseen by sixth-form prefects
- constructive use of free time (discouraged trespass)
- prevented illness and disease in schools
- seen as a valued recreational activity — character building, preventing drownings

Stage 3: the cult of athleticism

- schools now equipped for swimming events
- competitive inter-house and inter-school fixtures
- organised swimming lessons at schools
- physical endeavour via swimming— effort and prowess encouraged
- moral values via swimming — bravery, life saving, loyalty
- prestige of school reflected in quality of facilities

Athletics

Athletics in public schools also developed in line with the three stages of athleticism.

Stage 1: boy culture

- limited rules, for example in hare and hounds/paper chase
- organised by, and for, the boys themselves
- lack of control — unruly and violent mass races involving force, not skill
- took place in boys' free time
- valued as a fun, recreational activity
- simple and natural facilities

Stage 2: Arnold and social control

- some rules, for example the influence of Exeter College, Oxford, which held the first formal 'gentlemen's' athletics meeting in 1850

- still organised by the boys, but with more support from masters
- some inter-house competitions
- emphasis on social control and disciplining the boys
- promotion of Christian values
- some specialist facilities

Stage 3: the cult of athleticism
- full rules and the creation of NGBs
- full master support — sports days held annually in schools as important spectator events
- full games programme with inter-house and inter-school competitions
- emphasis on skill
- purpose-built facilities
- athletics seen to develop character, promoting leadership and sportsmanship

Tasks to tackle 3.5

Why did 'hare and hounds' decline in public schools following the era of 'boy culture'?

Football

Football and other team games such as rugby underwent a complete transformation in schools between Stage 1 and Stage 3, as shown in Table 3.4.

Table 3.4 A comparison of games (e.g. football/rugby) in public schools between Stage 1 and Stage 3

Stage 1	Stage 3
Flexible/localised rules	NGB rule structures
Uneven numbers	Regulated numbers
No officials	Referees/officials
No posts/pitch boundaries	Posts/lines
No special kit	Special kit worn
Violent	Limited violence
Emphasis on force	Emphasis on skill
Mob game	Association football/rugby games
Occasional intra-school matches	Regular inter-house and inter-school fixtures
Limited/natural facilities (e.g. the wall at Eton) and minimal specialist equipment	Purpose-built facilities and specialist equipment
No coaching	Specialist coaching
No spectators	Spectators
No age differentiation	Played in separate age groups

Cricket

Cricket in early nineteenth-century public schools differed from most of the other boys' sports and pastimes of the time. It was non-violent and a team game involving a group effort. It

focused on skill and was already codified. It was played in open areas of school grounds rather than in the relative wilds used for fishing and hare and hounds.

By the end of Stage 3, cricket fitted neatly into the ethos of the cult of athleticism:

- **Leadership and decision making** — the captain made significant decisions during a game, requiring leadership qualities. These skills were seen as transferable to life and personal organisation beyond sport.
- **Teamwork** — the game promoted loyalty and required players to help/respect each other, putting the team first.
- **Courage/bravery** — required when facing opponents (for example, fast bowling).
- **Endeavour** — even if facing a lost cause players were encouraged to never give up/do their best.
- **Morality** — the game promoted fair play, sportsmanship and honesty.
- **Physical skill** — cricket encouraged the development of prowess.
- **Health** — it offered relief from academia/stress relief.
- **Preparation** — for 'competitive' life ahead.

Tennis

Fives

The game of fives is ancient and informal in origin. Probably the best-known structured version is 'Eton fives' with its odd-shaped court, which is a modification of the space by the chapel steps at Eton. While fives became hugely popular in public schools in Stage 1, it had limited national development:

- It had a tradition of being played 'recreationally' in free time.
- Different versions continued to exist, such as Winchester fives and Rugby fives.
- It provided limited scope for 'character development'.

Racquets and squash

To start with, racquets was played informally by school boys on available walls. By the mid-nineteenth century, public schools such as Harrow had built standardised courts to play racquets on. As the game became more rationalised, it was played on a court with four walls (instead of one) and a roof to guard against bad weather. Many argue that racquets led to the invention of the more compact and less expensive game of squash. Boys at Harrow wanting to play racquets began playing outside and to avoid damage (such as broken windows) they used a less hard, more 'squashy' ball than for racquets. From the 1860s, purpose-built squash courts were common and boys took the game on to university and back to their country homes.

Emancipation:
freedom from
restrictions.

Key term

Lawn tennis

This game was invented by, and for, the middle classes, as a social experience. It also became an important vehicle for the **emancipation** of women.

However, the game was not welcomed by boys' public schools. In comparison with the team games favoured by the boys' schools, tennis:

- required less physicality/courage
- required less teamwork/cooperation
- provided fewer leadership/captaincy opportunities
- required a large space in order to occupy relatively few players
- (and fives) was regarded more as a social/recreational activity, with no fixtures to rival those of other games
- was associated with girls' schools
- was given lower value than cricket and rugby by parents and schools

Practice makes perfect

1 Define the term 'athleticism'. *(1 mark)*

2 Describe the 'sports characteristics' of public schools in 1870. *(4 marks)*

3 Explain why 'athleticism' was delayed in girls' public schools. *(4 marks)*

4 How did the provision and organisation of late nineteenth-century public schools promote sports and games? *(4 marks)*

5 Why did public school headmasters encourage boys to participate in, and excel at, team games such as rugby? *(4 marks)*

Chapter 4

Drill, physical training (PT) and physical education (PE) in state schools

What you need to know

By the end of this chapter you should be able to:

- describe the objectives, content and methodology of the 1902 Model Course, the 1933 Physical Training Syllabus and the *Moving and Growing* and *Planning the Programme* developments of the 1950s
- explain the reasons for replacing one approach with another and the effectiveness of such developments on increased involvement for all
- explain key developments in PE in the 1970s and 1980s, including a critical evaluation of the impact of National Curriculum PE in state schools

Development of state school education and physical activities

Table 4.1 An overview of the development of state school education and physical activities

Date	Developments in state schooling	Physical activities
Pre-1870	No formal state education — some patchy church provision	—
1870	Forster Education Act — foundations of state education	Drill training linked to Swedish gymnastics
1899–1902	Boer War — poor performance put down to lack of fitness/discipline in troops	Military drill to be introduced via the Model Course (1902)
1902–04	War Office exercises — Colonel Fox	The Model Course taught by NCOs
1904, 1909, 1919	Centralised government control of physical activity in state schools; Medical Board exercises — Dr Newman	Early syllabuses of physical training
1933	Last centralised syllabus of physical training ('watershed' between PT and PE)	Content more varied including gymnastics, small-sided games, etc.
1952, 1954	Influence of child-centred/self-discovery learning in primary schools (e.g. Laban)	*Moving and Growing* (1952) publication for primary schools, followed by *Planning the Programme* (1954)
1988	Education Reform Act — National Curriculum PE introduced	Wider range of activities to be taught with attainment levels in four key stages from 5–16 years of age

Before state schools

Prior to 1870, the working classes had no formal education other than that provided by some parishes. With the introduction of the Forster Education Act (1870), it was soon to become compulsory for all children to attend a state school. Note that this move was not immediately popular with the working classes as the children would no longer be working and families would lose vital income.

Early aims of state schools

The purpose of the state schools was to provide an education for the working classes. There were various reasons for this.

> **Top tip**
>
> For the OCR exam you need to be able to compare objectives, content and teaching methods at four key times in the twentieth century: the 1902 Model Course, the 1933 Syllabus of PT, *Moving and Growing/Planning the Programme* in the 1950s, and, finally, National Curriculum PE in the 1980s.

Many social reformers and philanthropists had worked to secure a better lifestyle for the working classes and to keep young children away from unsafe factory work, and employers were increasingly needing a more disciplined and educated workforce. The working classes needed to acquire basic skills: the 'three Rs' (reading, writing and arithmetic). The fourth R of religious education was an important part of state education for many years and was regarded as a way of instilling moral values, seen as important by the middle classes. The working classes were going to be the factory workers or soldiers, obeying commands from their employers or officers. Therefore discipline and obedience were important values for them to learn rather than the leadership and decision-making skills that were being promoted in the public schools for the middle and upper classes.

Characteristics of early state schools

Experiences for the working-class children in state schools were very different from those of the sons of the gentry in their public schools. Small, cramped spaces, with no recreational facilities, imposed restrictions on the activities state schools could offer. This was combined with the philosophy that the working classes at the latter end of the nineteenth century would have no need of recreation. These schools were built in local areas, were day schools and catered for both sexes. Most age groups were taught together. State schools were free of charge, in stark contrast to the public schools.

Physical activities in state schools at the turn of the twentieth century

Swedish gymnastics formed the basis of early state school physical activity. The Board of Education favoured the Swedish variety over the German style, which required gymnastic equipment. The Swedish exercises were free standing and free flowing and taught in an instructional style. The Swedish system was based on therapeutic principles, i.e. relating to curative practices to maintain health, and on the scientific knowledge of the body at the time. The link between exercise and health was a popular concept in the late nineteenth century when a direct link was made between lack of exercise and the poor health of the working classes.

Following the Boer War (1899–1902), the heavy losses suffered by the British troops were partly blamed on Swedish gymnastics for not being rigorous enough — physically or mentally. The system was not, it was claimed, sufficiently improving the health and fitness of the working classes or imposing a sufficiently strict sense of discipline.

The Model Course (1902)

Swedish gymnastics and the therapeutic approach were abandoned in favour of the Model Course in 1902. This new approach centred on military drill-style exercises taken directly from the War Office. Military needs had become more powerful than educational theory.

> **Key term**
>
> **Non-commissioned officers (NCOs):**
> low-ranking army officers who delivered military drill to large numbers of children at low cost.

The course was produced and imposed by Colonel Fox of the War Office and was taught by **non-commissioned officers** (NCOs), who were unpopular with the teachers. The children were taught in a command–obey style, with the NCO using an authoritarian teaching technique to make all the decisions and with no input from the group. The exercises were mainly free standing and static exercises, and the only items of equipment required were sticks or staves as dummy weapons in order to teach weapon familiarity.

With hindsight, the Model Course can be seen as a backward step educationally in comparison with Swedish drill. Girls and boys from all age groups were instructed together.

The highly regimented Model Course treated children like soldiers

The exercises were dull and repetitive — but, crucially, cheap as they catered for large numbers in a limited space. Overall, the Model Course lowered the status of sports in schools.

Main **objectives** of the Model Course:
- to increase fitness for military service ('fit to fight')
- training in handling of weapons (weapon familiarity)
- to increase discipline

Main **content** of the Model Course:
- military drill
- exercises in unison
- use of staves as mock weapons

Methodology of the Model Course:
- command–response via NCOs (for example, 'Attention!', 'Stand at ease!', 'March!', 'About turn!')
- group response — no individuality, as exercises were taught in unison, in ranks

The Model Course only lasted two years (1902–04). It rapidly became obvious that it had no educational focus, did not cater for children's needs and was questionable in its intention of improving the health and fitness of working class children. It was not considered right to treat children as 'little soldiers'.

> **Key terms**
>
> **Objectives:** reasons why different syllabuses were introduced and what they were trying to achieve (i.e. aims).
>
> **Content:** what was being taught in a lesson.
>
> **Methodology:** how a lesson was taught (and by whom, for example NCOs or teachers).

> **Top tip**
>
> The Model Course of Physical Training (1902) was produced by Colonel Fox of the War Office. It therefore had a military and disciplinarian emphasis.

> **Tasks to tackle 4.1**
>
> Outline the aims of the 1902 Model Course.

Syllabuses of Physical Training (1904–33)

The Model Course was replaced by the Syllabuses of **Physical Training** (PT) in 1904, 1909, 1919 and 1933. Each syllabus sought to stress the physical and educative effects of sporting activities. However, who was going to teach physical training? The NCOs were no longer being used in schools and the basic class teacher had no experience in teaching physical training. The government therefore needed to produce a highly prescriptive, **centralised** syllabus that a teacher could follow quite easily. Schools still had limited facilities and the working classes were still required to be obedient. Changes happened gradually over a number of years. Therefore, the style of teaching was still similar to drill but without the military content.

> **Key terms**
>
> **Physical training (PT):** physical training followed on from military drill as teachers and the military profession emphasised the need for young elementary children to experience a balanced set of therapeutic exercises.
>
> **Centralised:** under central control — the government directs policy across a country to seek some uniformity.

The last PT syllabus in 1933 involved more free movement, more creativity and some group work. Children were increasingly encouraged to use their imagination and there was a greater focus on the development of skills. There was growing interaction between the teachers and pupils and the influence of specialist teachers trained in the techniques of Rudolf Laban (see page 46) was being felt.

Early syllabus developments in PT (1904–09)

Main objectives of early PT:

- The 1909 syllabus emphasised the therapeutic effects of exercise (for example, on respiration, circulation and posture).
- Obedience and discipline were still considered vitally important.
- Enjoyment started to appear as an aim in lessons.
- Alertness, decision-making and control of mind over body were all emphasised.

> **Top tip**
> A key influence on the development of PT syllabuses was Dr George Newman, who was appointed as Chief Medical Officer within the Board of Education. As a medical man, he was interested in the health-giving/therapeutic effects of exercise.

Main content of early PT:

- The 1909 syllabus was more Swedish in character, with recreational aspects to relieve the dullness, tedium and monotony of former lessons.
- Dancing steps and simple games were introduced.

Methodology of early PT:

- The 1904 syllabus had 109 'tables' of exercises for teachers to follow.
- The 1909 syllabus reduced this number to 71 'tables'.
- Lessons were still formal and still in ranks with marching and free-standing exercises.
- Unison responses to commands were still required.
- There was a kinder approach by teachers, with some freedom of choice.

The 1919 PT syllabus

> **Key term**
> **Child-centred:** basing a programme of study around a child's physical, cognitive, social and emotional needs.

> **Top tip**
> Note that age differentiation started to appear following the introduction of the 1919 syllabus.

The drawing up of this syllabus was set against the huge loss of life from the First World War and the post-war flu epidemic. The syllabus was progressive in terms of its broader content and more **child-centred** approach.

Dr George Newman was still influential and eager to fight off accusations that PT was to blame for the lack of fitness of the working class. Newman also stressed the benefits of recreational activities for the rehabilitation of injured soldiers.

Main objectives of the 1919 PT syllabus:

- enjoyment and play for the under-sevens
- therapeutic work for the over-sevens

Main content of the 1919 PT syllabus:

- exercises performed were the same as in the 1909 syllabus
- a special section of games for the under-sevens
- not less than half the lesson was to be spent on 'general activity exercises' — active free movement, including small games and dancing

Methodology of the 1919 PT syllabus:

- more freedom for teachers and pupils
- less formality than previous PT syllabuses

The last PT syllabus (1933)

The industrial depression of the 1930s left many members of the working class unemployed. No state benefits were yet available. Against this background, the 1933 PT syllabus was well received and is viewed as a watershed between the PT syllabuses of the past and modern-day physical education (PE). The 1933 PT syllabus had one section for the under-elevens and one for the over-elevens. Although still set out in a series of 'tables' from which teachers planned their lessons, it was detailed and of high quality.

> **Top tip**
>
> The 1933 PT syllabus was a 'watershed', as it led to the PE of the future. For your exam, you need to know about early PT and the 1919 syllabus only as the forerunners of 1933.

This was the last syllabus to be published under the direction of Dr George Newman. It was also influenced by the Hadow Report of 1926, which had identified the continuing need to differentiate between ages for physical training.

Main objectives of the 1933 PT syllabus:

- physical fitness
- therapeutic results
- good physique/development of posture
- development of mind and body (holistic aims)

Main content of the 1933 PT syllabus:

- athletic, gymnastic and games skills
- group work

Methodology of the 1933 PT syllabus:

- set out in tables for teacher to select from
- still used a direct style for the majority of the lesson, mainly by teachers
- some decentralised parts to the lesson
- some group work and variation of tasks/activities
- encouragement to wear special clothing/kit during lessons
- many schools used the specialist facilities they now had available (for example, newly built gymnasia)

> **Tasks to tackle 4.2**
>
> Describe key features of the highly respected and well-received 1933 syllabus of PT.

Moving and Growing (1952) and Planning the Programme (1954)

The influence of the Second World War

The Second World War saw the destruction of some schools and the growing influence of female teachers as many male teachers enlisted in the war effort. The apparatus that was brought into schools following the war was a direct result of the commando training that had taken place during the war. The development of PE in the 1950s was greatly assisted by the extensive post-war rebuilding programme, which led to an expansion of school facilities.

As a result of changes in the way war was fought, troops needed to engage in a more mobile style of fighting and to be able to solve problems. The educational value of this type of activity was recognised and different styles of teaching emerged in order to develop children in a more positive way, with recognition of their physical, mental, social and emotional needs. This was reflected in the publication *Moving and Growing* (1952).

Changes in education

Moving and Growing was produced by the Education Department as a guideline for primary schools. Primary school teachers were still not trained specifically in physical education, so needed guidance when planning and delivering the subject. Note that the term 'physical education' had now evolved, giving a very different emphasis from the earlier term 'physical training'. Immediately, 'physical education' suggests that there was now a belief that the mind needed to be involved as well as the body. This was combined with the movement approach (as advocated by Laban) and saw the following developments in PE teaching:

- exploratory work
- problem solving
- creativity
- skill-based work

Top tip

Rudolf Laban influenced the development of state PE in the 1950s with his work in the late 1930s and post-Second World War linked to movement to music, educational dance and creativity. His work became highly influential in *Moving and Growing* (1952) and *Planning the Programme* (1954).

These developments reflected changes in educational thinking. There was now a more child-centred approach, with teachers being able to show initiative and autonomy. The teaching style changed from a command–obey style to one that was more heuristic or guiding. Heuristic teaching allows pupils to discover or reach an understanding of something through exploratory work or trial and error. Problems are seen as having open-ended possibilities rather than a pre-determined solution set by adults — therefore, a sense of success is more likely to occur. In guidance style teaching, the children are given a stimulus and they respond through movement within their own capabilities. This was particularly used in educational gymnastics — children were given a stimulus and used their gymnastic skills to answer a task according to their own ability — and dance.

Another key influence at this time was the (Butler) Education Act of 1944, which aimed to ensure equality of educational opportunity. It also required local authorities to provide playing fields for all schools and raised the school leaving age to 15 years.

Main objectives of PE in the 1950s:
- developing physical, social and cognitive skills/decision making
- variety of experiences in a fun and enjoyable atmosphere
- increased involvement for all at their own level of ability

Main content of PE in the 1950s:
- agility exercises, gymnastics, dance and games skills
- swimming
- movement to music

Methodology of PE in the 1950s:
- child centred and enjoyment orientated
- progressive
- teacher guidance rather than direction
- problem solving, creative, exploratory, discovery
- individual interpretation of tasks encouraged
- using apparatus in lessons (ropes, bars, boxes, mats, and so on)

The school sport experience in the 1950s to late 1980s had come a long way from the belief that the working classes had no need for recreation. Secondary school teachers were now fully trained and were therefore no longer dependent on following a syllabus drawn up centrally. Physical education teachers experienced about 40 years of a decentralised system where they had their own autonomy and could choose their own physical education programme.

Tasks to tackle 4.3

(a) Outline the aims of a lesson based on *Moving and Growing* or *Planning the Programme*.

(b) Make a table to summarise the development of state PE from the 1902 Model Course, to the 1919 and 1933 PT syllabus developments and on to PE in the 1950s. Summarise your information in relation to:
  (i) objectives
  (ii) content
  (iii) teaching method
  (iv) where it was delivered
  (v) its sociocultural determinants

Present-day physical education: National Curriculum PE (1988)

At the end of the 1980s, the government of the time introduced the National Curriculum (NC). This was because the government wanted:

- more control of education
- more teacher accountability
- national standards to be set for physical education
- a wider range of activities to be taught (i.e. more curriculum 'breadth')

This represented a return to a centralised approach towards education. All state schools now follow set guidelines about set subjects to teach, and are inspected by Ofsted.

As a result of the Education Reform Act (1988), physical education continues to be a compulsory subject that pupils must follow from the ages of five to sixteen. By including it in the National Curriculum, the government must consider physical education to be an important subject, so what are the aims of physical education that are viewed as important in a child's development?

The main objectives of National Curriculum PE are to:

- achieve physical competence (i.e. improve physical skills)
- improve self confidence/knowledge of strengths and weaknesses
- perform in a range of activities
- encourage active use of free leisure time
- improve health and fitness
- become a 'critical performer' (i.e. children should be encouraged to observe and be able to analyse physical activities in a knowledgeable way)
- learn how to plan, perform and evaluate
- improve cognitive skills/decision making
- improve social skills/leadership qualities

Key functions of the National Curriculum for individuals and society

Therapeutic functions

One of the main aims of the National Curriculum for physical education is to raise awareness in children of the need for a healthy lifestyle. Modern life tends to encourage children to be more inactive and sedentary; active play has been reduced in favour of the television and computer games. Increased safety concerns have led to fewer children walking to school compared with earlier generations and a fast food culture is leading to an increasing problem of obesity, which affects individuals and society alike.

Creativity

Since the middle of the twentieth century, children have been required by educationalists to be more creative and imaginative in their physical education lessons. With the advent of the

National Curriculum, this has been given even more importance as it is also assessed more formally.

Recreational breadth

During the twentieth century, the range of physical activities taught in schools gradually increased. The National Curriculum has made breadth a more formal requirement in trying to combat the potential problem of teachers only teaching a few activities. Schools have developed more facilities, greater use has been made of community facilities and since the 1970s there has been an explicit policy of educating people to use their leisure time effectively. The general idea is that the more activities you experience, the more likely you are to find one you enjoy and carry on into later life, with the benefits this brings to individuals and society alike.

School PE programmes promote healthy, active lifestyles:

- to counter health concerns for young people, such as obesity and declining physical activity levels
- to decrease the post-school gap (i.e. the sharp drop out from physical activity on leaving school at 16)
- as a required part of National Curriculum PE
- to increase pupils' knowledge of links between exercise and health

Critical performer

The National Curriculum aims to provide people with knowledge of additional roles in sport other than just as a performer. Involvement through officiating, coaching, spectating, leadership roles and so on encourages young people to appreciate physical activities in many different ways and possibly to take on some of these roles after leaving school at various stages of their lives.

Areas of activity experienced as part of National Curriculum PE

The current aims of physical education can be taught through a range of physical activities. The National Curriculum categories include:

- games
- athletic activities
- swimming
- gymnastics
- dance
- outdoor and adventurous activities (OAA)
- exercise activities

A broad and balanced physical education curriculum is encouraged. Obviously a school cannot possibly offer every sport available but there should be a balance between activities that are team-based and individual-based, competitive and non-competitive.

Extra-curricular school sport

As well as the core curriculum lessons, pupils are also offered other sporting experiences while at school. 'Extra-curricular activity' is the term given to the optional activities offered in schools during lunchtime and after school. These include purely recreational experiences as

well as competitive fixtures. Another term for this is 'school sport' and this should be viewed differently from 'physical education', which refers specifically to the compulsory core lessons. There is an overlap between them but their central focus is different. The hope is that physical education can provide the building blocks that the extra-curricular programmes can enhance, extending students' interest and aptitude.

Note that extra-curricular activities rely on the goodwill of teachers. Compare this situation with that in the USA (Chapter 6). This means that such activities have fluctuated over the years. In the 1980s, for example, there was a decline in the extra-curricular opportunities offered in the state school sector. Many factors affected the drop in competitive school sports:

- teacher strikes (based on contractual hours) reduced teachers' goodwill
- financial pressures on schools of running fixtures
- the competing leisure and employment options of teenagers
- some sections of the population (an anti-competitive lobby) were against inter-school sport, sports days, etc.

Evaluating National Curriculum PE

How does the National Curriculum for PE compare to the Model Course of 1902? While both of these had the aim of improving the health and fitness of children, it can be argued that National Curriculum PE is more effective in actually doing so because:

- it increases understanding of health and fitness and the links to nutrition
- it attempts to provide a wide range of activities to experience and therefore continue into later life
- it delivers PE in 'better facilities'
- it is taught by specialist teachers
- it links to clubs
- it contains more fitness-related activities

Table 4.2 considers whether National Curriculum PE has improved on its immediate predecessors.

Table 4.2 Has the National Curriculum improved PE in schools?

Yes	No
• Uniform experience as a result of centralised National Curriculum (clear aims/guidelines for teacher to follow)	• Less teacher initiative than the post-war curriculum developments (e.g. *Moving and Growing*)
• Gives a wide range of experiences in a variety of activities	• Compulsory for ages 5–16, but some groups are relatively low in terms of participation (e.g. Key Stage 4 girls)
• A variety of roles are experienced (e.g. performer, coach, official)	• Limited time for National Curriculum PE (2 hours a week as a guideline), and PE is often of lower status than 'more academic' subjects like maths and science
• Preparation for active leisure/lifetime participation	• Lack of specialist teachers/equipment/facilities to deliver certain aspects of National Curriculum PE (e.g. OAA)

Factors that influence PE/sport provision in schools

In the early twenty-first century, various factors can affect the quality of a pupil's PE/sport experience while at school. The impact of each factor can be positive or negative depending on the degree to which it applies in individual schools:

Tasks to tackle 4.4

List the similarities and differences between early twentieth-century PT and the later development of National Curriculum PE.

- Timetable restrictions — schools sometimes decrease the amount of time allocated on the curriculum to National Curriculum PE due to the competing demands of other 'more academic' subjects. PE may find itself marginalised, particularly at Key Stage 4 when the demands of GCSE examinations are particularly high.
- Lack of funding/resources — budgets may restrict the quality and breadth of a pupil's PE experience. For example, many schools find the funding of swimming and OAA particularly difficult, so these aspects of PE are often poorly experienced. Transport for fixtures may also be deemed to be too expensive and negatively affect inter-school sporting opportunities.
- Quality of staffing — PE teachers and external coaches vary in terms of their qualifications and degree of commitment to PE/school sport and this may well affect the quality of a pupil's early physical activity experience.
- Quality of facilities — the availability of specialist facilities for offering a range of PE/sport varies throughout the country.
- School–club links — links between schools and clubs are important as they can positively influence PE/school sport by improving a pupil's access to high-quality coaching, teaching and facilities.

Practice makes perfect

1 What were the main aims and characteristics of military drill? *(4 marks)*

2 What were the objectives and teaching methods of the approach to PE teaching during the 1950s? *(5 marks)*

3 Compare **(i)** the Model Course (1902) with **(ii)** PT syllabus developments (1904–33) and **(iii)** state PE in the 1950s with respect to objectives, content, and delivery methods. *(9 marks)*

Chapter 5

Sport in the UK

What you need to know

By the end of this chapter you should be able to:

- understand the historical and cultural context influencing the development of sport in the UK
- understand the current determinants of PE and sport in the UK, including geography, social aspects, government policy and sporting values
- understand the increased links between sport, sponsorship and the media in the UK
- demonstrate knowledge and understanding of health, fitness and obesity levels among young people and the general population in the UK
- outline current initiatives to promote sport in schools and in the wider community
- explain opportunity, provision and esteem in the UK in relation to sports excellence
- understand the importance of key sports excellence organisations and initiatives, such as UK Sport and UKSI
- explain how cricket, rugby league, rugby union and association football have evolved over time to their current status in the twenty-first century

UK sport in cultural context

The historical development of sport

Many sports in the UK can trace their origins back to the nineteenth century when many key influences were at work in society.

One major influence was the impact of public schools, which gave more structure and organisation to a number of sports. Dr Thomas Arnold, headmaster of Rugby School from 1828 to 1842, sought to reform public school life and improve the behaviour and morals of the boys who attended public schools. He saw organised games as a key vehicle for improving behaviour and establishing **social control**. By keeping the boys occupied in regular and organised games during their free time, social order was maintained.

Social control: occupying free time in a positive way via participation in physical activity to lessen the likelihood of 'bad behaviour'.

Key term

Under the influence of Arnoldian reforms, school sports developed technically, with more structure (such as rules to play to) allowing regular inter-house competition in games such as football and cricket. As the boys moved on to university there was a clear need for more widespread agreement on rules so that sport could be played more regionally and nationally. Ex-public school boys were prominent in the formation of many National Governing Bodies of sport (NGBs) in the second half of the nineteenth century, which **codified** many sports.

Codification: the setting of a nationally agreed set of strict rules to abide by in a sport.

Social class in British society

A strict class system underpinned British society following the urban and industrial revolutions. The social class an individual belonged to affected their health, housing and income, as well as the sporting opportunities available to them as a participant or, more likely initially, as a spectator.

The upper-class gentry had lots of free time, extensive grounds and plenty of money with which to participate in activities whenever they chose. The newly created middle classes were the self-made entrepreneurs aspiring to the upper regions of society. Both the middle and upper classes could afford to play sport for the 'love of it' as amateurs in a spirit of friendly competition. At the bottom of society, the working classes had very little time or spare cash to spend on leisure pursuits. In order to play sport, workers needed to earn an income to compensate for loss of earnings. The working classes were therefore associated with professionalism from an early stage in sports such as association football and rugby league.

The formation of National Governing Bodies of sport

Many National Governing Bodies (NGBs) for sport in England were formed during the late 1800s. The ex-public school boys who formed them were influenced by a number of factors including the need for codification to ensure that sports were played in a more uniform manner. With more fixtures and leisure clubs being formed, teams required not only rules but also competitions and leagues to play in. In addition, the development of professionalism and commercialism in sport in the late 1800s needed 'controlling', as the upper and middle classes wanted to maintain control of sport and preserve their amateur ideals.

The role of ex-public school boys who went on to universities and led the formation of many NGBs is of key importance.

Rationalisation case study: football

Key features of the new game of rationalised association football included:

- rule based and organised — NGBs developed, such as the FA
- respectable — accepted and encouraged by the middle classes
- clearly defined playing roles, including officials such as referees
- provision for spectators, such as the introduction of stands at grounds
- violence controlled by the laws of the game
- regular — played on a regional and national basis

There were many factors affecting the rise of rationalised association football as a game for the masses in late nineteenth-century Britain.

Improved working conditions:

- Regular working hours were now required by law.
- There was a decrease in the working week, for example Saturday half day.
- Workers had some spare cash to spend, paid to them on Saturdays, which was when matches took place (football was relatively cheap to watch). Broken time payments were offered to players as recompense for missing work.
- Football was seen as a good job to aspire to.

Urban expansion:

- Limited space in the cities led to a reduced and set playing area (i.e. pitch).
- The large numbers of people in towns and cities needed entertainment (i.e. spectatorism).
- Improvements in transport made it possible to 'follow a team'.

Influence of the middle class:

- The new rationalised, morally acceptable form of football was accepted by the middle classes and the Church.
- Running a football club offered a good potential business opportunity for the middle classes.
- Industrial patrons founded factory teams and paid for transportation of fans to away matches. Following a team was good for worker morale and therefore productivity.
- Ex-public school boys went on to universities and needed to unify the rules of their games. They were instrumental in the formation of the Football Association (1863).

Key terms

Amateurs: not paid for sporting involvement and tended to play for the love of it. Fair play and sportsmanship were more important than winning. Abiding by the spirit and the rules of the game were key qualities of the gentleman amateur.

Professionals: received payments for sporting involvements, via wagers or winnings, with extrinsic rewards an important motivator for participation. Initially, professionals needed another job in addition to sport, as earnings were not sufficiently high.

Soccer was played both as an amateur game for gentlemen as well as a professional game for 'the people' (working classes). Massive crowds and increased demand for regular matches led to professionalism being made legal in 1885 and the establishment of the Football League in 1888.

Amateurism and professionalism

In the eighteenth and nineteenth century, the 'gentleman amateur' was very wealthy and had plenty of free time in which to play sport. Sporting amateurs came from an elite social class group; they were highly respected members of society, with a public school background. Participation in sport was viewed as a character-building exercise and 'training' was frowned upon, as this would have constituted professionalism.

The middle classes who emerged as a result of the Industrial Revolution could not afford to take time off work, but at the same time did not want to get paid to play. They admired the high cultural values of the elite gentleman amateur and played sport in their free time according to similar principles of amateurism. The middle and upper classes used the 'amateur code' in most sports to effectively exclude the working classes, as this group could not meet the financial and social demands that the code required.

The working classes were the poorest members of society and therefore had to make money from sport, otherwise they could not afford to play. The working class professional came from a poor background and was perceived to be corruptible as he was controlled by money. He would, for example, take a bribe to throw a fight or lose a game on purpose. Early professionals included prize fighters and pedestrians (footmen of the wealthy used in long-distance running races). Early professionals were paid — by a patron or as a result of gambling — according to results, hence training was specialised and winning became the most important thing.

The differences over time in relation to how amateurs and professionals have been viewed when involved in sports are reviewed in Table 5.1.

Table 5.1 Summary of the differences between amateurism and professionalism

Amateurism	Professionalism
Came with the onset of the Victorian era (mid-nineteenth century onwards)	Slowly developed, with full onset coinciding with the commercialism/media coverage of sport in the late twentieth century onwards
High morality sportsmanship and 'gentlemanly' behaviour	Foul play, gamesmanship and cheating to gain an advantage
Games not taken too seriously; winning not important for upper classes	Win at all costs, high rewards at stake, pressure to succeed and to maintain lifestyle

Amateurism versus professionalism case study: rugby football

The status of amateurs and professionals in the late nineteenth century varied between sports. Rugby football, for example, was developed at Rugby School (one of the 'big nine' public schools — see Figure 3.1 on page 28). However, the game was so popular that workers in northern industrial towns adopted it, but needed to be paid to play or at least receive broken time payments. The rugby authorities, whose members believed in the amateur code, did not like this. Eventually, the disagreement led to a split in rugby: rugby union was played by amateurs from the south of the country; rugby league was played by professionals from the working classes, who had to miss work to play sport.

The professional/amateur division between the two rugby codes persisted until very recently. Ultimately,

Rugby league has used professional players since its earliest days

sports in the modern day need to be able to survive commercially, and money enables NGBs to promote the game and also finances coaching, competitions and facilities. Players who realised they could be paid a good income from rugby league were being tempted to play the professional game. Finally, in 1996, the union game turned professional.

Geographical determinants of sport in the UK

The 2001 census of the UK gave a UK population of 58 789 194. This rose to 60 587 000 in 2006, according to official estimates by the Office of National Statistics in 2006. The majority of the UK's inhabitants live in urban/suburban areas. Note that many urban areas in the UK are surrounded by protected green zones, or greenbelts, which may be available to the local community to use for healthy physical outdoor activities. In comparison with the USA and Australia, the UK has a much higher density of population, as illustrated by Table 5.2.

Table 5.2 Population densities for the UK, the USA and Australia

Rank	Country	Population	Area (km²)	Density (population per km²)
51	UK	60 776 238	242 900	250
180	USA	301 140 000	9 629 991	31
235	Australia	21 050 000	7 682 000	2.7

The well-established motorway and public transport networks mean that most places in the UK are accessible within a day for both participants and spectators alike.

Climatic conditions in the UK can be described as 'variable', but are generally temperate with warm summers, cold winters and lots of precipitation throughout the year. Average total sunshine hours in the UK are just under 30% of the maximum possible. The UK is therefore not blessed with the ideal climate to attract people to participate in the great outdoors, unlike Australia, which we will consider in Chapter 7.

The geographical features of the UK, such as those outlined above, impact on PE and sport in a number of ways:

- Lack of space and a wet climate decrease the range of sports available.
- A high urban population concentration gives potential for mass spectatorism in inner cities and towns.
- Well-established transport systems covering a relatively small geographical area enable ease of access for players and spectators.
- PE programmes have been traditionally linked to the seasons, for example an emphasis on winter games such as football, rugby and netball switching to summer sports such as cricket, rounders and athletics.

Tasks to tackle 5.1

Explain the influence of each of the following determinants of sport in the UK:
(a) historical development of the UK
(b) the climate of the UK
(c) transport in the UK
(d) the population of the UK

Government policy on sports participation in the UK

Sports policy in the UK has traditionally been set via a decentralised system of administration, with several autonomous bodies making their own minds up about the direction sport should take. Until the advent of the National Lottery in the late twentieth century, funding of sport had been relatively low on the government's agenda. Following the successful bid to host the London 2012 Olympics, government/Lottery funding of sport at all levels is deemed much more important. The government's aim is for Britain to finish as high as possible in the medal table in 2012, and for the London Olympics to leave a lasting legacy of higher levels of mass participation in the general population.

> **Top tip**
> To keep up to date with UK Sport Olympic funding, visit www.uksport.gov.uk/news/.

Sport England

In June 2008, Sport England announced a new strategy aimed at getting one million additional people to participate in sport by 2012. In addition, Sport England made a commitment to reduce drop out of sport by 16 year olds and make a contribution to the delivery of the government's 'Five Hour Sport Offer' for children and young people. The list of targets set included increasing people's satisfaction with their experience of sport. In delivering the strategy, partnerships were created between Sport England, NGBs and local authorities.

Sports Coach UK

As a partner of Sport England, Sports Coach UK invests via NGBs in 'Coaching for Young People'. Its aim is to increase coaching for young people in key sports at an early age to help deliver the 'Five Hour Sport Offer'. As part of an effort to attract and retain more volunteers in community sports, a 'Recruit to Coach' initiative has been designed to increase the voluntary coaching workforce by 4000 people, with another 4000 to be found by working with the Youth Sport Trust.

Commercialisation of sport in the UK

The UK is a mixed economy, with elements of both a **public sector** and a **private sector**. The twenty-first century has seen strengthening links between sport and big business (i.e. the private sector) as evidenced in football, cricket and many others. Multinational companies compete for exclusive rights to fund high-profile sports, teams and individuals in return for high media exposure. This mutually beneficial relationship between high-level sport, sponsor-

> **Key terms**
> **Public sector:** local authority/ local government provision.
> **Private sector:** provision via businesses that are out to make a profit.

ship and the media is sometimes known as the 'golden triangle'. While minority sports such as netball and hockey miss out on the pot of gold, football is very much cashing in with fame and fortune available to a limited few.

A more detailed consideration of how various case study activities have been affected by the increased commercialisation of sport from the late twentieth century onwards is given at the end of this chapter.

Social determinants of sport in the UK

The UK has a long tradition of 'Sport for All' since the original Sports Council campaign bearing the same name started in 1975. Initiatives designed to raise participation levels in **minority groups** have been ongoing ever since.

As we continue into the twenty-first century, there are still issues negatively affecting participation by members of minority groups. These include:

- reduced opportunity to participate, for example through lack of money
- poor provision, for example lack of access to facilities, clubs or coaches to meet specific needs
- low esteem, for example lack of belief/ self-confidence in their ability to take part

> **Key terms**
>
> **Minority groups:** in a sporting context, this means groups identified by social class, race, gender, age or ability with low levels of participation. There is a key focus on identifying any discrimination leading to the relative lack of participation of minorities.
>
> **Discrimination:** where prejudice leads to negative treatment of an individual, often from a minority group.

Sporting values in the UK

The UK is a democratic society with personal freedom to choose as a key principle in life. Unfortunately, many individuals are choosing to live very inactive lifestyles and eat very unhealthy diets, as illustrated by rising levels of obesity in the UK (see below). On the other hand, sports participation has a long tradition in the UK, with many positive values to be gained via participation:

- Teamwork — developing the ability to work as part of a team is seen as a positive value of sport/PE.
- Individuality — the UK has a long tradition of autonomy, with sports organisations and individuals free to make their own decisions on participation. Individual efforts may be rewarded in certain sports, with high rewards in high-profile sports if successful.
- Fair play — this tradition, which emphasises high moral conduct in the sporting arena, is of importance in the UK.
- Competitiveness versus participation — taking part has traditionally been seen as more important than winning. The UK may be said to lack competitiveness, with less of a win ethic than other countries, such as Australia.
- Overcoming discrimination — society strives to overcome inequality in general via sport programmes/initiatives, which often include anti-discrimination schemes (for example, Kick it Out in football).

PE/school sport and mass participation in the UK

PE/school sport in the UK

PE programmes in UK schools generally consist of compulsory PE lessons following National Curriculum programmes of study between the ages of 5 and 16. In addition, there are extra-curricular opportunities that pupils can choose to participate in — also known as 'school sport'. These may involve competitive sport within a school, for example inter-house or inter-form competition, as well between different schools. Such extra-curricular activities have traditionally been at the discretion of teachers — staff are not paid for their time and effort — and have varied in quantity and quality as a result. In the 1980s, for example, a wave of industrial action by teachers against newly imposed working conditions led to the loss of many extra-curricular sporting opportunities, with staff very unwilling to run them.

Such reluctance has led various British governments and local authorities to introduce initiatives designed to counter the decline in availability of school sport. These include sports colleges, School Sport Coordinators (SSCos) and Sports Development Officers (SDOs). Such initiatives all involve more importance being placed on sporting opportunities for pupils than has been the case in the past. The emphasis in extra-curricular sport is placed on participation rather than results, with the ethic of fair play (a legacy of public school tradition) still very much encouraged by PE staff today. There is also a strong continuing tradition of focusing on team games, such as football, rugby and netball. More recently, as part of the government's health and fitness agenda, there have been more varied extra-curricular programmes offered in an attempt to promote lifelong involvement in physical activity.

Health, fitness and obesity levels in young people in the UK

In its *Foresight Report: Tackling Obesities — Future Choices* (2007), the Department of Health predicted that 60% of adults and a third of children will be classed as obese by 2050. The Information Centre for Health and Social Care at the NHS published some statistics on obesity, physical activity and diet in England in 2006. The findings included worrying statistics on rising levels of obesity in young children. In boys and girls aged 2–15, the proportions who were classified as obese were as follows:

- for boys — proportion increased from 10.9% in 1995 to 18% in 2005
- for girls — proportion increased from 12% in 1995 to 18.1% in 2005

Physical activity levels indicated that in 2002, 70% of boys and 61% of girls met current physical activity guidelines for children, indicating that a significant number of young people were not active enough. This was particularly the case for young girls.

It is therefore apparent that health and fitness levels are in decline among young people in the UK, with obesity levels increasing as a consequence of relative inactivity. High-profile initiatives such as Ian Wright's 'Fit Kids' and the Leeds Metropolitan University 'Fat Camps' reflect the need to redress the balance and encourage healthier, more active

Key terms

Health: the World Health Organization defines 'health' as a complete state of physical, mental and social well-being, and not merely the absence of disease.

Fitness: the ability to meet daily demands without undue fatigue.

Obesity: an excess proportion of total body fat, usually due to energy input exceeding energy output. For males this proportion is set at greater than 25% body fat and for females it is above 35% body fat.

lifestyles. To aid this process, the government is investing millions of pounds into school PE/sport with one key objective: to foster a culture of healthy physical activity from an early age and continue this into adulthood.

Initiatives promoting PE and school sport in the UK

In the UK, PE and school sport have traditionally been kept apart, but there has been a growing awareness of the need to bring the two closer together. A number of initiatives have been put in place to try to achieve this.

> **Key term**
>
> **Sports colleges:** part of the government's specialist schools programme, sport colleges are secondary schools that have achieved specialist status for sport.

> **Top tip**
>
> The best way to keep up to date with school PE/sport initiatives is via the Youth Sport Trust website (www.yst.org.uk). This includes information on the development of PESSCL into PESSYP (Physical Education, School Sport and Young People).

Physical Education, School Sport and Club Links (PESSCL)

The Physical Education, School Sport and Club Links (PESSCL) strategy contained a number of different 'sub-programmes' to help achieve its aim of increasing the uptake of sporting opportunities by 5–16 year olds so that at least 85% of them experienced of a minimum of 2 hours high-quality PE and school sport each week.

One of the key aspects of PESSCL was the development of specialist **sports colleges**. Sports colleges are key players in helping to deliver the government's targets for school PE and sport, as they are designed to provide high-quality sporting opportunities for young people in the community they serve. Sports colleges have the important aim of raising standards in PE and sport for all their students and are regional focus points for:

- promoting excellence in PE and sport in the community
- extending links between schools and the community they serve
- helping young people to progress on to careers in sport

Hundreds of 'school sport partnerships' have also been set up in England, seeking to improve opportunities for pupils to experience different sports, access high-quality coaching and engage in competition. In September 2004, the then Prime Minister Tony Blair announced that 'competition managers' would be added to the network of school sport partnerships to plan, manage and implement a programme of inter-school competitions across their school sport partnership.

Other key strands of PESSCL included:

- the Youth Sport Trust, a key organisation with responsibility for the development of school PE/sport. It is involved with many initiatives such as TOPs programmes, which support the delivery of National Curriculum PE particularly at primary school level.
- Sportsmark/Sports Partnership Marks — a reward scheme for good practice in PE/school sport.

- Step into Sport — a Youth Sport Trust coordinated scheme to increase the number of sports leaders in the 14–19 age range.

Five Hour Sport Offer

At the start of the twenty-first century, the government expressed a strong belief in the power of PE and sport to improve and enrich people's quality of life as well as improve the health and fitness of individuals and society in general. In 2007, Prime Minister Gordon Brown announced the 'Five Hour Sport Offer' — a £100 million campaign to give every child the chance of 5 hours of PE a week. The £100 million allocated was designed to fund:

- provision of up to 5 hours of sport per week for all pupils and 3 hours for young people aged 16–19
- a new National School Sports Week championed by Dame Kelly Holmes, when all schools will be encouraged to run school sports days/inter-school tournaments
- a network of 225 competition managers across the country to work with primary and secondary schools to increase the amount of competitive sport they offer

Lifelong learning

This is a key government policy, which aims to enable people to take part in physical activities that will improve their quality of life. It involves school PE departments offering more varied activities to encourage lifetime participation, such as aerobics and badminton.

> ## Tasks to tackle 5.2
>
> The government has set a number of PE/school sport targets, including a required minimum of 2 hours a week of National Curriculum PE for each child by 2008. Why might some schools find it difficult to make such provision?

UK participation/fitness levels

In 2002, UK Sport and Sport England released *Participation in Sport, Past Trends and Future Prospects*. This report showed that the number of people participating in sport in England was likely to fall by almost half a million by 2026 unless positive action was taken to address the situation. Using population projections for different age groups over three decades through to 2026, the research estimated how many people would be participating in sport in the future. The data predicted that if participation rates follow the same trends as they did between 1990 and 1996 for adults, and between 1994 and 1999 for young people, by 2026 the overall participation rate will have fallen from 52.5% to 46.3%.

Fitness levels among individuals in the UK have reached an all-time low according to a survey by gym chain LA Fitness. It published a poll in December 2007, which reported that over half of respondents could not touch their toes and nearly 70% could not manage to do 20 sit ups! Two thirds of those who participated in the survey confessed to not having done any 'fast paced' exercise such as running/cycling in the previous 12 months.

Sport England's new strategy to raise participation was launched in June 2008. It is committed to meeting various targets by 2012/13. These include:

Top tip

To find out more about sports you might be interested in pursuing visit www.activeplaces.com.

Tasks to tackle 5.3

Sporting Champions is a Sport England initiative that brings world-class athletes face to face with young people to inspire and motivate them to participate in sport.

Visit **www.sportingchampions.org.uk** then:
(a) explain what the scheme entails
(b) list its main aims

- one million more people doing sport
- a measurable increase in people's satisfaction with their experience of sport
- playing a key role in the delivery of the Five Hour Sport Offer for children and young people

In July 2008, Sport England welcomed the news that promoting participation in sport was one of the top 20 priorities for local authorities in England. This meant that millions of pounds would be invested by local authorities in sports provision, including training coaches, improving facilities and awareness of activities, and providing a range of activities for individuals to access.

The pursuit of sporting excellence in the UK

Individuals need to have the opportunity to achieve **excellence**. For many aspiring athletes, this opportunity is connected directly to the financial support available. Such support tends to initially come from parents, but more formal financial support systems have been put in place for aspiring athletes in their quest for excellence. These include the Talented Athlete Scholarship Scheme (TASS), the World Class Performance Programme, Lottery funds, sports college scholarships and SportsAid funding.

Key term

Excellence: describes a high/elite level of performance in sport.

In addition to financial support, aspiring performers also need appropriate provision for:
- top-level coaching
- high-quality facilities to train in
- sport science analysis, support, physiotherapy
- expert advice on personal life, career development

With appropriate finance and support systems in place, it is also important to develop the esteem of elite performers so that they strongly believe that they can compete with the best in the world and beat them. Specialist training camps and elite training groups bring like-minded individuals together and provide the high-level competitive opportunities necessary to develop such self belief and confidence.

UK Sport

UK Sport is the key organisation responsible for elite sport development in the UK, including for young people. It improves opportunity by funding elite-level athletes via NGBs and also via its 'no compromise' World Class Performance Programme, which enables performers to devote themselves full time to their sport in their quest for global sporting success.

In July 2007, UK Sport and SportsAid revealed a plan to offer support for emerging athletes across over 30 sports in the build-up to London 2012. From 2008, UK Sport and SportsAid allocated millions of pounds to Talented Athlete Scholarship Scheme (TASS) performers to maximise their sporting potential without compromising their academic careers.

UK Sports Institute (UKSI)

In the spring of 1999, UK Sport, the four home country sports councils and the Department for Media, Culture and Sport initiated the foundation of the UK Sports Institute (UKSI). This consists of 10 regional centres in England, with separate national centres in the home countries.

The UKSI network has been important in establishing world-class facilities for performers to train and compete in, along with provision of coaches, sports scientists and medical professionals. The UKSI network also coordinates research and development, drawing upon best practice from across the world and applying this to UK sports and elite athletes.

Case study activities

Cricket

Cricket was played in English villages from the early eighteenth century. From the start, social classes played together as a reflection of a village's class structure, with the gentry employing some workers specifically for their cricketing prowess. From an early stage there were also freelance professionals who played in a 'servant role' to their 'employer'. Such interest and patronage from the gentry led to the relatively early standardisation of rules. The first 'Articles of Agreement', for example, were written in 1727. Spectatorism and wagering at cricket matches were also evident from the latter half of the eighteenth century.

Cricket has long been associated with public schools as an inter-house/inter-school game, with professional coaches employed to raise standards and increase the prestige of the school via success in cricket fixtures.

In the late nineteenth century, county cricket took over as a spectator attraction from professional touring teams such as the William Clarke XI (see page 24). County committees accepted the need for professionals in the game of cricket but 'kept them in their social place'! There were, for example, separate travel, eating and changing arrangements for the different classes. The captain was typically a university educated 'amateur' man and there were clear distinctions

> **Mythology of the Ashes**
>
> On 19 August 1882, an Australian touring party had the audacity to defeat England at the Oval. Following the defeat, an obituary for English cricket was published in the *Sporting Times*. This included a statement that English cricket had died and 'the body will be cremated and the ashes taken to Australia'.
>
> The following winter saw the balance of power restored when England beat Australia in a three-match series 'down under'. Some female Australian supporters burnt a bail, placed the ashes in a small urn and presented them to the winning captain from England. Whenever cricketing rivalries are resumed between the two countries, the 'Ashes' are now at stake!

Twenty20's shorter game play and razzmatazz break with tradition

between the professionals (i.e. 'players') and amateurs (i.e. 'gentlemen'). The distinction between gentlemen and players was not abolished in English cricket until 1963.

New challenges are facing English cricket in the twenty-first century as the sport has increased its media profile and commercial attractiveness. This is particularly the case with twenty20 cricket (a 20-over per side variant of the longer game). The advent of an Indian Premier League/English Premier League in twenty20 cricket and Stanford's 'twenty20 for 20' (an annual match between England and the West Indies for a winner takes all $20 million) illustrate the tremendous earning potential of this form of cricket. However, many traditionalists view the relative demise of test match and county cricket as a threat to fair play and sportsmanship, regretting the win at all costs ethics linked to twenty20's high rewards.

Rugby league

The late nineteenth century saw an increasing need for professional rugby players, particularly in the north of England. Players could not afford to take time off work without payment, or afford to be injured and unable to earn a wage. So the game of rugby was split in two, with the Northern Football Union (formed in 1895) allowing official payments for loss of earnings, while southern clubs maintained their amateur tradition.

Rugby league is still very much dominated in England by northern clubs, but there have been attempts to spread its appeal. Creation of the Super League, for example, marked a switch in the playing season from winter to summer, allowing a better quality product away from the competition of football, in particular. The Super League brand expanded into a franchise system from 2009, including clubs in London, Wales and France, and has certainly created demand from television and sponsors.

Rugby union

By excluding manual workers in the late nineteenth century, the southern rugby clubs cemented the tradition that the game of rugby union was for gentleman amateurs only. Such a belief lasted for the next 100 years. The game only turned professional in 1995, so has only recently begun to exploit the commercial opportunities available to it.

England winning the World Cup in 2003 raised UK participation levels in the sport. In a BBC Sport Academy website survey following the World Cup success, 80% of respondents said that watching the event had made them want to play the game. The World Cup win also increased the earning potential of the game as a whole and its star performers, such as Jonny Wilkinson, in particular. The BBC Sport Rugby Union website reported a £10 million price tag for UK television rights to screen the World Cup and Wilkinson's potential earnings from sponsorship topping £20 million. Merchandising soared as a result of the win, with Nike replica England shirt sales up more than 200%.

Association Football

In 1863, public school old boys from Oxford and Cambridge Universities formed the Football Association (FA). Before this, the dribbling game of soccer and the handling game of rugby had existed together. The 'hackers and handlers' then moved away from the 'dribblers' to form the Rugby Football Union (RFU). At this time, soccer became both an amateur game for 'gentlemen' and a professional game for the working classes.

Football quickly became a regular spectator attraction on a Saturday afternoon with the foundation of the Football League in 1888 heralding the further development of football as a professional sport for the working classes, which the FA reluctantly accepted. The game was particularly popular in the northern industrial towns, as it could be played in the limited space available in the limited free time workers had on a Saturday afternoon. It was also relatively cheap to watch.

The public school old boys fought back against the wave of professionalism and working class dominance of soccer with 'amateur only' leagues, an amateur cup and amateur international fixtures. They were, however, fighting a losing battle.

As the influence of the cinema and, later, television grew in the post Second World War period, so did the status of the professional footballer as a sports and television personality who could sell commercial products. In 1951, Stanley Matthews received £20 a week from

The fees payed to football stars such as Cristiano Ronaldo are fuelled by television rights and commercial sponsorship deals

CWS (Cooperative Wholesale Society) for wearing the company's football boots — no mean amount of money in those days. Of course the 'new commercialism' in football looks very different from earlier versions. You could argue that the effects of commercial interests accelerated in England in the 1960s with the rise in popularity of television, the removal of the maximum wage for players and the successful hosting of the 1966 World Cup as a major global television event.

Today, billions watch the World Cup finals when they are staged every 4 years. The English Premiership is now viewed as the most successful league in the world, due in no small part to the riches on offer to players. Television companies such as Sky and Setanta paid $3.1 billion for the Premier League contract running from 2007/08–2009/10. Together with associated sponsorship deals, these sums make the Premier League a commercial success with vast global appeal.

Practice makes perfect

1 List different initiatives designed to increase participation in sport by school-aged children. *(3 marks)*

2 Creation of the UKSI is viewed as an important development in Team GB's successful Beijing Olympics where they reached fourth in the Olympic medal table. How are national institutes of sport such as the EIS helping in the development of elite performers? *(3 marks)*

3 Why did 'amateurs' have higher social status than professionals in nineteenth century Britain? *(2 marks)*

Sport in the USA

What you need to know

By the end of this chapter you should be able to:

- understand the historical and cultural context influencing the development of sport in the USA
- understand the current determinants of PE and sport in the USA, including geography, social aspects, sporting values and government policy at federal, state and local level
- understand the highly commercialised nature of sport in the capitalist system of the USA
- demonstrate knowledge and understanding of health, fitness and obesity levels among young people and the general population in the USA
- outline current initiatives to promote sport/outdoor education in schools and in the wider community and show how equality in participation is achieved in the USA
- explain the pathways available to professional sport, such as the college system, scholarships and the pro-draft system
- explain how the 'big four' American sports originated, evolved and developed into highly commercialised products in the twenty-first century

US sport in cultural context

Historical determinants

Following the Declaration of Independence in 1776, the American colonies achieved their objective of freedom and independence from Britain. The first independent American government was anxious to detach the new nation from the British elitist 'closed social class' system, which effectively excluded the majority of the population from advancing in society, as they did not possess the preferred social status.

> **Top tip**
> It is important to relate back to knowledge about the UK as you work through this section on the USA. Such comparisons *will* form the basis of questions in Unit 3.

As a 'new world' culture, the USA therefore pursued a policy of 'isolationism', distancing itself from the previous system of power to produce a new identity and escape from the imposition of British culture. Such isolationism spread into sport with the rejection, or at least marginalisation, of British sports such as cricket and rugby. There were many reasons for this:

- The games lacked popularity with Americans.
- Americans do not like the idea of a 'drawn game', which often happens in cricket.

The Super Bowl is an all-American, all-action spectacle

- The games lacked the dynamic/all-action spectacle Americans demand when watching sport.
- Many British sports reflected British middle class values/traditions, which did not suit Americans who tended to have a more egalitarian/individualistic philosophy.

Therefore, while sports such as cricket and rugby union are very much at the margins of American society, the big four sports of basketball, American football, baseball and ice hockey are highly promoted and at the forefront. American football developed from rugby and baseball developed from children's activities, such as rounders. Basketball was invented by James Naismith in 1891 as a competitive game to suit his nation's new world culture and independence.

The highly competitive nature of top-level sport in the USA can be seen as a reflection of 'frontierism' — the **pioneering spirit** that characterised the American migration west during the nineteenth century and which was epitomised by the way pioneers stood up to the harsh environment. The legacy of the frontier spirit has shaped the ideology of the USA today and is viewed as an important part of national character. Modern-day frontier spirit is reflected in toughness, endeavour and a strong work ethic. Sport is regarded as the 'last frontier' by many Americans and the frontier spirit can be seen reflected in the aggression and violence of American football and ice hockey.

Key terms

Frontier: an imaginary boundary between civilisation and areas unoccupied by pioneers.

Frontier/pioneer spirit: toughness, determination and rugged individualism — all needed to survive in an alien environment and now evident in modern-day American sports such as American football.

Geographical determinants of sport in the USA

The USA has a population of approximately 300 million, following rapid acceleration from 1850 onwards, and continues to grow with individuals from a variety of racial backgrounds. It is made up of 50 separate states and is vast in size (the whole of the UK is only about two thirds the size of the single state of California).

The USA has a population density of about 70 people per square mile. It contains some areas of 'wilderness' (i.e. uninhabited remote areas), but also others that are vast urban sprawls (such as Los Angeles) with serious pollution and congestion problems. The majority of the population live in cities and urban areas. Reflecting such contrasts, the large unpopulated areas of wilderness have helped to generate an interest in the **Great Outdoors**, while the densely populated areas have become hotbeds for the development of new world urban sports like American football and basketball.

North America covers a huge geographical range in terms of both latitude and altitude, creating a wide spectrum of climatic zones. It is very cold in Alaska but semi-tropical in Florida. The terrain also varies markedly, from wide, open plains to desert and high mountain ranges.

In comparison with the British, Americans are prepared to travel great distances across the vast country by car. This is helped by an advanced network of interstate highways and direct urban freeways. Interstate air travel is widely available, while, as in the UK, rail links are well established and played a key role in the early development of structured competitive sport from the late nineteenth century onwards.

> **Key terms**
>
> **Great Outdoors:** American term for the natural environment, such as the mountains, particularly where outdoor and adventurous activities can be pursued.
>
> **Federal:** a form of government or a country in which power is divided between one central and several regional governments.
>
> **Decentralisation:** the power base for government lies within the state and not with the central or federal government.

Government organisation

Following its emergence as an independent nation in the late eighteenth century, America founded a new government with a **federal** constitution, effectively creating a republic.

As a republic it has an elected President but, unlike the UK, it has never had a monarchy or privileged class with the power to determine or strongly influence opportunities available. There is also a tradition of self rule for each state made possible by the federal administration policy of **decentralisation**.

A federal constitution is where the powers of government are divided between national and state governments and decentralisation allows power to be distributed throughout the USA. This is reflected in the way education and sport are administrated.

> **Top tip**
>
> It is important to be aware that education in the USA is decentralised. There is also a strong link between decentralisation and capitalism. Such a distribution of power gives the opportunity for free enterprise, reflecting individual effort and offering rewards as 'appropriate' for such efforts.

Sport and commercialism

Professional sport is highly organised in America as a commercial industry. Most Americans have contact with professional sport via the medium of television, with major television companies screening hundreds of hours of sport on a daily basis.

America is a highly competitive capitalist society where individual endeavour is seen as a desirable characteristic. **Capitalism** drives both society and sport in America. For the most successful, in the highest profile sports, the 'Golden Triangle' (i.e. mutually beneficial link between sport, sponsorship and the media) means that fame and vast fortunes are attainable. For example, in late 2007, the New York Yankees agreed a deal with player Alex Rodriguez for $275 million over 10 years, with a multi-million dollar bonus written into the contract for breaking the all-time home run record as a Yankee.

Key terms

Capitalism: an economic system based on private ownership and free enterprise.

Discrimination: unfair treatment of an individual/section of society.

Hegemonic: when one social group dominates.

Top tip

See www.bankofamerica.com/sponsorship for more detail of the Bank of America's sponsorship of sport.

Multinational corporate sponsors pumped nearly $10 billion into sports sponsorship in 2007. The New England Patriots are among the top five American football teams in terms of sponsorship revenue and provide some representative statistics. The team's official bank is the Bank of America, its official soft drink is Pepsi and numerous other household names, all with official product endorsements, pay for an official link to such a prestigious product. In 2004, the Bank of America also became the first ever company to be recognised as the official bank of Major League Baseball.

Social determinants of sport in the USA

The world's population can be divided into different races, or ethnic groups. Some races stand in a position of superiority, for example in terms of economic attainment, and this may provoke ideas of racism towards other, 'inferior' races. When such beliefs lead to actual actions, racial **discrimination** occurs. In the UK and USA, white ethnicity forms the **hegemonic** group.

Stereotypical views, i.e. negative generalisations, may exist towards ethnic groups. For example, a stereotypical view might group all black sports performers together and suggest that black players are best suited to roles in a team requiring physical rather than mental qualities. For example, black players have been allocated in large numbers as running backs in American football and to outfield positions in baseball. The disproportionate concentration of ethnic minorities in certain positions in sports teams is known as stacking. This can exclude these groups from prestigious or judgement positions. Such pivotal positions are known as 'centrality' positions and require decision making and leadership, qualities ethnic minorities are stereotypically viewed as not possessing. Stacking is not as prominent in basketball, where centrality positions such as 'point guard' are frequently occupied by black players.

The objective measurement of success in sports like athletics, where there are clear winners, diminishes the possibility of racist opinions that may appear in more subjective activities. African-Americans have been channelled into sports such as athletics as well as American football, basketball and baseball. Consequently, these sports feature black role models who can motivate children of all ethnicities.

Historically, black people have not been channelled into sports like tennis and golf. However, Tiger Woods has destroyed the myth that black people cannot be elite golfers. Likewise, the Williams sisters have shattered the stereotypical view that black people are not able to succeed at tennis. Therefore, while centrality does exist, there are increasing opportunities for ethnic minorities to succeed in a wider variety of sports.

Values of sport in the USA

The USA is a democratic, capitalist nation where many ideologies (i.e. beliefs, values and attitudes) influence participation and progression in sport.

Provision of opportunity

As the **land of opportunity**, opportunity is theoretically available and open to all in America. Everyone is given the chance to succeed within the capitalist system, and freedom is given to all individuals to pursue the wealth and happiness that can be gained from capitalism. Individuals theoretically require only hard work, effort and sacrifice in order to achieve success.

'The American Dream' is a strong belief that happiness is secured through the generation of wealth. However, the pursuit of that dream has resulted in a highly competitive society, where failure to win results in dismissal. An example is the 'hire and fire' policy of employing sports coaches, whereby lack of success soon leads to dismissal.

Pluralistic versus hegemonic culture

As stated above, the USA believes itself to be the land of opportunity, but to what extent is this true? The decentralised distribution of power in the USA gives the opportunity for free enterprise and reflects individualism, allowing some institutions to become wealthier than others. The freedom to seek wealth actively is the whole idea of capitalism and is the perfect example of the spirit of the USA. However, the facts of actual wealth distribution in the USA tell a different story.

Some see the structure of the USA as reflecting **pluralism**.

Key terms

Land of opportunity: a name given to America because of the belief that anyone can 'make it big' in the USA. Sport can be a vehicle to bring success and wealth, and take someone from 'rags to riches'.

Pluralism: the theory that society is made up of several autonomous, but interdependent groups, each having equal power and with all opinions considered before decisions are made.

In a pluralistic society:

- no one particular group dominates
- each culture retains its own identity and cultural norms
- each culture has the opportunity to influence the operation of the country
- liberty, justice, equality and opportunity are freely available to all cultures and individuals

Others claim that the USA is hegemonic. Under this system:

- a single group dominates — in the USA this group is known as the **White Anglo Saxon Protestants (WASPs)**
- the dominant group controls the economy and political institutions
- the dominant group uses its influences to shape attitudes, values and cultural norms within society
- other groups become convinced that the dominant group is right and just, which spreads conformity throughout the whole society
- the dominant group tells everyone else that the country lives by, and supports, the pluralist image

Key terms

White Anglo Saxon Protestants (WASPs): this group dominates wealth in the USA. 40% of wealth is concentrated in 1% of the population, 31% by the next 9% and 29% by the bottom 90%.

Lifetime Sport: a sports initiative that focuses on sports that can be played into middle and older age.

Top tip

WASPs form a small hegemonic group, which nevertheless provides the focus for the rest of society and continues to perpetuate competition via the capitalist system.

Other sporting values that you need to be aware of include the **Lombardian ethic**, which emphasises winning as the main motive for participation. This 'win at all costs' attitude is named after Vince Lombardi, an American football coach during the 1960s who was famous for his motivational skills. He is credited with having said: 'Winning isn't everything; it's the only thing'. Lombardianism dominates in inter-scholastic, inter-collegiate and professional sport. It is often linked with profit-making and commercialism.

By contrast, the **counter-culture** approach has an anti-competitive focus and emphasises the intrinsic benefits that can be derived from sports participation. An extreme example is eco-culture, which involves fun and health promotion in the outdoor environment. This emphasis on participation as opposed to results is more like the traditional British approach.

Finally, the **radical ethic** can be seen as 'the middle way', with both winning and the process involved seen as important. This ethic prevails in intra-mural college games and is associated with **Lifetime Sport**, which is the equivalent of the UK Sport Council's Sport for All initiative.

Tasks to tackle 6.1

Many American team sports are violent in nature. Using examples from American football, explain how this links to American culture.

PE/school sport in the USA

The USA has a strong tradition of state autonomy and this is reflected in a decentralised education system — i.e. each state has control of its own education. Such decentralisation distributes control and gives power to the body that is directly in charge. This has the advantage of being more likely to meet the needs of each state as considerations of wealth and climate can be catered for. In the USA there are two types of high school: local public schools, where education is free, and private schools, which involve paying fees to attend. A high proportion of high school students progress to degree courses at college (around 75%, compared with less than 50% in the UK).

Unlike in the UK, the majority of schools in the USA do not train students for externally set exams, although some states have introduced a high school 'exit exam'. Completion of studies at high school to a 'pass standard' leads to the award of a High School Diploma, which is the accepted requirement for a college degree course.

The concept of a National Curriculum does not exist in the USA. There are a number of core subjects, with PE among them. Although there is an element of consultation within a school, PE programmes are designed and regularly inspected by a superintendent of the school board. The teacher is therefore accountable and is required to work through set programmes while assessing student performance.

At high school level there is a strong emphasis in the PE programme on delivering fitness and direct skill learning. This system of organisation allows for variations between schools and ensures that the programme is delivered effectively. However, while there is a framework for progression in place, the nature of this focus restricts opportunities for 'creative teaching' or any inclusion of counter-culture activities (see above).

PE assessments are mainly of a practical nature, linked to skills and fitness levels, with a written input into the final assessment for the purpose of the High School Diploma. Fitness testing tends to suit a culture that is based on objectivity and a determination to excel.

Top tip

In one sense, the USA school system is similar to that in the UK, where local authorities have some input. However, teachers in the USA do not have the same amount of freedom as British teachers in choosing their teaching programme. The superintendent of the local school board draws up a programme, which the teachers implement. Thus at local level it is more centralised.

Top tip

Until around the mid-1970s, daily PE lessons were compulsory for all ages in USA schools. Today, this is not necessarily the case. PE teachers in the USA are separate from sports coaches and generally have a lower status.

The decline of school PE in the USA

PE is facing something of a crisis in the USA. Following abolition of military conscription in 1970, all states became less stringent in enforcing compulsory PE. At the turn of the century in 2000, Illinois was the only state enforcing the subject, but since then it has withdrawn this policy. Millions of dollars are saved each year by making PE optional, particularly in grades 11 and 12 (i.e. for 16–17 year olds).

PE in the USA faces competition from other 'more academic' subjects for curriculum time, particularly with the need to effectively prepare children for state achievement tests.

In 2006, a survey of PE coordinators in the education agencies of all 50 states and the District of Columbia (i.e. the Washington DC area) was conducted by the National Association for Sport and Physical Education (NASPE) and American Health Association. Its findings illustrate the low status of PE in many schools in the USA, with consequent health and obesity issues. For example:

- a number of states have no laws requiring any PE classes in elementary, middle and high schools, for example Colorado and Wyoming
- most states do not set a specific time allocation for PE
- 12 states allowed PE credits to be earned via online classes, with no real accountability for students being active and actually learning skills

The President's Council on Physical Fitness and Sports currently quotes a range of physical activity statistics (see: www.fitness.gov/resources_factsheet.htm) from publications prepared for the US Department of Health and Human Services. These include the fact that 16% of children and teenagers (aged 6–19) were overweight in 1999–2002, which was triple the amount in 1980. Equally as worrying was the fact that 25% of US children spent over 4 hours watching television on a daily basis and were therefore at particular risk of developing obesity as they grew older. In addition, only 28% of students in grades 9–12 participated in daily school PE in 2003, which was down from 42% in 1991.

The participation rate in PE for all students was about 70% in the 1980s but fell to below 60% by the turn of the century. The greatest decline was beyond sixth grade as pupils progressed on to Junior High. Such a decline led to a warning by NASPE that PE is now being seen as an expensive luxury rather than a necessity.

The decline in the amount of PE and consequent engagement in physical activity has raised many concerns about health and fitness levels. Indeed, obesity concerns are increasing in all affluent countries. Low levels of fitness and obesity in teenagers has been an ongoing issue in the USA since military recruitment was made necessary in 1942. In 2003, 44 million Americans were registered as obese, which was an increase of 74% in 10 years.

Strategies to improve school PE

Some strategies are now being put in place to try to reverse the decline of PE and improve the quality of pupils' timetabled PE experiences, which many including the NASPE believe to be essential for the promotion and living of healthy active lifestyles. Tens of millions of dollars have been invested into a programme called Physical Education for Progress (PEP). Local school districts and community organisations can access grant funds to promote activities, develop the curriculum, purchase equipment and train teachers to deliver PE more effectively.

One interesting, but slightly controversial, initiative was the McDonald's 'Passport to Play' scheme. Launched in 2005, this initiative centred on a PE programme for third through to fifth graders, which included games and activities from around the world. McDonald's claimed that 31 000 public elementary schools with 7 million students signed up for the scheme in 2005. The initiative came at a time when nearly a third of all children aged 6–19 were classified as overweight or at risk of becoming so. Some of the blame for this childhood obesity epidemic has been assigned to fast-food diets. Many were critical of the involvement of McDonald's in such an initiative, but others pointed to the possible advantages (such as marketing power) and to the quality of the product. Passport to Play has the support of NASPE, which had an input into the development of the new programme.

Equality in PE and sport in the USA

The USA has a very active policy of sports provision for different sections of society, particularly for disabled individuals. Federal law states that PE must be provided for students with special needs and disabilities. The provision made for these children is called 'adapted physical education' and involves diverse programmes that have been modified to enable full participation. In order to raise the quality of experience while at the same time increasing awareness of disability, pupils with special needs are integrated into the mainstream high school curriculum.

Title IX

Title IX was passed as law in 1972 and is an example of central legislation (i.e. it was government imposed). It addressed the issue of gender equality in all areas of education. In terms of sport, the law was not primarily concerned with opening up the traditional male-dominated physical contact activities like American football to more female participation. Instead it focused on participation for women in general. Although it was a general entitlement, Title IX focused on sports opportunities rather than daily PE at high school and college.

Prior to Title IX, opportunities were severely restricted for female inter-scholastic and inter-collegiate sports participation. Indeed, women's sport was segregated and often confined to inferior facilities. **Athletic** scholarships for women were rare. As a result, men tended to believe that women would lower the status of sport and they perceived competitive sport as 'unfeminine' and lacking in dignity.

> **Key term**
>
> **Athletic:** in the USA, the term athletic is used to describe high-level competitive sport and is synonymous with the Lombardian ethic.

The necessary upgrading of women's facilities has inevitably impacted positively on the curriculum subject. It certainly led to a dramatic increase in female participation in sport among girls at American high schools. In 1971 (the year before Title IX) there were 294 015 girls participating in sports across the USA, compared with 2 990 836 in 2002.

TopFoto

Top tip

Title IX was highly influential in increasing female participation. It led to hundreds of lawsuits and civil rights complaints being settled in the favour of women, resulting in many women's teams being reinstated where they were due to be cut, as well as equal pay for female sports coaches.

Women's soccer is hugely popular in the USA

Title IX has increased standards in women's sports, with raised performance levels in soccer and track and field widely celebrated by American society.

Critics of Title IX claim that money used to support women has been taken directly from men and that minority sports are being withdrawn from high schools and colleges for political and financial reasons.

Extra-curricular sport in US high schools

In contrast to the provision of daily PE, **inter-mural** (or inter-scholastic) sport in the USA is very strong. Most major sports are represented in high schools, with an emphasis on American football, basketball and baseball for boys, and track and field, volleyball and soccer for girls. The State High School Athletic Association (SHSAA), a national advisory body with branches in each state, controls inter-scholastic athletic competition.

Specialist coaches and assistant coaches are employed to take charge of school teams and are accountable to the athletic director of the school. The athletic director manages both

Key terms

Inter-mural: organised sport programmes between different schools/colleges.
Intra-mural: organised sport programmes within a school/college.

Top tip

For exam questions, it is important that you are aware of the contrasts between sport/PE in the USA and the UK. In the UK, for example, PE has high status as a compulsory National Curriculum subject while extra-curricular sport has been in decline.

OCR A2 Physical Education

overall PE and inter-scholastic sport. High school sport has a high status, with thousands of spectators attending fixtures played in high-class facilities. It is keenly followed by the local community. It is also expensive and is paid for by gate receipts, sponsorship, media payments and alumni donations (i.e. funds from past students/friends of an institution).

Certain schools, such as Mission High in Texas, have a strong tradition in sport and are seen as centres of sports excellence, operating as the first step in progressing individuals towards more elite levels. There is a strong tradition of Lombardianism in school sport with coaches fired if the team is unsuccessful. Players also have a strong desire to win as college athletic scholarships are on offer.

It is evident that American ideologies are very much reflected in inter-scholastic sport. There is opportunity for all to play and excel, but only the elite performers with a strong desire to win achieve athletic scholarships, bringing professional status and the ultimate 'American Dream' a step closer. While school and college sport is the main route to a career in professional sport, it should be noted that it is very elitist with only 3% moving from school to college teams and in basketball only 1 player in 10 gets into the pro-draft (see pages 81–82).

> **Key term**
>
> **Athletic scholarship:** a grant of free education given by a college/university to top performers only. The talented student follows an 'academic course' but is virtually contracted to play sport for the college, which can involve many hours of training and playing matches each week.

Intra-mural sport does exist and is where players of a 'lower standard' play for fun. It is very low profile and often occurs late at night after the college teams have finished their training.

Outdoor education

Several youth agencies, such as the YMCA, sponsor outdoor activities and some schools offer programmes of 'low-risk' adventure. Outward Bound, Project Adventure and Wilderness Encounter are examples of packaged adventure programmes that have become popular. The Outward Bound Association is the largest of these organisations and works together with senior high schools to offer wilderness experiences and proficiency courses in outdoor skills and leadership.

Summer camps for young people

Since the mid-twentieth century, the number of camp schools for young people has significantly increased. These camps take place in the summer holiday and can last from just a few days to up to eight weeks. There are different types of camps, such as:

- state-sponsored camps for the underprivileged — these enable poor children to have a basic outdoor experience and aim to give inner-city children a break from the urban environment
- sports camps and outdoor adventure camps
- special needs camps — for those with learning or physical disabilities, or for people who are overweight (known as 'fat camps')
- camps sponsored by businesses, or ethnic or religious groups

- commercial camps — these can be expensive (run on a profit-making basis) and are therefore only available to rich families. This exclusivity reflects the discriminatory nature of a capitalist economy such as the USA.

Children working as a team on an obstacle course at an adventure summer camp in Connecticut, USA

To ensure the widest opportunity for participation there are 12000 camps in the USA: 8000 are residential, while 4000 are day camps. A camp is chosen on the basis of the experience required by the child and on what a parent can afford to pay. The most popular specialist activity camps include outdoor adventure and sports camps. Most camps have a mission to continue a patriotic culture, for example a bugle sounding the morning waking call, and the stars and stripes flag formally unfurled and displayed. Evening sees campfire rituals enjoyed by the children. Such features reflect a military ethos and the spirit of frontierism, both of which underpin national pride.

Tasks to tackle 6.2

(a) How do American high schools influence the development of sports talent?

(b) Give reasons to account for the lack of status given to PE in American high schools.

(c) Why has female participation in US high schools significantly increased since the late twentieth century?

(d) Explain possible benefits a child might gain as a result of attending an American summer camp.

National fitness levels and rates of participation in the USA

The USA has a low emphasis on mass participation for adults. Instead, there is a danger that it is becoming more of a spectator society. In 2006, the National Center for Health Statistics stated that just over 30% of adults engaged in regular leisure time physical activity, meaning that around 70% did not. Only three in ten adult Americans get the recommended amount of physical activity (i.e. 30 minutes, five times a week, of pulse-raising, aerobic activity).

Such inactivity is a major contributory factor to the development of heart conditions. Heart disease is now the leading cause of death among men and women in the USA. Obesity is another associated major health issue, with nearly 60 million Americans classified as obese and 108 million classified as either obese or overweight. Therefore, 60% of Americans carry an unhealthy amount of excess weight.

It is important to be aware that there is very little provision by amateur sports clubs to enable general participation in a variety of activities. Where provision does exist, memberships are expensive. This contrasts directly with the strong tradition of voluntary sports club provision in the UK where the emphasis is on providing opportunities for club members to participate, with fees set to cover costs rather than profit being the motive.

Contemporary initiatives/strategies to promote participation in the USA

- The President's Challenge is a 6-week programme designed to challenge all Americans to make physical activity part of their everyday lives. The 'Challenge' includes the 'Presidential Active Lifestyle Award' for performing regular activity beyond the daily activity goals set for each individual.

   See www.presidentschallenge.org for more detail on this initiative.

- USA Swimming's Make a Splash initiative attempts to decrease the disparity in overall swimming participation between different ethnic groups.
- In ice hockey, the OneGoal initiative attempts to increase the understanding and awareness of youth hockey so that people will find it less intimidating to participate in the sport or join a club.
- Midnight Basketball Leagues were set up on outdoor asphalt surfaces with a key aim of improving/controlling behaviour and increasing physical activity among inner-city ethnic minorities in particular. The success of this scheme has led to the African-American domination of basketball in the USA.

Tasks to tackle 6.3

(a) Give reasons why Midnight Basketball Leagues have been established in American inner cities.

(b) What are the main reasons for the lack of participation in sports by the general population in the USA?

The pursuit of sporting excellence in the USA

Little League

Little League involvement is very popular and caters for 7–16 year olds. Sports teams involved in Little Leagues, which form the foundation of most American sports, are coached and managed mainly by volunteers such as parents. While there is a strong moral philosophy, with an emphasis on safety, the Lombardian ethic is evident from the outset. Some specialist coaches are used to raise standards of performance and increase the chances of success. Little League formats reflect the professional game, for example the mini 'Super Bowl' finals; these inspire competition and attract interest from sponsors and the media.

The Little League promotes competitive sport from an early age

Pathways to professional sport

In 1906, the National Collegiate Athletic Association (NCAA) was established to control and create order in **collegiate** sport. The system of inter-collegiate sport became based on a number of divisions, as follows:

OCR A2 Physical Education

- **Division 1** is for top-level performers and is run as an entertainment and a business. Training is given for professional and high-level amateur sport, such as the Olympics.
- **Division 3** is for small institutions where sport is an integral part of students' lives.
- **Division 2** is a transition ground between the two. The lack of an effective club structure in the USA makes the college route an important one for individuals wishing to pursue a career in sport.

Athletic scholarships in most major sports are available to elite high school performers so they can progress on to colleges in the USA. A scholarship is worth upwards of around $10 000 a year, with this amount granted by the college to pay for meals, accommodation and tuition fees. They are binding contracts, which require the recipient to train for long hours and play sport for the college.

Athletic associations govern college sports and set the rules governing scholarships. It has been apparent over the years that college administrators have enrolled students who are excellent players but who lack academic qualities. Such leniency in recruitment allows a college to compete and remain at the highest sporting levels to maintain their commercial viability. The NCAA has stated that 20% of football and basketball players enter through 'special admit' programmes. These allow students to attend a college and follow a course because of their sporting prowess, despite not having the necessary qualifications.

Problems in varsity sport occur when coaches, in their quest for success, exert excessive pressure on students and sport loses its value as an educational process. Problems can also arise when media rights to games are bought and sold, so that the academic progress of players becomes less of a consideration than profit.

College athletes do not complain about the scholarship system, which critics view as exploitation, for a number of reasons:

- The opportunity to play college sports is a dream come true for many, giving the chance to perform in front of many thousands of people.
- There is honour and social status for an athlete attending a major university.
- Most athletes have been conditioned from an early age to willingly accept the disciplined/conformist approach necessary for sports success and experienced at college.
- The prize of entering the pro-draft is a huge motivator.

The pro-draft system acts as the bridge between the college system and professional leagues. Professional clubs choose the best college performers when they become available on graduation. Professional teams in each of the major professional

Tasks to tackle 6.4

(a) What are the benefits to children of taking part in 'Little League' sports in the USA?

(b) Why might a successful American high school performer accept a scholarship at an American college despite little financial benefit, and high demands being placed on them?

(c) How does the USA's college system of sport develop sports excellence?

sports are ranked at the end of each season. Ranks are also given to outstanding college players. The lowest ranked club has the first choice of the highest ranked players so that, theoretically at least, some form of parity is maintained in American sport.

Equality and discrimination in American pro-sport

Segregation and inequality have been features of organised sport since the nineteenth century. Black players were excluded from Major League Baseball until 1947, but since this time gradual integration has occurred. To understand the reasons for such exclusion it is necessary to be aware that American society is organised not only by wealth but also by race.

Being the first group to become established in the 'New World', the WASPs have retained domination and form the controlling hegemonic group. After African-American players had broken into white professional sport in the 1950s, a period of **tokenism** followed. As we have already seen, when more black players entered professional sport, they were stacked into positions that required physical, rather than decision-making, skills (see pages 70–71).

Further integration and a more even positional distribution have taken place in the twenty-first century. Major League Baseball now has 20% African-American players, while the National Football League has 70%. Only about a fifth of players registered with the National Basketball Association are white, which represents an exit of WASPs from the game. The exit of white players in basketball is termed **white flight**.

It would appear that American ideologies of having freedom and the opportunity to pursue the American Dream are becoming increasingly available to women and ethnic minorities in sport. Success in sport has become significant to ethnic minorities in their pursuit of the **glass ceiling**.

The ability and potential of ethnic minorities to achieve success in sport is reinforced through the achievements of role models such as the Williams sisters, Tiger Woods, Michael Jordan and many more. Increased belief and self esteem has resulted in those from ethnic minority groups now having the confidence and motivation to strive for recognition in sports, including those that were traditionally seen as the preserve of the dominant white cultural group.

> **Key terms**
>
> **Tokenism:** a limited number of vacancies were made available to African-American players so that a non-discriminatory policy could be claimed.
> **White flight:** white players have withdrawn from the game of basketball in America, which is increasingly perceived as belonging to African-Americans.
> **Glass ceiling:** the imaginary level to which certain groups aspire.

Case study activities

There are four major sports popular in the USA: American football, basketball, baseball and ice hockey. Sport in these instances has become big business and athletes are marketed as assets who can help to generate funds and advertise products through their skills, showmanship and positive health images. These sports are packaged and presented to the public. They tend to be loud, brash, energetic and involve huge production costs — a show as much as a game!

Baseball

In comparison with the other three major sports, baseball is not a 'territorial' game and is not governed by time. Its roots are rural, it has a slower pace and more of an individual focus. It is thought to have evolved from the game of rounders, though it has left this game far behind in the modern-day sports world. It began as a working-class sport and developed in inner cities; as such, it has parallels with soccer in England, with more aggressive supporters than are found in American football.

American football

American football sums up the country's character: technological, territorial, violent and intimidating, displaying a team effort and individual specialisation. It originated from the game of rugby in Britain, but developed along different lines in its new culture. It developed further in America's elite colleges and universities and was therefore historically seen as a middle-class game. Its development reflected America's attempts to develop a new identity, separate from Europe, and the game was influenced by many different cultures. American football has never been constrained by amateur traditions and the 'win ethic' emerged along-side professionalism.

Basketball

Basketball has more potential for improvisation than either baseball or American football due to its fluidity of play. Players are free to execute their own individuality and

can perform cunningly deceptive moves. It was deliberately created, rather than gradually evolving (like baseball from rounders and American football from rugby), by James Naismith to channel young men's energies and develop their moral character. Basketball has more recently become a symbol of black identity and social power.

Ice hockey

Ice hockey is the most violent of team games — fighting is part of the action, and is expected by the crowd! The physical speed of the game and the use of sticks have made it fast and brutal. Team members play in a confined area with highly vocal supporters close to the playing area. In contrast to basketball, ice hockey is predominantly a white game.

Ice hockey is fast and brutal

Beyond the big four

Soccer is striving to become the fifth big game in America and attendances are starting to increase with the 'Beckham influence' increasing its media profile and sponsorship opportunities. One reason for its relative lack of popularity is the concept of **sport space**. However, in a market of around 300 million people it is difficult to see why soccer has not gained a higher profile. One possible reason for this could be that soccer has lost its compatibility with a 'new world' culture, which has long since shaken off its colonial roots.

Practice makes perfect

1 How have 'cultural factors' influenced the development of professional sport in America? *(4 marks)*

2 How does extra-curricular sport differ between the USA and the UK? *(4 marks)*

3 Explain how the nature of professional sport deters participation in the USA. *(5 marks)*

4 Give reasons why ethnic minority achievement in sport is increasing in the USA. *(4 marks)*

Chapter 7

Sport in Australia

What you need to know

By the end of this chapter you should be able to:

- understand the historical and cultural context influencing the development of sport in Australia, particularly the concept of the UK as its 'motherland'
- understand the current determinants of PE and sport in Australia, including geography, social aspects, government policy and sporting values such as the legacy of 'bush culture' and 'land of the fair go'
- understand how sport in Australia has become increasingly commercialised
- demonstrate knowledge and understanding of sport participation levels among young people and the general population in Australia, and in Victoria in particular
- outline current initiatives to promote sport and outdoor education in schools and in the wider community, for example SEPEP and PASE
- understand the structure and functions of the Australian Institute of Sport (AIS) and national strategies to encourage excellence
- explain how cricket, rugby league, rugby union, association football and Australian rules football have originated, evolved and developed into highly commercialised products in the twenty-first century

Australian sport in cultural context

Background information

The British established a colony in Australia in 1788. Independence from the UK was gained in 1901. Unlike the USA, however, Australia has maintained its links with its former **motherland** and throughout the country there is continued evidence of colonial roots. Many aspects of its education system, sports ethos and general traditions, for example, are similar to those of the UK. The monarch of England is still Australia's Chief of State.

Colonial links to the past mean that sporting relations between the UK and Australia are still close, with regular Test series in sports such as cricket, rugby league and rugby union.

Key term

Motherland: term used to describe one's country of birth or a country that is the source of one's structures, values, etc. The term generally has positive overtones but in the context of colonialism often has an underlayer of antagonism. Australia particularly loves to beat its 'motherland', England, at sport (i.e. 'Pommie bashing').

Australia has a federal parliament based in the capital city of Canberra with an elected Prime Minister as Head of Parliament selecting a ministerial cabinet. Three levels of government exist:

- central government at a federal level
- six states and two territories (state governments all take an active role in promoting sport and PE through set policies and programmes)
- local government in each state (the local level plays an important role in delivering initiatives such as 'Active Australia', meeting the needs and interests of its local community)

Top tip

It is important to understand that unlike those who emigrated to the USA, the British who settled in Australia readily continued traditional sports from the 'old country' such as cricket and rugby, which gained a firm foothold.

Australia has a decentralised system of government, giving autonomy to each state. This means that provision for sport, education and PE, as well as sport in the community, is different in each state.

Twenty-first century Australia aspires to be an inclusive, pluralistic society. Its ideology focuses on being a democratic and capitalist society of the 'Western model'. A strong egalitarian ethos is present. It is considered as a 'land of opportunity' as epitomised in the phrase 'land of the fair go' (i.e. everyone has a chance to succeed). Australia has a strong sense of nationalism and sporting success is greatly valued by its patriotic population.

Climatic conditions in Australia are highly favourable and support outdoor activities in all seasons. This, combined with a reputation for encouraging community participation in all forms of sport, has resulted in a sports-obsessed nation. Australia has over 120 national sports organisations, and it is estimated that around a third of its population are registered members of sports clubs.

Sport in Australia is used to try to shed the image of 'bush culture'. 'Bush' or 'outback' is the name given to the wilderness areas of the continent. The concept of bush culture links to nineteenth-century frontier ideals of individuality and ruggedness — created when early settlers explored the outback — which led to male domination and gender discrimination. Such an image of Australia does not fit its more egalitarian, twenty-first-century ethos.

Transport systems in Australia are well developed, with an extensive network of roads along the coast, modernised train services and internal air transport systems. The development of satellite television has allowed access to previously remote areas and sports coverage from all around the world.

With the advent of such technological developments in the media, Australian sports have become increasingly commercialised as sponsors have grown more interested in using sport to promote their products. As a result of increased television and sponsor interest, more and more sports have turned professional and new organisations have been set up to cater for such developments (for example, the Australian Football League and National Soccer League).

A number of private sports management companies have emerged, such as International Management Group (IMG), to secure sponsorship deals, advise on marketing strategies, and negotiate television rights and endorsement contracts.

Geographical determinants

Australia is a 'young' country. The population is growing at a rate of 1.4% a year and hit 21 million in 2007. Most Australians are descended from colonial era settlers and pre-federation immigrants from Europe. According to the Australian Bureau of Statistics, in mid-2006 there were 4 956 863 residents from outside Australia, partly due to government-sponsored emigration from the UK in the mid-twentieth century, which made 'Brits' by far the biggest immigrant group. The influx of individuals from the UK as well as other European nations brought a tradition of soccer to Australia, which has now got over some early problems and is increasing in popularity.

The population of Australia is relatively small and largely settled around eight cities — around 85% of its population live in just over 3% of the nation's land area. Though it is a vast and diverse country, the majority of Australians live on low-lying coastal plains around the south and east coast. These areas have a temperate climate that is highly favourable for sports in the outdoors. It also means that a large percentage of the Australian population lives close to thousands of miles of coastline, providing free and accessible facilities for a range of activities.

TopFoto

Young people learn lifeguarding skills on Bondi Beach

It is important to understand the size of Australia. Vast distances separate the eight major cities. This gave problems for the initial development of sport in the nineteenth century before communication and transport systems improved.

PE and school sport in Australia: a case study of Victoria

PE is compulsory in all Australian schools, although there is variation in content and scheduling across the states. The education department in each state is responsible for all educational matters, though in the case of PE and school sport the education department often works closely with the state's department of sport and recreation.

Following a government examination of participation patterns in the late twentieth century into declining standards of skill and fitness levels, changes have taken place in the delivery of PE and sport in schools. Victoria state responded to the government enquiry by setting up the Victoria School Sports Unit to introduce strategies and ensure that programmes were being delivered effectively. The unit operates within the Department of Education and is controlled by the state government. PE and sport education programmes were made compulsory for pupils up to Year 10 and included the Curriculum Standards Framework, which comprises eight compulsory 'key learning areas' to be delivered to pupils up to Year 10.

Top tip

Australian school education is the responsibility of the state government, not federal government.

Sport Education and Physical Education Project (SEPEP)

Edith Cowan University in Western Australia presented a model as a suggested guide to the teaching of physical activities, called the Sport Education and Physical Education Project (SEPEP).

SEPEP is a 'loose' framework. Although it provides a structure and is available to all throughout the Australian PE system, it forms only a small part of curriculum delivery. Teachers are free to adapt and innovate their own programmes to accommodate variations in the ability of pupils, teaching environments and the specific expertise of a PE department.

SEPEP places an emphasis on intra-school and inter-school competition, as well as broadening the range of activities experienced as pupils mature. In primary schools (Years 1–6), the focus is on increasing competence in fundamental motor skills as opposed to games strategies. The logic of this approach is that if skill levels are developed, children will enjoy participating and become less likely to withdraw from sport in later life.

Sports played in Years 7 and 8 tend be of a traditional nature, for example, football, cricket and netball, with a variety experienced across the four-term year. Sports are initially played on an intra-school basis with progression on to inter-school competition in the final few weeks of term. Matches between local schools take place in school time and include all children in order to maximise participation. They are played on a 'round robin' basis with the most successful schools qualifying for the state finals (i.e. progression to a higher level). Selection for state teams begins at inter-school level.

Further motivation to participate comes from the possibility of selection for the Pacific School Games, which take place every 4 years and involve thousands of able bodied and disabled pupils from primary and secondary schools. These Games serve to encourage participation and achievement in education and sport.

> **Top tip**
> SEPEP is a suggested framework for PE in Australia and can be adapted by teachers. Unlike in the UK, there is no National Curriculum PE or OFSTED inspection service. Teachers therefore have professional autonomy.

Inter-school sport continues during Years 9–10, but traditional sports give way to allow more choice, including the possibility of pursuing activities such as aerobics, surfing and badminton. Electives are available to broaden experiences and prepare older pupils for active leisure. This trend is continued for senior pupils who can become involved in administration, coaching and officiating.

Australian schools emphasise enjoyment and maximise participation, as illustrated by the 'Active Australia/More Active Australia' initiative (see page 92), which encourages participation by as many people as possible and has its foundations in teacher-delivered skill-based PE programmes.

One programme that influences PE/sport for young people in Australia is the 'Victoria model' which has a number of important features:

- 100 minutes of compulsory PE each week
- 100 minutes of compulsory sport education each week
- all school teams play in school time
- government schools can access further training free of charge

Sport education in Australia is non-elitist. Pupils who demonstrate a high level of talent are directed towards club participation. In addition, the Department of Education has implemented a 'Sports Linkage' policy involving schools and clubs sharing facilities to benefit the wider community.

Fitness standards are assessed in secondary schools via tests designed by the Australian Council for Health, Physical Education and Recreation (ACHPER). ACHPER researches and develops health-based initiatives and school programmes to improve participation standards in PE/sport.

Results showing a percentile reading in relation to the rest of Australia enable personal goals to be set rather than making direct comparisons within a class of pupils. The main reason for testing is to promote healthy lifestyles and educate pupils in ways of improving fitness. At one time, these fitness statistics were monitored by the Australian Institute of Sport (AIS) and those with exceptional readings were selected for special training. This process of 'Sports Search' was particularly effective for endurance-based events such as rowing but was less effective in predicting games potential.

The Victoria School Sports Unit also commits to the training of non-specialist teachers. Primary school teachers tend to take courses in PE, while secondary teachers focus more on sport education professional development. Courses are intensive and are placed under the all-embracing title of **Physical and Sport Education (PASE)**. All such professional development is financed through the government. High-quality online resources share good practice in teaching and provide further support for staff.

Forty schools in Victoria have earned the status of government **exemplary schools**. Teachers from these schools deliver professional development and share good practice with neighbouring institutions. Grants are given to cover the cost of teacher release and there is considerable prestige associated with such 'exemplary' status.

Victoria has committed to raising the profile of PE and sport. Indeed, teachers themselves raise their own profiles as role models by engaging in the Teachers Games. These are residential competitive sports experiences, but their main aim is to provide network opportunities and endorse the participation ethic (participation is the main focus in Australian PE/sports education).

Victoria acknowledges its high achievers in sport with awards for fair play. For example, the de Coubertin awards are presented to students who have made an outstanding contribution to administration, coaching and other important roles beyond that of a participant. The award reflects the original spirit of the modern Olympics that taking part is more important than winning.

Examples of other sport/PE initiatives include the following:

- The Schools Network was set up for schools across Australia that share an interest in the contribution of sport and physical activity to the overall health and well-being of young people and communities. Over a thousand schools are involved. They aim to improve the quality of their sport and PE programme, improve links to the community, provide opportunities outside of the scheduled classes and create a school environment that supports and encourages sport and physical activity.

- The Active After-School Communities programme is a national initiative that provides primary school-aged children with access to free, structured physical activity programmes in the after-school time slot of 3 p.m.–5 p.m. It encourages traditionally non-active children to engage in structured physical activities and involves them more with sports clubs.

- Aussie Sport was developed by the Australian Sports Commission (ASC) in 1986 to overcome the lack of games skills in youngsters and improve their participation in sport, for example via the use of modified games such as Netta Netball.

Outdoor education in Victoria

Outdoor activities are the 'norm' in Australia, with its highly favourable climate and concentration of population near to the coast. Schools generally have good facilities, including playing fields, swimming pools and outdoor gymnasia. Swimming is a very popular sport with a high emphasis placed on it in the school curriculum.

There is a high level of interest in the international Outward Bound movement and the Duke of Edinburgh scheme. However, outdoor education relies on government support and staff goodwill and initiative.

There are different types of residential centre operating in Australia. These include:

- Outdoor Schools — extensions of classrooms where students get first-hand experiences of the natural environment
- Environmental Centres — focusing on environmental studies
- Outdoor Pursuit Centres — containing field centres and the opportunity for students to participate in a wide range of outdoor and adventurous activities

> **Tasks to tackle 7.2**
>
> **(a)** Summarise the key features of the Sport Education and Physical Education Project (SEPEP).
>
> **(b)** Give examples of PE/school sport strategies and initiatives in Australia.

Mass participation in Australia

Federal government figures suggest that there are 6.5 million registered 'players' in Australia affiliated to over 30 000 sports clubs, indicating a good basis for long-term participation. The **Australian Sports Commission (ASC)** and state government agencies responsible for sport and recreation annually collect information on participation patterns in the 15+ age group. This is achieved via the Exercise, Recreation and Sport Survey (ERASS). In 2006, 66% of people aged 15 and over (i.e. 10.9 million) participated in exercise at least once a week, with 42.8% participating in sport three or more times a week. The three most popular activities were walking, fitness activities like aerobics and swimming.

> **Key term**
>
> **Australian Sports Commission (ASC):** the Australian government body that manages, develops and invests in sport at all levels.

When Australia experienced a dismal Olympics in Montreal in 1976 there was a clear need to develop a national sports policy for all levels from mass participation to sports excellence. An important part of this new policy was the creation of the ASC. The purpose of the ASC is to administer and fund sport nationally on behalf of the federal government. It is central to an integrated national sports policy, which encourages sport and physical activity for all

Australians. As such, it works closely with a range of national sporting organisations, state and local governments, schools and community organisations to ensure sport is well run and accessible to all. Administration of the ASC is based in Canberra at the AIS Bruce Campus. The ASC has spread its operations throughout Australia with close to 60 Active After-School Communities offices across the country.

The ASC's current framework is its Strategic Plan 2006–09. There are a number of 'critical result areas' against which it assesses the implementation of the plan. These include:

- sustained achievements in high-performance sport by Australian teams and individuals
- maintaining the AIS as a world centre of excellence for the training and development of elite athletes
- growth in sports participation at grass-roots level, particularly in youngsters, indigenous Australians, women and people with disabilities
- increasing opportunities for children to be physically active
- increasing adoptions of fair play, self improvement and achievement

Sport is widely recognised in Australia as an integral part of life and the Australian government provides funding for sport as an investment in the community, both at grass-roots level and through to the elite level. The AIS has a key responsibility for the training and development of elite performers, while the Sport Performance and Development Group has responsibility for increasing participation. It has resulted in a number of innovative programmes.

More Active Australia

This initiative has been developed with the aim of increasing participation at grass-roots level via PE programmes and initiatives that encourage 'self-initiated' participation. It has a particular focus on increasing active membership in sports clubs throughout Australia via national and state sporting associations. In addition, More Active Australia seeks to promote social, health and economic benefits of participation so that more individuals are encouraged to take part in healthy sports pursuits and increase their fitness levels. For individuals with particular talents, the scheme emphasises the importance of linking them to clubs to assist in developing their talents to the full.

Tasks to tackle 7.3

(a) What are the main aims of the More Active Australia initiative?

(b) Why have initiatives like More Active Australia achieved national importance?

Sportit!

Sportit! was designed to develop basic motor skills used in the major sports of Australia. Its aim is to help encourage children to become involved in physical activity from an early age. Support packages have been designed to help teachers deliver lessons more effectively.

Modified Sport Programme

This programme changes the nature of adult sports for young children, for example by modifying equipment and rules. Modified versions of sports include Netta Netball and Kanga Cricket.

'MILO Have-a-Go'

This programme is a Cricket Australia initiative that delivers an introductory cricket programme to 5–8 year olds, developing basic skills and principles involved in cricket, with an emphasis on fun and safety.

The pursuit of sporting excellence in Australia

The AIS

The Australian Institute of Sport (AIS) leads the development of elite sport and is widely acknowledged both in Australia and internationally as a world best practice model for elite athlete development.

The AIS is based in Canberra in the suburb of Bruce. In terms of structure, it is decentralised — each state has a replica AIS academy. Each academy currently has its own specialist sports, although they are becoming more multi-sport based.

The stated functions of the AIS are to:

- allow top performers to train in world-class facilities
- give top performers access to high-quality coaches
- undertake sport science research to further improve elite-level performances
- give sports medicine support to get athletes back on track as soon as possible
- provide educational support and lifestyle advice to support performers
- use elite performers as role models in sports clubs and schools to inspire others (for example by giving presentations and signing autographs). The Sports Person in Schools project and AIS Connect programme aim to increase the profile of the AIS and its athletes.

Top tip

Following Team GB's success in moving from 10th to 4th in the Olympic medal table between Athens and Beijing, the Australian Prime Minister Kevin Rudd stated that Australia should consider using Lottery finance for elite sport, as in the UK.

National talent search

The ASC uses the National Talent Identification and Development Programme (NTID) to identify and fast track Australia's next generation of talented athletes who have potential to win medals at major global sports events. The Australian Government committed $20 million from May 2006 to May 2010 to fund and support the delivery of NTID initiatives, including national talent identification networks/initiatives, and talent identification schemes focusing on the unique potential and needs within the indigenous population. Such talent identification programmes (TIPs) will help to broaden Australia's sporting base and maximise its relatively small talent pool of about 280000 athletes (compared with 16 million in China and 1.2 million in the UK).

The 'draft' system

A 'draft' is a process used in both the USA and Australia to allocate certain players to sports teams. In a draft, teams take it in turns to select from a pool of eligible players. When a team selects a player, the team receives exclusive rights to sign that player to a contract, and no other team in the league may sign the player.

The best-known type of draft is the 'entry draft', which is used to allocate players who have recently become eligible to play in a league. Depending on the sport, the players may come from college, high school or junior teams. The entry draft prevents excessive bidding wars for young talent and ensures no one team can cream off all the best talent, making the league uncompetitive. To encourage parity, teams that do poorly in the previous season usually get to choose first in the post-season draft.

The Australian Football League Draft is the annual draft of new unsigned players by Australian rules football ('Aussie Rules') teams. In the AFL Draft, the order in which teams select from the pool of players is based on the position in which they finish in the league during the season — teams at the bottom of the league take first pick.

Equality and discrimination

Sport and gender

Early colonialist attitudes, including the frontier spirit, led to male domination and high levels of discrimination towards women in Australian society, including in the sporting arena. Australia was founded on a pioneering ethic that encouraged a flourishing masculine culture, while social etiquette restricted women to 'parlour games'. As in the UK, historically, femininity and fertility were thought to be under threat if women participated in all but the most mild of activities. It was not until the mid-twentieth century that female sports performers began to emerge in athletics, swimming, and other sports. Even then, if female performers exhibited too much aggression or competitiveness they were deemed to be 'butch' or 'too masculine' and often had their sexuality challenged.

The second half of the twentieth century saw a gradual change in attitudes, with women successfully competing in a wide range of activities. Nevertheless, in a country where women are in the majority, sports representation is still disappointingly low.

Top tip

The many Australian women who have become champions in their sport have triumphed over a system that has largely worked strenuously against them.

Australian 400 m star Cathy Freeman was hugely influential as a female role model in the 1990s

In the 1980s, government moves helped to open the door for more women to participate. In 1984, the Commonwealth Sex Discrimination Act was passed, followed by several state-level equal opportunities Acts. The main Act made it unlawful to discriminate against a person on the grounds of sex, marital status or pregnancy. Sporting clubs were forced to open an option of full membership to women.

In order to achieve more success in elite sport, Australia is realising it needs to promote and develop more equality in sport, for example via mixed-sex school PE programmes, and the use of female role models in a promotional manner in clubs and schools. The Women and Sport Unit of the ASC is involved in the research, identification and development of innovative policies that address gender issues in sport and increase the likelihood of both boosting participation as well as raising the success levels of female elite performers in Australia.

Disability sport in Australia

Sports CONNECT is an initiative designed to create sporting options for people with disabilities. It focuses on finding ways to include more people with disabilities in sport and recreation, in different roles and at different levels. It also aims to promote understanding among disability groups of the many benefits of sport and to demystify any perceived difficulties regarding getting involved.

Key term

Sports CONNECT: a national programme coordinated by the Disability Sport Unit, with the aim to ensure that all Australians with disabilities have opportunities to participate in sporting activities at the level of their choice.

Paralympic sport in Australia

Paralympic sport is gaining increased prominence in Australia, as illustrated by its raised profile in the media. The Australian Broadcasting Corporation (ABC) and the Australian Paralympic Committee (APC) announced a collaboration to bring the 2008 Paralympics into every household in Australia. ABC television broadcast more than 100 hours of live and highlights coverage across ABC1 and ABC2 during the Games. The president of the APC, Greg Hartung, said that it was fitting that Australia's largest ever 'away team' was followed by the most extensive Paralympic Games coverage by a television network in the world.

The APC sent 170 athletes and 123 officials to the Beijing Paralympic Games in September 2008. Its raised media profile was assisted by Australian Government funding to ensure quality television coverage, with a particular focus on Australia's female Paralympians (as recommended by a governmental enquiry into women in sport in Australia in September 2006). In 2008, 72 women competed for Australia at the Beijing Games, making up 45% of the team. This improved on the 40% representation in Athens.

Case study activities

Cricket

Cricket was the first sport to come to Australia from the UK in the early nineteenth century. It remains to this day a mass spectator sport, uniting and generating confidence in Australia as the number one in the world game. The structure of the game was imported into Australian culture with no changes from the English version previously played, but it was far more integrated among the different social classes in Australia. A home victory in what is regarded as

Top tip

To understand the development of sporting activities in Australia, it is important to be aware of the strong influence the UK has had on such developments. Australia's major games are mainly straightforward adoptions from the motherland (such as rugby union and league).

Australian players celebrate a South African wicket in the 3 mobile series third test, January 2009

the first cricket Test match in 1876 and success in England in 1882 created the Ashes phenomenon (see page 63).

Towards the end of the twentieth century, cricket developed as a commercial product. In 1977, the Australian television magnate, Kerry Packer, introduced World Series Cricket, taking power away from the International Cricket Board and having a major impact on the world game. World Series Cricket offered highly lucrative financial contracts to the world's best players. However, taking part in the 'cricket circus' led to subsequent bans for players representing their countries. The first World Series, hosted by Australia, featured floodlights, rule changes and coloured clothing — all of which increased the entertainment value of the game and made it more attractive to sponsors and television networks alike.

The twenty-first century began with another revolution in world cricket. Twenty20 cricket is a much shortened version of the traditional 5-day Test match, and offers high-level entertainment for spectators from all sections of society. This shorter, more televisual format has increased the attractiveness of cricket to television and sponsors, raising the profile and marketability of the game and its players. Massive financial rewards are on offer, such as the $20 million prize money for the winning team of Stanford's Super Series in the West Indies in 2008.

Rugby league

In 1907, at a meeting in Bateman's Crystal Hotel in Sydney, New South Wales, the New South Wales Rugby Football League (NSWRFL) was formed as a professional organisation. Players were immediately recruited for the new game, and despite the threat of immediate lifetime expulsion from the rugby union establishment, the NSWRFL managed to recruit Herbert Messenger, the most famous rugby footballer in Sydney at that time.

Rugby league is traditionally seen as a working man's sport, with its roots in the state school system, while rugby union has more of a middle/upper class image with its roots in the prestigious 'private school' system. Such a class divide can be traced back to a similar schism that occurred in Britain, and for similar reasons (see pages 55 and 64).

'League', as it is now commonly known, is one of the most popular team sports in Australia. It is the dominant winter sport in the states of New South Wales and Queensland, which comprise around half of the country's population. The elite club competition is the National Rugby League (NRL), which features 10 teams from New South Wales, three teams from Queensland, and one team each from Victoria, Australian Capital Territory and New Zealand.

State of Origin

The Rugby League 'State of Origin' is an annual series of three inter-state rugby league matches between the Queensland Maroons and the New South Wales Blues. The State of Origin series is one of Australia's premier sporting events, attracting a huge television audience and usually selling out the stadiums in which the games are played. Origin games are traditionally hyped to be the toughest, hardest-fought matches played in Australia, with both teams maintaining a fierce effort right to the end of the game.

Some demographics of rugby league

The ASC's Exercise, Recreation and Sport Surveys have produced a range of statistics, including some related to rugby league. In 2006, a total of 371 557 Australians participated in rugby league, which was a sharp increase from 223 204 in 2005. Gala days and coaching clinics were successful initiatives in raising participation among all sections of the community. The vast majority of these participants were male (approximately 95%).

There is an Australian Women's Rugby League. It was formed in 1993, and achieved affiliation with the ARL in 1998. It is not customary for girls over 11 to continue playing rugby league against boys and the exclusively women's clubs have a relatively small profile compared with the local boys' clubs. However, at a junior and local level there are many women involved in volunteering positions. Women form a very important part of the local club structures.

New South Wales and Queensland account for almost 85% of rugby league participants nationally. Per capita figures show that Queensland and the Northern Territory rate ahead of New South Wales. Rugby league enjoys only minor participation in other states of Australia due to competition with Aussie Rules. The reason for such state divisions is the promotion of Aussie Rules in the late-nineteenth and early-twentieth centuries. In those times, Aussie Rules was expanding throughout southern and western Australia.

Top tip

The NRL is very important for the Australian television scene, providing not only the highest rating programme in Australia (the NRL Grand Final) but also six out of the top seven and 78 out of the top 100 programmes on subscription television.

Media coverage of rugby league

Due to the widespread interest in rugby league, including the State of Origin series, comprehensive match reports are carried by many Australian newspapers. All premiership games are broadcast on television. Interest in rugby league is highest in the eastern states. High levels of media coverage ensure commercial interest in rugby league.

The NRL is a corporate sporting competition, with sponsors' logos appearing on everything from the ball itself, to the playing field's surface and most parts of the players' and officials' kit. Since 2001, the NRL Premiership has been sponsored by Telstra. Other notable sponsorships include Coca-Cola Amatil for ball sponsorship, Bundaberg Rum for Monday night football and TAB Sportsbat as the official betting agency of the NRL.

Rugby union

Historically, the first rugby football club that was established in Australia was at Sydney University in 1864. A decade after the first club was formed, a body called the Southern Rugby Union was formed as a result of a meeting at the Oxford Hotel in Sydney. A Sydney competition was established, which was administered from England Rugby Headquarters at Twickenham. 1876 saw the first games of rugby played in Queensland. With its origins, image and administration anchored in England, supporters of rugby saw the game as a symbol and reminder of their Englishness or colonial roots.

A National Governing Body was established in the late 1940s and in 1949 the Australian Rugby Union joined the International Rugby Board. In 1987, the first ever Rugby World Cup was held in Australia and New Zealand.

With rugby union becoming an openly professional sport in 1995, after more than a century of a strictly enforced amateur code, major changes were seen at both the club and international levels. The Super 12 rugby competition was born that year. The tournament involved 12 provincial sides from three countries — Australia, New Zealand and South Africa. The year also saw the Tri Nations Series commence between these three countries.

Australia were Rugby World Cup winners in 1999, claiming their second William Webb Ellis trophy. In so doing they were the first multiple winners of the tournament. The tournament was staged in Australia in 2003. It was hailed a great success, with an estimated 40000 international spectators travelling to Australia for the event. An estimated $100 million was injected into the Australian economy as a result of hosting the World Cup. Indeed, the Australian Rugby Union said that revenues exceeded all expectations and a tournament surplus of $44.5 million was made. The hosting of the World Cup also saw an increase in Super 12 crowds and raised levels of junior participation in the sport.

> **Top tip**
>
> The focus of rugby league and rugby union remains in New South Wales and Queensland and, unlike in the UK, rugby league tends to be the more popular version.

Association football (soccer)

Australia's first football club, called Wanderers, was founded in 1880 by a teacher in New South Wales. The early governing bodies of the sport in Australia had to distinguish themselves from Aussie Rules and rugby football — both rival sports that had become very popular during the late-nineteenth century. Today, soccer is a popular recreational sport in Australia, although on a professional level it remains less popular than the two other dominant codes (Aussie Rules and rugby league). The fully professional A-League domestic competition has only been operating since 2005.

In the late twentieth century, while native-born Australians overwhelmingly played and watched Aussie Rules or either code of rugby football, interest in association football increased due to the influx of immigrants from Britain and other southern European countries. These migrant communities expanded rapidly during the 1950s and 1960s: Croatians, Greeks, Italians and Serbs gave rise to most of the larger clubs. At the time, the game served as a bonding force between ethnic minority communities, and as a point of identity between them and the wider Australian community.

There were a number of reasons why Australian soccer experienced an initially slow development and was not accepted by much of society:

- Soccer was branded a British game or was associated with ethnic migrants.
- There was anti-British feeling from Australians who wanted their 'own game'.
- Ethnic rivalry led to spectator and player violence.
- Ethnic connections meant low-level interest from the media and potential sponsors.

Some of these problems are now being overcome for a variety of reasons:

- Soccer administrators made an effort to 'de-ethnicise' the game and some ethnic team names were banned — for example, Sydney Croatia is now Sydney United.
- Ethnic connections have decreased with more media and sponsor interest in soccer as a product.
- Soccer is being increasingly seen as a social unifier.

The successes of the Australian national football team have done a great deal to raise the profile of the game. At the 2006 World Cup, matches versus Japan and Italy were the top rating television programmes in their respective weeks.

Pay television is the main outlet for both domestic and international football in Australia. Following a $120 million, 7-year deal between the Football Federation of Australia (FFA) and Fox Sports, Fox Sports gained exclusive rights from 2007 to all home internationals, all A-League and AFC Asian Cup fixtures, as well as the FIFA World Cup qualifiers. It represented the most significant television rights agreement for football in Australia, but is still relatively small compared with the English Premier League deal with BSkyB.

Australian rules football

Details of the game's origins in Australia are obscure and still cause a great deal of debate. Australian rules football became organised in Melbourne in 1858 with a series of experimental rules in a bid to keep cricketers fit during the winter months. The early connection with cricketers may be responsible for the shape and size of the field of play — a large oval, essentially a cricket ground rather than the rectangular pitch more usual in other types of football. In fact, many sports 'ovals' in Australia double as cricket and Aussie Rules grounds. Gradually the game, known first as 'Melbourne rules' and 'Victorian rules', became 'Australian rules' following its spread from Victoria into other Australian colonies.

In 1982, in a move that heralded big changes within the sport, one of the original Victorian Football League clubs, South Melbourne, relocated to the rugby league stronghold of Sydney to become known as the Sydney Swans. The national league changed its name to the Australian Football League (AFL) following the 1989 season, gaining its first South Australian team (Adelaide) in 1991. The AFL has 16 member clubs and is the sport's elite competition. It is the most powerful body in the world of Aussie Rules and continues to look for further opportunities to expand its product into new markets.

Aussie Rules has attracted more overall interest among Australians (as measured by the *Sweeney Report, 2006–07*) than any other football code. In fact, when compared with all other sports throughout the nation it has consistently ranked first among the winter sports. As a football code it is the most popular form in the Northern Territory, South Australia, Tasmania, Victoria and Western Australia. It is less popular in New South Wales and Queensland. The AFL teams from Brisbane and Sydney have attracted a strong increase in crowds, television audiences and participation since they both recently won premierships.

Key term

Indigenous: the Aborigines were the original indigenous population of Australia before the British colonists arrived.

The game is particularly popular among indigenous Australian communities. Indigenous Australians are well represented among professional AFL players: while only 2.4% of the population is of indigenous origin, 10% of AFL players identify themselves as such.

Aussie Rules is the most highly attended spectator sport in Australia: government figures show that more than 2.5 million people attended games in 2005–06, when the AFL was one of only five professional sports leagues in the world with an average attendance above 30 000. (The others are the NFL and Major League Baseball in the USA and Canada, and the top division soccer leagues in Germany and England.)

Aussie Rules action

In 2006, a total of 615 549 registered participants played Aussie Rules. ASC statistics show a 42% increase in the total number of participants over a 4-year period from 2001 to 2005. This increase has resulted from a number of initiatives designed to increase interest and enjoyment in playing the sport (for example, Kick-to-kick, Auskick, Women's Rules Football, Masters Australian Football). Each state has its own local league for Aussie Rules with recreational, young children's, elderly people's and women's competitions all provided.

Tasks to tackle 7.5

Explain the development of Australian rules football into a 'game of the people'.

Top tip

Professional sports leagues in Australia use a model based on franchises, as is standard in North America. The European system of promotion and relegation is foreign to Australia.

Practice makes perfect

1 Using the following headings, explain a range of factors that have influenced the development of sport in Australia:
   (a) social factors
   (b) ideological factors
   (c) traditions
   (d) geographical factors *(8 marks)*

2 How are schools in Australia helping to develop talented sporting individuals? *(4 marks)*

3 Compare school sport programmes in Australia with those in the UK. *(5 marks)*

4 How does the Australian government increase active sports participation among the adult population? *(3 marks)*

Chapter 8

Individual influences on the sports performer

What you need to know

By the end of this chapter you should be able to:

- describe the influences on the formation of sporting personalities
- say what attitudes are and how they can be formed and changed
- identify the causes of aggressive behaviour in sport

Personality

Believe it or not, you are unique. Personality is defined as the unique psychological and behavioural characteristics of an individual. In sport, personality affects the way that each individual performer approaches competition. Both Roger Federer and John McEnroe have been successful Wimbledon tennis champions yet have very different personalities (on court at least). Federer is calm and assured, McEnroe was volatile and temperamental. What makes Federer and McEnroe so different? Three major theories outline how a personality develops. These three theories — trait theory, social learning theory and the interactionist approach — are very important because they form the basis not only of personality development, but also of many other topics that you will see in sports psychology.

Trait theory

Trait theory states that we are born with certain personality characteristics, or **traits**, that influence the way in which we behave. These inherited characteristics are fairly stable, in that they stay with us for quite some time. Trait theory therefore suggests that it might be possible to predict the way in which a sports person will behave. For example, an aggressive football player might be prone to commit fouls in a game in which the referee has lost control. It may be a good idea, therefore, if in such a game the coach substituted that player to avoid a sending off. Inherited traits include **extroversion** (being loud and confident) or **introversion** (being shy and quiet). These two opposing traits should be viewed on a sliding scale or continuum since individuals can have a mixture of extroversion and introversion.

> **Key term**
>
> **Trait:** an innate characteristic that could predetermine behaviour.

Personality traits are, at least in part, a function of our biology. The reticular activating system (RAS) regulates the amount of arousal experienced by the brain (see page 139). Extroverts, whose characteristics include the need to affiliate to other people and social situations, prefer high arousal situations because their RAS operates at comparatively low levels of activity. To this group, high arousal situations are stimulating and enable them to drive towards their goals. Introverts, who do not seek social situations, prefer low arousal conditions because their levels of internal arousal are comparatively high and they do not require the extra external stimuli for drive or motivation.

Other examples of traits include **stability**, which is consistent behaviour, and **instability** which is neurotic behaviour. Again, individuals have a mix of both characteristics but some tend to be more towards one extreme than the other. Figure 8.1 shows how personality can be viewed on a sliding scale.

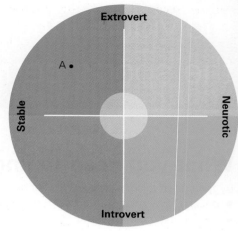

Figure 8.1 A matrix of personality traits — 'stable extrovert' (e.g. point A) describes a personality that is consistently loud and bright

Narrow band

The narrow band approach is a trait theory that groups personality characteristics into two types. **Type A** personalities lack patience and tolerance; they are anxious, but they tend to continue with tasks such as training schedules, even when they feel tired. **Type B** personalities are more relaxed and tolerant and suffer less from anxiety.

Data collection and trait theory

Attempts to **profile** sporting personalities using trait theory have, however, been largely unsuccessful. In sport, personality can change with the situation. In a game of rugby, for example, a player could be performing with

> **Key term**
>
> **Profile:** a short description of personal characteristics.

control and clear thinking until he is fouled by an opponent and then his behaviour could change to become aggressive. It is also possible for sporting personalities to behave very differently outside the sporting arena. A boxer may be calm and sociable in his home life yet in the boxing ring he is assertive and highly motivated. It is also true that many of the methods used to measure sporting traits — including questionnaires, observation and physical tests — have rendered the research unreliable, invalid and inconsistent.

Questionnaires can be very quick and yield a lot of information in a short space of time. Examples include the Sport Competition Anxiety Test (see Chapter 10). The problem with such questionnaires is that respondents may fail to understand the question asked or may be tempted to give the answer they feel they ought to give rather than the truth. This may result in a biased response.

Observing the behaviour and recording the characteristics of the subject can give a true-to-life picture. However, if the subjects realise that they are being watched, their behaviour can change. This is also a very subjective way of assessing personality characteristics and the observers need to be trained so that consistent results can be found. After all, two people watching the same game can have very different opinions on the reasons for success or failure!

Some researchers have suggested that sport can affect personality. For example, physical education instils social qualities, and builds teamwork and leadership skills. There may be a link between physical exercise and psychological well-being.

Physical testing for personality includes the measure of heart rate, for example, to assess anxiety and stress. Such measures are factual and objective, which means that there can be valid comparison between results. However, quite often sports performers do not like to be wired up with assessment equipment during an event, because it is so restrictive to their movement. It has therefore been very difficult to get a true measure of anxiety during a real-life game, such as a cup final, and most results have been recorded during training situations.

Therefore, in terms of the reliability of the research into personality traits, it can be said that the results may:

- lack consistency (for example, due to subjective observation)
- lack internal validity (for example, due to untruthful questionnaire results)
- lack external validity (for example, when physical testing environments do not match the wider sporting environment)

Trait theory is therefore a poor predictor of behaviour and it can be argued that the need to take account of personality *change* is more important. Social learning theory tries to address this problem.

Tasks to tackle 8.1

The following table shows the main methods of collecting information on personality. Copy and complete the table by suggesting at least one advantage and at least one disadvantage for each method in the appropriate column.

Method	Advantages	Disadvantages
Questionnaire		
Observational		
Physiological		

Social learning theory

Social learning theory states that instead of remaining stable, personality characteristics develop over time. Individuals learn from sporting situations and other experiences (the environment) and also copy other people who are held in high esteem. Such people are known as **significant others**. Significant others include sporting icons or role models and they may also include the people we associate with, such as our friends, our parents and our teachers and sports coaches. If your parents have been involved in sport and introduce you to an active and healthy lifestyle you are much more likely to develop sporting characteristics than if you had not been exposed to such competitive situations. Think of some of the parent and child combinations that have featured in professional sport. For example, former county cricketer and Leeds rugby player Liam Botham is the son of Sir Ian Botham, who played cricket for England.

> **Key terms**
>
> **Significant others:** people we hold in high esteem.
> **Socialisation:** the process of associating with others and accepting their behaviour as the norm.

We learn personality characteristics by a process called **socialisation**. We associate with significant others and begin to accept and display their behaviour. For example, if our friends all play in the same junior football team then it is a good bet that during break at school, the same friends will end up playing football together in the school playground. The social learning process often follows the pattern:

observe → identify → reinforce → copy

In other words, we see behaviour, realise what it is and if it is successful, we will try it ourselves. Individuals are likely to copy behaviour that fits in with their own age, gender, ability and values. Behaviour tends to be copied if is high profile, powerful, consistent, successful and reinforced. For example, the goal scoring celebrations of professional football players that are highlighted in the media are often copied by youngsters because of the high status value of the football role model to the youngster.

TopFoto

Judy Murray, mother of Britain's tennis number one Andy Murray, is a leading tennis coach

The interactionist approach

The interactionist approach encompasses the best of both worlds by combining the features of trait theory and social learning theory. It suggests that an individual's behaviour is a result of both personality *and* the influence of the environment. This is summed up by the formula:

$$B = f (P \times E)$$

Top tip

Exam questions, particularly longer ones, may ask you to discuss all of the psychological theories dealt with in this chapter. Make sure that you give all of the conflicting views, and note that it is the interactionist approach that students tend to forget.

This means that behaviour (*B*) is a function (f) of personality trait (*P*) and environmental situation (*E*). In other words, people are born with stable personality characteristics, but these characteristics are then adapted to suit the situation. For example, a hockey captain may act as a calming influence to settle the team's nerves before a big game, but in the closing stages of that game if the team is a goal down the same captain may use all her powers of motivation to drive the team on to score the equalising goal. This theory accounts for changes in behaviour and is perhaps more applicable to modern-day sport because it takes into account how behaviour can change during a game.

Achievement motivation

Achievement motivation is a concept of personality that looks at how individual athletes approach a competitive situation. Some players welcome the challenge and feel very confident as they approach a big game or are asked to do a demanding task. Some do not welcome competition and will be tempted to leave to others those tasks that present a risk of failure. Those who welcome competition and seek out a challenge are said to be motivated by the 'need to achieve', and display **NACH characteristics**. Those who avoid competition and are not willing to accept a challenge are said to display the 'need to avoid failure', or **NAF characteristics**.

The features of a NACH personality are as follows:

- The athlete is very competitive and welcomes a challenge.
- Risks are taken, even if there is a chance of failure.
- The performer is keen to see feedback on the outcome.
- Confidence is displayed.
- Personal responsibility is taken for the result.
- The athlete blames internal reasons, such as his/her ability, for success.

The features of a NAF personality are as follows:

- Challenge is avoided and the athlete may seek easy targets.
- Lack of confidence may be present.
- Feedback is unwelcome.
- External reasons are blamed for lack of success.

The adoption of these NACH or NAF characteristics can depend not only on the performer, but also on the situation. Sometimes an athlete feels confident and prepared to have a go while at other times he/she may prefer to leave the challenge to someone else.

Naturally confident personalities — those said to display trait confidence — will be likely to show a competitive approach. Those who have had experience in a similar situation before, especially if they have succeeded, will also be likely to show NACH characteristics. A young performer at school, for example, might relish the chance to show his classmates the advanced gymnastic skills that he has developed already at gym club.

One of the most important influences on the adoption of a NACH or NAF approach concerns how much the task means to the individual. In other words, what is the incentive? A task that can be achieved easily offers little incentive for the performer and no sense of satisfaction when it is completed. A task that is hard to achieve, one where failure is possible, offers much more personal incentive and a sense of achievement when completed. Imagine going mountain walking and finding two routes you can take: an easy stroll that you are guaranteed to finish, and a hard three peaks challenge that not everyone completes. Which one would you do? Which offers the greatest incentive? The harder route is taken by those who have a need to achieve and who wish to gain satisfaction from completing the task.

Coaches want their players to maintain a competitive approach and to show the need to keep on achieving. To help maintain motivation, the coach should set targets that can be achieved in the early coaching sessions and then make these targets more difficult as the players improve. Any success achieved by the players should be rewarded with praise and positive feedback and the players should be made to feel that they are responsible for any success achieved. The coach could point out role models who have similar ability to their own players and who have achieved success. The challenges faced by the players should be hard enough to offer an incentive but not so impossible to achieve that confidence is lost. In such a way, motivation to compete can be maintained.

Attitudes

An attitude is the way a person views something or tends to behave towards it. You may have heard someone described as having a bad attitude in class, for example because he/she does not like doing written work. In sport, both negative and positive attitudes exist and there are a number of ways that such attitudes are formed.

An attitude is made up of three parts, referred to as the triadic model:
- The **cognitive component** relates to what we think or believe. In sport, the cognitive part of attitude is shown by a belief in the benefits of exercise, for example the knowledge that going to the gym is healthy.
- The **affective component** relates to feelings and emotions. For example, when we go to the gym we may enjoy it and show enthusiasm towards our training.

Key terms

Cognitive: describes a thought process or belief.

Affective: describes an emotional feeling or interpretation.

Behavioural: describes an action — a physical response to a situation.

Tasks to tackle 8.2

Give an example from sport that shows each of the three components of an attitude. You can use examples from your own experience if you wish to show how you may have shown a cognitive attitude, an affective interpretation and a behavioural response.

- The **behavioural component** relates to what we do and how we behave. For example, going to the gym three times a week is an indication of a positive behavioural attitude towards exercise.

Forming attitudes

There is a link between all three parts of an attitude. However, the cognitive component (what we think) it not always reflected in the behavioural component (what we do). If you posed the question 'Is going to the gym good for your health?' most people would answer 'Yes'. But not all those people would actually go to the gym on a regular basis. They would use the affective part of the attitude to justify their actions: 'I don't go to the gym because I do other forms of exercise like walking the dog and I like the fresh air.' It is the affective, or emotional, part of the attitude that often determines our actions. Attitudes, therefore, do not always predict behaviour, although they can predict specific responses to attitude objects if all three components of the attitude are similar. Other influences, such as personality traits, may also mean that attitudes alone are not a good means of predicting behaviour.

Attitudes are formed from an individual's beliefs, influences and experiences — they are learned responses. It is important to note that such influences can be either positive or negative, and so attitudes can also be either positive or negative.

We have already seen how people held in high esteem, in other words significant others, are a major influence on an individual's beliefs and attitudes. Significant others include parents and friends, teachers and sports coaches and, very importantly, role models that we may look up to. Such role models do not necessarily have to be elite performers at the top professional level (sometimes we may feel that we will not be able to match such talent); they may be people of our own age who have worked hard to reach a good level of performance or who simply enjoy taking part. A youngster with sporty parents, who has been encouraged to take up a sport by being taken to early coaching sessions, may begin to enjoy the activity and then develop positive attitudes. On the other hand, a child whose parents are not sporty and who refuse to get involved in sport may not develop positive attitudes to any sporting activity.

Key term

Role models: people we regard in high esteem who set targets and abilities we would aspire to match.

Individuals' past experiences may influence their future attitudes. If, for example, we attended a gymnastics class as a youngster and stretched too far, causing an injury, we may have developed negative attitudes to gymnastics. If we went to the class and enjoyed it, we may have developed positive attitudes towards gymnastics.

The media have a powerful influence on the development of sporting attitudes. When the England cricket team won the Ashes against Australia in 2006, the sport enjoyed far more extensive and enthusiastic media coverage than usual. The media hype surrounding that win led to very positive approaches towards cricket and a lot of young players were attracted to the sport. A few months later, in early 2007, the same cricket team went to Australia, lost the series after a spate of poor performances, and were subsequently 'slated' by the press. Negative attitudes towards the team began to develop and the positive thoughts regarding cricket became more negative. This may have been partly why no terrestrial channel bid for coverage of live test cricket when the rights were redistributed in mid-2008.

> **Top tip**
>
> Questions on attitudes often ask for the ways in which attitudes are formed. Remember that the influences on the formation of attitudes can be positive or negative. For example, a role model can be a positive sporting icon who demonstrates fair play, but role models can also be negative and promote hostile behaviour.

Such a turn around in attitudes in such a short space of time suggests that attitudes can be readily changed. From a coaching point of view, it is desirable to change negative attitudes into positive ones.

Changing attitudes

One way to change an attitude is to use the simple technique of persuasion. Persuasion is most effective when it is carried out by an expert. For example, persuading someone that it might be a good idea to go to a fitness class, despite their reservations, might be easier if the advice came from a fitness conditioner or health expert.

Another way to change a negative attitude into a positive one is to use the concept of **cognitive dissonance**. This is a process that challenges existing beliefs. Imagine a rugby prop forward being told that as part of his training he has to take part in some aerobics. The prop may believe that aerobics is for girls and refuse to take part. The coach could challenge this cognitive part of the attitude by suggesting that aerobics is a good measure of stamina and only the fittest people can maintain a constant work rate for a full hour. In response to the challenge the prop may then go and do his aerobics session.

Other ways in which negative attitudes can be changed include making the training sessions fun and enjoyable, with variety in practice, so that the affective part of the attitude is developed in a positive way. Giving young players early success will help them to develop a belief in their ability and foster a positive approach. For example, young tennis players play a half court version of the game with a sponge ball to allow early success and enjoyment. The use of rewards and plenty of positive reinforcement will help to promote confidence and

Successful coaching offers youngsters the possibility of early success to promote positive attitudes

enjoyment. The cognitive part of the attitude could be developed by simply pointing out the benefits of exercise to the performer.

Sometimes attitudes can become very strong and an expectation develops. Extreme attitudes can develop into a prejudice — a generalising assumption that may not be correct. Undesirable and prejudicial attitudes can be formed on the basis of race, gender, age or physical ability, and even against sporting officials.

Imagine that your favourite football team is playing in a cup semi-final. The referee gives the opposition a penalty when it is clearly shown in television replays and in newspaper photographs that the foul was committed outside the penalty box. The opponents score from the spot kick and your team is out of the competition. A few weeks later, the same referee is due to officiate at your team's next home game. As he runs out onto the field he is greeted by a chorus of boos from the home fans. In fact, every referee who has taken charge of home games has been ridiculed in the last few weeks by the home fans. All referees are bad, aren't they? In this example, a prejudice against match officials has been formed on the basis of one bad experience. The referee perhaps had a good game apart from that one error, but the influence of the media has focused attention on the official. When the home crowd starts to boo the referee, everyone seems to join in, perhaps because of a need to fit in with the crowd and not be left out.

The above example shows how a prejudice can be formed from a past experience, by the influence of the media and by fitting in with the norm of group behaviour. Historical influences and cultural differences can also be responsible for the formation of a prejudice. Few England football fans think positively of the Argentine player Diego Maradonna since his infamous 'hand of God' goal that knocked England out of the World Cup in 1986, even though it was a long time ago and he was a great player.

To counter a prejudice, coaches use some of the methods involved in promoting positive attitudes. Persuasion by an expert or the use of cognitive dissonance will help to change a prejudicial view. A coach can also prevent a prejudice from developing by reinforcing fair play in training and punishing behaviour that may be seen as being unfairly biased. Most professional sports have a fair play charter by which any racist or sexist comments result in a ban from playing or watching the sport. The media can further prevent prejudice by highlighting the positive aspects of fair play and equality that frequently happen in sport. The coach can point out positive role models who play the game in a fair and balanced fashion.

Attitudes — since they are specifically directed at attitude objects — can theoretically be used to predict behaviour. It may be possible to predict how someone with a negative attitude will behave in a specific situation. For example, a jockey may not be expected to try his best in a game of rugby. Yet behaviour is unpredictable, and the jockey might do his best in the rugby session just to show what he is capable of. We should note that the cognitive part of the attitude does not always reflect how we behave and therefore using attitudes to predict behaviour is not always reliable.

Attitudes can be measured by questionnaires in a similar way to personality (see pages 104–05). Attitudes are measured on 'attitude scales', such as the Likert scale, on which the subject has to state the extent to which he/she agrees or disagrees with a statement. Attitudes can also be measured by observation of behaviour.

Attitudes are very important in sports performance because they affect effort and motivation. Promoting positive attitudes is a way of encouraging participation in sport.

Aggression in sport

While watching a game on television you may have heard the commentator describe one of the players as being very 'aggressive' when making a hard tackle. If the player concerned was trying to win the ball and played within the rules, then the tackle was not actually aggressive, it was assertive. **Aggression** is defined as an intent to harm. An aggressive act is outside the rules of the game and is often prompted by reactive behaviour that is out of control. For example, a rugby player who is pulled back when chasing a kick might react by punching the offender. **Assertion** is within the rules of the game and is well-motivated behaviour that is more in control, such as a hard yet fair tackle during a game of rugby.

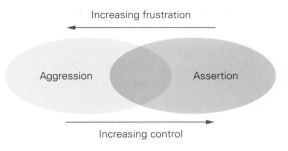

Increasing frustration

Aggression   Assertion

Increasing control

Figure 8.2 Aggression and assertion

Hostile aggression: an intent to harm; a reaction to mounting anger and frustration.
Instrumental aggression: no specific intent to harm another person, but a purposeful action aimed at breaking the rules or abusing equipment.

There is an overlap between the definitions of aggression and assertion as shown in Figure 8.2. In the example of the rugby tackle above, there may be fair contact but there may also be intent to make sure the ball carrier feels the impact!

Hostile aggression is a specific intent to harm another person. Sometimes the aggression shown in sport can be very hostile — for example, when a reaction to a foul is designed to inflict injury on another player. **Instrumental aggression** is less personal and lacks the intent to injure someone else but it is aimed at breaking the rules or abusing the equipment, for example a tennis player shouting at an umpire to dispute a line call.

Tasks to tackle 8.3

There is some overlap between the definitions of aggression and assertion. Use your knowledge of aggression in sport to construct your own diagram, Powerpoint or Word document to show some of the main features of an aspect of aggression. Use this example to help you.

Type of sport — Contact — Unfair decisions — Frustration — Losing

Importance of event — Over arousal — **Aggression in sport** — Personality traits — Expectations

Social learning — Environment — Stress — Intimidation — Blow to self-esteem

There are four theories that explain why aggression happens in sport.

Instinct theory

This theory states that we are all born with an aggressive instinct that will surface under provocation or threat. The nature of this theory lies in evolution, which teaches that humans once had to be naturally aggressive hunters and defenders of territory. The aggressive instinct can be manifested on the pitch when defending a goal or reacting to a foul, for example. Some players only need a slight provocation to react in a violent manner, while others need much more intimidation before losing their cool.

Frustration–aggression theory

Aggression can be caused in sport by the frustration of being prevented from achieving what we want to achieve. For example, an ice-hockey player prevented from reaching the puck by a defender's illegal use of the stick might take out his frustration on the defender by lashing out. This tendency to react aggressively when our goals are blocked is called the frustration–aggression hypothesis, or F–A hypothesis. The F–A hypothesis suggests that aggression is inevitable once an individual is stopped from achieving his/her aim, and aggression will immediately develop in response to the mounting frustration. The hypothesis also states that if the individual can let this aggression out, perhaps by retaliation, then the inclination to be aggressive will be reduced. If, however, the player is unable to get rid of his/her frustration, then the aggression will become more intense and lead to even more frustration and subsequent aggression.

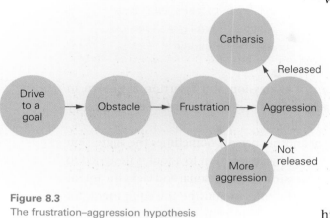

Figure 8.3
The frustration–aggression hypothesis

The release of aggression is called **catharsis**, literally meaning 'cleansing the emotions'. It is common to see players in a game get wound up and indulge in pushing and shoving, only to calm down once their little spat is over. If those players were unable to indulge in the pushing and shoving, they could harbour the aggression for the rest of the game. Holding on to the aggressive inclination is seen in this theory as a form of punishment.

> **Key term**
>
> **Catharsis:** a reduction in frustration or anger as a result of releasing aggressive inclinations or 'letting go'.

> **Top tip**
>
> A nature versus nurture debate runs through the personality, aggression and attitude theories. The nature approach, exemplified by the instinct theory of aggression and the trait theory of personality, supports the view that behaviour is innate, consistent and predictable. The nurture approach is based on social learning theory, and suggests that behaviour is learned from significant others and from our experiences, especially if such experiences are reinforced. The interactionist view combines the nature and nurture approaches by suggesting that behavioural change is a result of differing situations. You may find it helpful to group the theories into nature and nurture when answering exam questions.

Aggressive cue theory

While the first two theories of aggression suggest some natural aggressive inclination, the next two suggest that aggression is nurtured.

Associated with the work of Berkowitz, the aggressive cue hypothesis proposes that aggression occurs as a result of a learned cue or trigger. This trigger could be something that has developed in the past. A player who has an existing rivalry with a particular opponent, for example, will perhaps only reach certain levels of aggression when confronted by that rival, who acts as the cue. The cue could be self-activated. Think of a boxer grinding one fist into the other glove as though in anticipation of making contact with the opponent. Alternatively, the cue can be learned from, and sometimes activated by, the coach. In boxing, coaches at the ring-side can be seen urging their athletes to direct their aggression towards the target — in this case, the coach acts as the cue.

Social learning theory

Aggression can also be nurtured by learning from other people — social learning. In the same way that personality traits are in part learned from significant others, such as friends and our peers, then aggressive acts can be copied from sporting role models and fellow players. Aggression will be copied especially if the aggressive act is successfully reinforced. In a game of basketball, if the captain fouls an opponent and the foul prevents the opponent from scoring, other players may be tempted to copy this unacceptable behaviour in order to win the game. Aggressive acts are more likely to be copied if they are consistent, performed by someone of our own age and if they are powerful.

Controlling aggression

Aggression is not desirable in sport because it can cause injury, and because players who are aggressive tend to be stressed and unable to perform at their best. Coaches and players therefore have a responsibility to reduce aggression. This can be done in a number of ways.

The coach could substitute players who behave aggressively on the pitch, or punish players with fines if they get sent off. In training, aggressive acts should be criticised and non-aggressive acts should be encouraged with praise. The coach could introduce cognitive techniques, such as imagery and mental rehearsal (see Chapter 10), to lower arousal and stress, and the responsibility of the player to the team should be emphasised by pointing out that giving away penalties for foul play is letting the team down.

Players should learn to walk away from aggressive situations and calm down by focusing on the game and not on retaliation. Players could **channel** the aggressive response into more assertive behaviour and use physical relaxation techniques before high-pressure games to make sure they stay in control. Players can also help each other to avoid the consequences of aggression by using peer group pressure — in other words, they could remind each other not to get involved in irresponsible aggressive acts.

> **Key term**
>
> **Channelling:**
> re-directing the drive caused by increased frustration into an assertive, rather than an aggressive, response.

The referee can play an important role in reducing aggression by applying the rules in a consistent and fair manner so that frustrations are reduced. The referee should punish acts of aggression so that standards are set for fair play and any sanctions handed out by the referee should be immediate. The referee could prevent aggression by simply talking to players to calm them down before they commit a foul.

Practice makes perfect

1 The performance and behaviour of a sports performer may be affected by his/her personality. What is the trait theory of personality? *(3 marks)*

2 Some performers show a negative attitude to training and playing. How could a negative attitude be changed into a positive one in sport? *(4 marks)*

3 Aggression is an unwelcome feature of sports performance. What can a coach or player do to reduce the aggressive tendencies that sport can sometimes generate? *(4 marks)*

Playing in a team

What you need to know

By the end of this chapter you should be able to:
- understand the dynamics of group performance
- define the factors that affect group performance
- understand how the role of the leader is important in helping the team

Team dynamics

A group is a collection of individuals who work together to achieve a common goal. In sporting terms this could mean your hockey team, which trains and plays together each week in the hope of winning the league. According to Steiner, the success that such a team achieves is based on the following formula:

actual productivity = potential productivity – faulty processes

Actual productivity refers to the result; potential productivity is the best performance the team could achieve if everything went just right; and the faulty processes are the factors that make things go wrong. In other words, the 1–0 win in our last league game (actual productivity) is based on our best possible performance (potential productivity) minus all the things that went wrong during the game (faulty processes).

The potential of the group could be improved by simply having the best players, but the coach should remember that it is how such players interact and work together that produces the best results. Some teams get fantastic results with average players who give their best and work for each other, while other teams have great players but do not always win. Faulty processes affecting a team include coordination problems, lack of cohesion and lack of motivation from some team members.

Top tip

Learn your definitions. Many short exam questions will ask for the meaning of such terms as potential productivity and actual productivity.

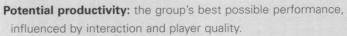
Key terms

Actual productivity: the result; the level of attainment on the task.

Potential productivity: the group's best possible performance, influenced by interaction and player quality.

Faulty processes: the factors that reduce group potential, such as poor coordination, social loafing (page 121) and the Ringlemann effect (page 121).

Stages in group formation

According to the psychologist Carron, a group or team is formed over time by passing through four stages, sometimes known as antecedants:

- The **forming stage** — members of the group develop an affinity with each other based on their desire to share a common goal. In sport this could happen, for example, at the first training session undertaken by a group of players who are hoping to be selected for the college rugby team. After the first training session, the players might begin to socialise with each other when they meet in the college recreation area and a bond between them begins to form.
- The **storming stage** — differences of opinion and conflicts within the group may begin to surface. In the college rugby team example, it may emerge that two players are trying to get into the team in the same position and a rivalry develops between them.
- The **norming stage** — the group or team members begin to resolve their differences and settle down into a team with long-term potential. The two players trying out for the same position might solve the problem by agreeing that one of them should play in a different role, a role with which they are now familiar.
- The **performing stage** — finally, the team begins to fulfil its potential and concentrate on achieving its goals. Regular fixtures are fulfilled and the team members enjoy playing their chosen sport.

Tasks to tackle 9.1

The four stages of group formation are forming, storming, norming and performing. Imagine that you are about to join a local hockey team. Describe the characteristics of each of the four stages of formation that you may experience from when you first join the team.

Cohesion and coordination within the team

Coordination problems — seemingly small issues relating to timing and effective communication — can have a significant impact on sports performance. A defender who fails to communicate effectively with fellow defenders might end up leaving an attacker free and giving away a goal. Poor tactics and strategies also result in coordination problems. For example, the players in a basketball team might be instructed to use a one-on-one defence when the individual speed of some of the opponents means it would be better to operate in a zone.

Coordination problems within the team affect group cohesion. **Cohesion** is defined as the degree to which members of a team unite to achieve a common goal. There are two types of cohesion:

- **Task cohesion** involves the group members working together to achieve a goal.
- **Social cohesion** is about how individual team members get on.

Key terms

Interaction: working together to achieve a goal.

Coordination: work and effort that is timed and matched to produce success.

Cohesion: the degree to which members of a team unite to achieve a common goal.

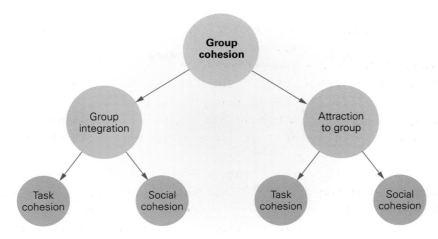

Figure 9.1 The task and social cohesion of individuals combine to give group cohesion

Generally, the best results are achieved when both task cohesion and social cohesion occur, and there is little doubt that successful teams show a high degree of cohesion. Nevertheless, even if some members of the team do not get on socially, they can still produce excellent results with task cohesion alone. Personal differences can be put aside in order to achieve results. Social cohesion does, however, help to promote group interaction.

Both types of cohesion are involved in attraction to a group, and integration within it. Figure 9.1 shows how a player could be attracted to a team for social reasons, to meet and work with others, and for achievement reasons — they like working as a team and think this team will be successful. Once in the group, the player has to integrate with other team members to get the task done — a defensive player needs to communicate with fellow defenders to make sure no goals are conceded, for example.

Influences on cohesion

There are a number of factors that affect both group cohesion and coordination. These factors may be seen as the forces acting on the group that keep the group together.

The type of sport is important in this regard. Sports such as marathon running depend on the individual

Top tip

More advanced exam questions might ask you to account for the influence of task cohesion and social cohesion on team success, so make sure you can describe the importance of both. Remember that task cohesion alone can produce results, but is best accompanied by social cohesion.

Tasks to tackle 9.2

Make a list of the factors that you think could affect team cohesion. For each factor that you identify, state whether you think it affects task cohesion, social cohesion or both. For example, the personality of the players in the team is a factor that could influence social cohesion.

Chapter 9   Playing in a team

Some sports require high levels of coordination to avoid both failure and injury

athlete and do not need much coordination with others. Team sports such as netball, on the other hand, require a high degree of coordination and cooperation and the interaction of team members is important. There is also more potential for things to go wrong in a team because it is more likely that someone will make a mistake. Sports that are performed in a pair, such as tennis doubles, require interaction and cohesion. Think how vital it is for a double sculls rowing pair to get their mutual timing right. Timing is also important in team coordination. When a set move is performed in rugby it is important that all the players time their runs to perfection.

The personalities of the players also influence cohesion. It is important that the members of the team get on socially and that their personalities 'gel'. Imagine a group of extroverts all vying for attention within the group — a mix of both loud and quiet personalities is better for group harmony.

The rewards on offer can affect team morale and motivation. The desire to win a major cup game will tend to bind the team together in the drive for success. Personal differences are often forgotten in order to achieve success. In other words, the cohesion related to the task is stronger than the cohesion related to social aspects.

Cohesion and coordination are also affected by past success and the probability of future success. If a team has already beaten a particular opponent in the cup, then the players may well look forward with confidence to playing the same opponent again in the league — the good chance of a win will bring a desire to play.

Leadership can also affect team coordination. The captain should encourage and reward the team, with player of the match incentives for example.

Social loafing

A lack of effort by individual team members is called **social loafing**. This can have an effect on team cohesion and performance because it reduces the motivation in the team as a whole. Social loafing can occur when:

- an individual player feels that his/her efforts are not being recognised. This is known as a lack of performance identification. Players might give up if they think that their efforts will not change the result. If the team is losing 5–0 with only a couple of minutes to go there might be no point in trying.
- there is no reward on offer, such as a player of the match award. If the players lack confidence or motivation they might be more prepared to leave it to others to do all the work.
- the players perceive that others are not trying. They might think 'If she isn't putting any effort in, why should I?'
- the team captain is a poor leader and fails to encourage the team
- there is a perceived lack of ability. If a player feels that he/she is not as good as some others in the team, there may be a tendency to leave the majority of the work to the better players.

Social loafing is not desirable within a team so the coach should employ tactics to reduce its effect. The best way to prevent social loafing is to highlight individual performance and one of the best ways to achieve this is to use statistics. The number of tackles, the number of assists and the success rate of shots are all examples of data that players can be given after the game to provide feedback and show that they have been noticed. The coach should also make sure that players are encouraged and motivated during the game and that suitable rewards are on offer. Most clubs have a player of the year award to maintain motivation throughout the season. Confidence could be raised by pointing out the contribution players have made to the result and making them feel responsible, at least in part, for any success. In other words, success should be attributed internally.

Finally, the coach should set goals for the players and perhaps give them a specific role to play in the game, such as marking a certain opponent or playing in a wider position. Any goals that are set should be realistic and achievable and may represent an improvement on the last performance, such as to make three more tackles.

> **Top tip**
> Extended exam questions may ask you to suggest factors that influence a group's potential or to account for faulty processes. Make sure you understand the concept of social loafing and the factors that influence cohesion.

The Ringlemann effect

This theory suggests that the larger the group the less the collective group effort. Ringlemann performed an experiment using a 'tug of war' trial and discovered that a team of eight did not pull eight times harder than one individual. This suggests that there might be motivational problems in a team when players think that they can leave it to others to cover for them and hide within the team.

Ultimately, cohesion in sport is affected by a constantly changing mix of influences.

Leadership

Some of the most successful teams in sport have won major cups and trophies because they have been managed, coached or captained by an influential leader. Think of the success of Manchester United under the 23-year reign of Sir Alex Ferguson from 1986 until the time of writing.

A leader is someone who can influence others towards achieving goals. There are two types of leader in a sports group:

- An **emergent leader** is one who comes from within the group and assumes responsibility for the role or can be elected by the members of the club. In a sixth-form rounders team it could be that the captain is chosen by the players and coach. He/she is usually a player from year 13 who has played for the team in year 12 and already knows how the team works best. Although unity and the status quo is maintained, there might be a lack of fresh ideas.

- A **prescribed leader** is appointed from outside the group, in the way that the English Football Association appointed Fabio Capello as England manager in 2007. Such a leader may bring a fresh approach and give new impetus to the team, but could disrupt team unity and cause a few upsets. Sometimes players leave a club when a new prescribed leader is appointed.

> **Key terms**
>
> **Emergent leader:** a leader appointed from within the group.
> **Prescribed leader:** a leader appointed from outside the group.
> **Leader characteristics:** the qualities that facilitate good leadership.

Leaders will emerge or be appointed because they have **leader characteristics**. A good leader will have motivational skills to encourage the team to keep playing when they are losing or are involved in a difficult game. A leader usually has charisma and is well respected by the team. Sometimes the leader needs the ability to empathise — to listen to the needs of the group and to operate with the consensus of opinion. A leader must have good communication skills, so that tactics and strategies are adhered to by all the players. Usually leaders are experienced in their chosen sport and can pass this experience on to others. Finally, a leader should be able to adjust his/her style of leadership to suit the task in hand. There are a number of styles to choose from.

Leadership styles

The **autocratic** or task-oriented style of leadership is when the leader takes charge and dictates to the rest of the group, who have no say in the way the task is undertaken. By contrast, in the **democratic** or person-oriented style of leadership, the leader empathises and listens to the group members before making a decision on how the task should be done.

> **Key terms**
>
> **Autocratic style:** the leader makes all the decisions and gives the group formal instruction.
> **Democratic style:** the leader listens to the group members and involves them in decision making.

Fiedler's contingency model is summarised in Figure 9.2. According to this model, the choice of either the autocratic or the democratic style depends on how good or how favourable the situation is, and the leader should therefore choose the correct approach according to the situation.

The autocratic style is best when the situation is highly favourable and also when the situation is highly unfavourable. In a favourable situation, the leader is strong and well respected, the task is clear and the team members get on well and understand each other's play. There is no need to spend time discussing tactics, the team accepts and gets on with the decision of the captain. For example, if a netball team has a set play for moving the ball up towards the opposition goal and all the players know this well-rehearsed play, individuals will simply obey the captain's call to execute this move.

An unfavourable situation is one in which the team cannot agree on the tactics to be used, does not follow the instructions from a weak leader, or the task is unclear. A team facing unknown opponents in a hostile away game needs a strong leader to tell them what to do. A group in which the players are uncertain or arguing among themselves may need to be told the best strategy to adopt.

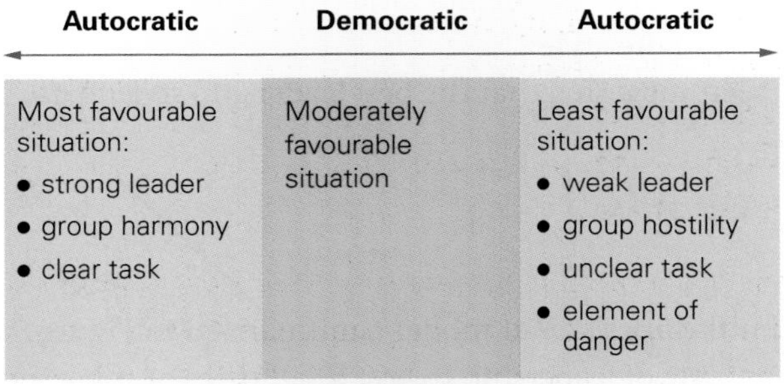

Autocratic	Democratic	Autocratic
Most favourable situation: • strong leader • group harmony • clear task	Moderately favourable situation	Least favourable situation: • weak leader • group hostility • unclear task • element of danger

Figure 9.2 Fiedler's contingency model

The democratic approach is best in a moderate situation, where a group is well established but there is scope for new ideas. In this case it may be best to sit down and discuss tactics with the team before a match.

Other styles that the leader can use include the **rewarding style**, when the leader gives incentives such as a player of the match award to motivate the team. Praise and encouragement may also be used to keep the team playing to the best of its ability. A **social support style** involves the coach or captain offering individual advice or feedback to particular players to help them improve their game.

During training sessions, a coach may put the players through their paces by setting up and

Top tip

Many exam questions on team dynamics are based on diagrams. Make sure you know and understand the diagrammatic models based on the work of Fiedler and Chelladurai and that you can explain the key phases of each model.

organising a number of specific skills and drills. This structured and often essential part of leadership is called a **training and instruction style** of leadership.

Sometimes the leader may find it appropriate to take a step back and just let the group get on with it. This laid-back approach is called a **laissez-faire style** of leadership. It can be used when the team members are experts in the task and know exactly what they are doing, or when a new coach has been appointed to lead a team and needs to stand back and assess what level his/her new charges are at.

One of the essential qualities of leaders is that they can adapt their leadership style to suit the situation. We have already seen how leaders might choose either the autocratic or the democratic style according to how favourable the situation is, but they may also need to take into account the features of the group or individual they are coaching as well as their own characteristics and preferences before choosing the style in which they want to operate. For example, in a dangerous situation, such as when coaching a contact skill such as a tackle, the leader may want to use an instructive and autocratic style to ensure correct technique and reduce the risk of injury. With beginners, to make sure they learn the basics, the style may be instructive and autocratic, motivational and rewarding. With experts, the leader may step back a little and ask for the democratic input of the group or even let them get on with things in a laissez faire style.

It has therefore been suggested that the best leadership style to use depends on three main influences:

- the situation
- the leader
- the group

Chelladurai's multi-dimensional model (summarised in Figure 9.3) suggests that if the leader can adapt the style of leadership to best fit all three of these influences then it is more likely that a rewarding and satisfactory performance will result. In other words, if the style of leadership chosen is equal to the requirements of the group and the demands of the situation, the better the performance is likely to be.

A final consideration of leadership in sport is the debate over whether leaders are born or made. This debate reflects a nature versus nurture approach to sports psychology. Some argue that people are born with characteristics, such as charisma and motivational skills, that make them

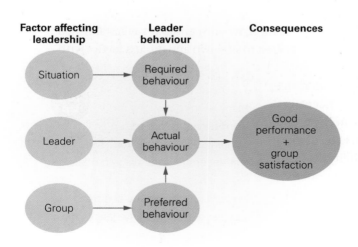

Figure 9.3 Chelladurai's multi-dimensional model of leadership styles

almost natural choices as captains or coaches. Others argue that such characteristics are learned and that good leaders are usually those with experience of the game. Perhaps the best approach is to accept a combination of both nature and nurture theories — that leaders are indeed born with essential leadership characteristics and that these characteristics are used in accordance with the circumstances under which the group will operate.

Tasks to tackle 9.3

Look again at the styles of leadership listed on pages 122–24. For each style, give a sporting situation in which you would use that style, and give a reason for your choice. For example, you might choose to use an autocratic style of leadership in a dangerous situation, such as swimming, especially if you were coaching beginners.

Top tip

It is essential that you know the situations in which autocratic and democratic leadership styles are used and that you can describe what you mean by a favourable and an unfavourable situation. Make sure that when you answer a question on the factors influencing leadership style you include not only situational factors but also the influence of the group and the leader's characteristics. Make sure that you give an example and an explanation from each of the three influences on leadership according to Chelladurai, namely situation, leader and group.

Practice makes perfect

1 Elite performers sometimes train on their own and sometimes as part of a group. How would you distinguish between a group and a collection of individuals? *(3 marks)*

2 Team players are often influenced by a leader who helps them to achieve an active and healthy lifestyle. Distinguish between a prescribed and an emergent leader and describe the characteristics that may be necessary for effective leadership in sport. *(5 marks)*

3 (a) Look at this model of group performance:

actual productivity = potential productivity – faulty processes

What is meant by the term potential productivity? *(1 mark)*

(b) What are the influences that can combine to produce faulty processes in a team? *(3 marks)*

Chapter *10*
Emotional control of sporting performance

What you need to know

By the end of this chapter you should be able to:
- say how confidence can affect sporting performance
- describe why and how coaches set goals for their performers
- understand the importance of controlling emotions such as anxiety and stress in sport

Confidence in sport

Confidence can be defined as a belief in your ability to master a particular situation. There are three factors that affect the level of confidence shown by a sports performer: personality, experience and situation. For example, a professional footballer playing in a European cup competition may be worried if his team is due to play the away leg of the cup tie at a ground at which he has never played before. The situation may be new to him; however, his experience of playing in many European competitions may help to reduce such lack of confidence, especially if the player is **competitive** and has a naturally confident personality. In other words, these three major influences on confidence can combine to produce a level of confidence in any given sporting situation.

Confidence in sport takes two forms:
- **Trait confidence** is innate and some sports performers remain upbeat in most situations even when the going is tough. Trait confidence is general and consistent.
- **State confidence** occurs in a particular situation, for example a penalty shoot out. For some players, such a high-risk part of a match can influence performance.

Key terms

Competitiveness: the degree to which challenging situations are welcomed.

Trait confidence: an innate degree of self-belief in being able to master a situation.

State confidence: a temporary degree of self-belief in a given situation.

The psychologist Vealey suggested that confidence is interactive and influenced by a number of factors, as shown in Figure 10.1. This model shows that a player will approach any situation with a pre-determined level of confidence based on his/her natural inclinations (trait confidence) and a level of competitiveness related to the goal. He/she will therefore have a level of state confidence in any situation, such as the penalty shoot out. Once the task has been performed, the player will evaluate how successful the performance has been and this judgement will then give rise to a new level of confidence in future similar situations. A player who has taken a penalty and scored may well be prepared to take part in future penalty shoot outs; if the penalty was missed and the shot was poor the player may be reluctant to take penalties in future. Naturally confident players who have trait confidence may simply offer to take a shot whenever the situation arises. Confidence can therefore affect the level of competitiveness shown in sporting events. Confident players will show a greater willingness to take part and attempt more difficult and challenging skills. They will show the 'need to achieve characteristics' that were discussed in Chapter 8.

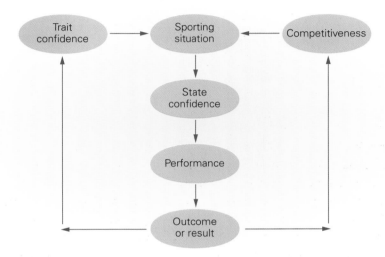

Figure 10.1 The factors affecting confidence — Vealey's model

Self-efficacy theory

While confidence refers to a general predisposition, confidence in any given sporting situation can be referred to as **self-efficacy**. The psychologist Bandura suggested that self-efficacy depends on four factors:

- **Performance accomplishments** — this refers to the amount of success that performers have achieved in the past on a similar task. For example, at an athletics meeting, a high jumper who has cleared 1.25 m in a recent training session will be confident of clearing the bar that is currently set at 1.10 m.
- **Vicarious experience** — this relates to players seeing others, especially their peers, perform a task similar to the one they are about to do themselves. Essentially, if someone else can do it, so can you! For example, at a junior school swimming lesson, the children may be apprehensive of diving in at the deep end despite the expert instruction of the teacher who is building the dive up from a sitting position. However, when one of the class attempts the dive successfully, the rest may be less apprehensive about having a go.

- **Verbal persuasion** — this relates to the amount of encouragement received from significant others, such as a coach, friends or family members. For example, you might feel a lot calmer when approaching a major event if your coach comments on how well you have been doing in training and that he/she knows you can perform well on the day of the event.
- **Emotional arousal** — this refers to the level of anxiety that a player may experience leading up to a big game. Ways of controlling such high levels of anxiety are discussed later in this chapter.

Top tip

The theory of self-efficacy is a popular theme for examiners. It is a good idea to learn the four factors that influence self-efficacy and to link these factors to the methods that coaches can use to improve confidence.

Figure 10.2 Bandura's self-efficacy theory

Bandura argued that if the four self-efficacy factors are positive, the performer will believe that he/she can do well and will succeed.

Improving self-efficacy

A lack of confidence can lead to anxiety and nervousness in sport, and performance can be adversely affected if confidence is low. In order to improve the confidence levels of players in their charge, the coach might adopt a number of strategies related to the theories of both Bandura and Vealey.

To promote confidence relating to performance accomplishments, the coach can highlight a player's past successes and the performance failures of the opposition. For example, the coach of a football team about to play the second round of a cup may point out that the opposing team has already been beaten in the league this season. When coaching beginners, the coach should make sure that success is achieved at an early stage by setting tasks that are within the capabilities of the players. For example, when coaching passing skills in team games, the coach might ask for the pass to be practised without any opposition in a static situation before introducing the pressure of an opponent in the passing drill.

An accurate demonstration of the skills and tactics to be used in the game can increase confidence relating to vicarious experience. The coach may also point out other players who

Junior versions of sports ensure successful performance accomplishments

are successfully performing similar tasks and these players can be used as **role models**. The coach should be careful to use role models to which the players in their charge can aspire. If top-class professionals are used as role models for beginners, the beginners might think that they could never be that good and actually lose confidence.

Positive verbal persuasion can be used by the coach in the lead-up to a game. Offering encouragement and praise, and telling performers that others think they will succeed can often help to improve confidence. The coach can also offer encouragement through rewards and incentives, such as player of the match awards. A final way to promote confidence is to make it clear to the players that any success achieved is down to them rather than due to any external influences. Success at an athletics meeting could be attributed to the effort put in by the athlete rather than the below-par performance of his/her competitors.

To promote confidence, the coach should lower the anxiety and emotional arousal felt by performers. A good way to do this is to practise mentally before the competition (see page 134), allowing the players to go through the performance in their mind several times before the big day. A gymnast might mentally run through the sequence of the routine before performing in a competition to

Tasks to tackle 10.1

List the four considerations that make up self-efficacy theory. For each factor that you list, suggest a method that the coach could use to develop and promote its influence.

make sure that the order of skills is correct. Emotional arousal and anxiety can also be controlled by muscular relaxation techniques (see page 135).

Goal setting in sport

Various research studies into sports psychology have found a positive link between goal setting and improved performance. Players who set themselves achievable targets or who have goals set by their coach generally produce better results. The specific boundaries established by such targets give players something to aim for, so that personal motivation is provided and a sense of satisfaction is felt when that target is achieved. Confidence will improve once a goal has been reached, allowing a more difficult target to be set to allow further improvement. Goal setting also has an important role in lowering anxiety and reducing the stress of performing at a high level.

The goals set by coaches and players can be long term or short term. Long-term goals are concerned with the end result of a lengthy period of work and are sometimes called **outcome goals**. For example, an outcome goal for a swimmer may be to qualify for regional team selection. Short-term goals are the stepping-stones towards meeting long-term targets. **Performance goals** are short term and are judged against a past performance. For example, an attempt by a swimmer to beat her personal best time by the end of next month might be a step towards meeting the regional target time. **Process goals** are concerned with technique and are also short term. For example, in order to achieve a personal best, the swimmer must work on improving her exit from each turn.

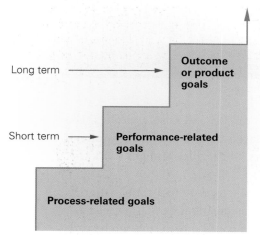

Long term ⟶ Outcome or product goals

Short term ⟶ Performance-related goals

Process-related goals

Figure 10.3 A summary of the types of goals that can be set by players and coaches

It is important that goals do not focus solely on winning. In an athletics race, for example, there can only be one winner and performers who fail to meet that target may lose motivation and suffer stress. It is more important to set goals that can be achieved, such as those that focus on personal improvement and technique. Personal goals provide intrinsic motivation and a sense of satisfaction from doing your best. An athlete may not win the race but can still gain a personal best time and show improved technique.

Other factors that a coach might consider when setting goals are summed up by the **SMARTER** principle. This is a set of guidelines that should be taken into account when setting goals. Goals should be:

Key terms

Outcome goals: the end result after a lengthy period of work.

Performance goals: targets related to improvement and enhancing current standards.

Process goals: targets related to improving technique.

OCR A2 Physical Education

Specific — 'going up one level on the bleep test' is a specific goal, 'improving fitness' is not.

Measured — statistics or a stopwatch should be used to inform performers about their achievement.

Agreed —players should sit down and discuss the goals with the coach, so that they are involved in the goal-setting process.

Realistic — the goals should offer a challenge but be achievable.

Timed — a goal should be long term or short term, and preferably have a specific date, in order to help keep the performer focused.

Exciting — players work harder for something they are interested in.

Recorded — progress should be written down to allow for evaluation.

If the SMARTER principle is followed, then improved performance and confidence should follow.

> **Top tip**
>
> Maximising the effectiveness of goal setting is a popular topic with examiners. Do learn the SMARTER principle, but don't forget that effective goal setting does not always mean setting a target to win — performance and process goals are also important.

> **Tasks to tackle 10.2**
>
> Goal setting is an important technique that coaches and players can use to improve their performance. In your own sport, think of a long-term objective or outcome goal that you would like to achieve this season and then suggest some shorter-term goals that would help you to achieve your aim.

Anxiety and stress in sport

One of the most common reasons for failure in sports performance is stress and high anxiety levels in the athlete. In simple terms, when you are nervous your performance is not as good. In sports psychology it is important to look at the causes of stress and anxiety to see if anything can be done to prevent or reduce the symptoms of stress.

The terms stress and anxiety are linked. **Stress** can be defined as the response of the body to a threatening situation. The causes of stress, known as stressors, may be perceived by the performer either positively or negatively, and it is the performer's **perception** that dictates the response to the threat. For example, at the start of a race, an athlete becomes aware that some of the runners have faster personal best times than he does. The response to this competitive threat could be positive: 'I've been training well and I think I can use the faster pace to improve my personal

> **Key terms**
>
> **Stress:** the response (not always negative) of the body to a threat.
> **Perception:** what we think might happen; not necessarily what does happen.

> **Top tip**
>
> Know the difference between anxiety, stress and arousal because these basic definitions are often required in the exam and they can gain you a couple of easy marks.

best.' However, the response to this threat could be negative: 'These runners have got really fast times and I've got no chance of winning today!'

Such positive or negative responses determine the confidence and motivation levels of the athlete. A positive response to a stressor could actually improve motivation and result in an enhanced performance, so stress should not always be viewed negatively — it can help to produce better results. When the response to a stressor is negative, it becomes anxiety. **Anxiety** is the negative aspect of stress characterised by irrational thinking, worry and loss of **concentration**.

In sport, stress — and by consequence anxiety if the stressor is perceived in a negative way — can be caused by a number of influences. Highly competitive situations can be stressors, such as playing in a cup final or a major event such as a regional championship. Performers may be aware that higher levels of effort and technique are needed in order to succeed. Are they up to the task?

Stress and anxiety can also be caused by the anticipation of conflict in sport. For example, the possibility of being marked by a strong and robust player who is known to play to the limit of the rules may cause apprehension before the game starts. Frustration is another stressor, often caused by the same factors that lead to aggression in sport, perhaps by being fouled, not playing well or losing. Such frustration causes the blood pressure and heart rate to go up. Another cause of stress is climatic influences. Playing a fast, physical sport in very hot conditions increases heart rates and levels of fatigue. Rugby league, for example, is played in the summer months when temperatures can reach over 40°C.

> **Key terms**
>
> **Anxiety:** the negative response to a threat, including irrational thinking and worry.
>
> **Concentration:** the ability to maintain attention on the required task.

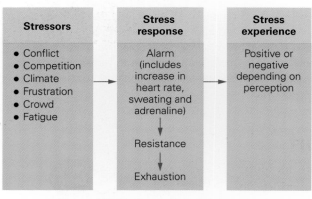

Figure 10.4 Features of stress in sport

Remember that in all these stressful situations it is the players' perception of how they can meet the demands of the situation that is important. If they think they can match the threat, then a good performance should result; if they feel they are unable to match the threat, then anxiety and an inhibited performance may occur. Figure 10.4 shows that the stressors discussed above can cause an athlete some initial shock or alarm but then it is the athlete who determines whether to treat the stressor in a positive or negative way.

Anxiety

Anxiety is an unwelcome feature of sports performance. Performers may view a situation negatively and begin to think irrationally. Worrying thoughts may enter their mind, such as 'What if I get injured today playing against this overly physical team?' or 'If I miss this penalty

I will let everyone down'. They might worry about events well before the game takes place, such as not meeting the demands of the training schedule, or even about matters unconnected with sport, such as family concerns. The effect of all this is that they begin to lose concentration on the task and become tense and lacking in confidence.

Anxiety may be experienced in two ways. Anxiety that occurs in the mind, or psychological anxiety, is known as **cognitive anxiety**. Physiological anxiety is known as **somatic anxiety**. Somatic anxiety is characterised by the physical responses of the body to stressors such as an increase in heart rate, a rise in adrenaline levels, increased sweating, muscular tension and poor coordination.

Reducing cognitive anxiety

Cognitive anxiety can be controlled using various techniques, such as:

- visualisation
- imagery
- mental rehearsal
- positive self-talk
- thought stopping
- goal setting

Key terms

Cognitive anxiety: psychological anxiety, worry in the mind.

Somatic anxiety: physiological anxiety, physical symptoms of stress.

Visualisation: creating a mental picture of a successful attempt to complete a task as if in a real situation.

Imagery: recreating a mental picture of a task that has been successfully completed in the past.

Visualisation involves picturing yourself doing the skill that you are practising in a competitive situation. For example, a football player might be taking free kicks successfully in practice, but when it comes to the actual game on a Saturday afternoon those free kicks are not as good. What the player needs to do is to imagine during the training session that the free kicks are being taken for real, perhaps

Top tip

Visualisation, imagery and mental rehearsal are similar, so make sure you know how to differentiate between them.

when there is more pressure, more fatigue and in the presence of a crowd. The player needs to feel any anticipated sources of anxiety and overcome them so that when it comes to actually taking the free kicks for real, any stressors have been dealt with in practice. A successful attempt in training should be locked into the thoughts of the player so that it can be repeated for real. Having dealt with the anxiety already, the player should maintain confidence and produce better end results.

Another method of controlling cognitive anxiety is **imagery**. This is similar to visualisation in that the performer pictures in his mind a successful attempt at the skill. This time, however, the performer looks back at an earlier task or game, one in which he/she performed well — perhaps a cup-winning performance or a game that led to the award of player of the match. The key is to try to recreate the sense of pride gained from a past success so that more confidence and less anxiety is felt at the present time. The idea is to tell yourself 'I did it before, so I can do it again'.

Mental rehearsal involves going over a practised skill, drill or routine in the mind without physical movement so that the sequence of actions is stored firmly in the memory. Mental rehearsal is very useful when performing serial skills involving a sequence of well-learned movements, such as those required when performing a gym routine. Such movements are performed in a set order and this set routine can be rehearsed before competition. Closed skills, when the sequence of movements is not likely to change, are well-suited to mental rehearsal since it is unlikely that the performer will have to alter the pre-learned sequence.

Mental rehearsal: going over a performance in the mind repeatedly.

Key term

Mental rehearsal can be used by both novice and experienced players. In the case of a novice, the coach could use mental rehearsal in small chunks as part of a distributed practice session. For example, when the player is resting the coach could remind him/her of basic techniques to run through in their mind. In the case of an expert, the coach might allow the player time to devote to the whole task or sequence, concentrating on detail and repeating the finer aspects of the task in the mind over and over again.

In all three cognitive management techniques mentioned above there are considerations that both coaches and players should note to make the techniques successful. First, the coach should take into account the level of experience of the player, so that the mental techniques can be applied in a different manner for the novice and the expert, as explained above. When any of the cognitive techniques are used they should always concentrate on success. The player should visualise performing the task with a successful end result or imagine a previous winning performance. Players should use real time when using mental rehearsal. Real time refers to the actual time it takes to perform the task in competition, so that if a gym routine lasts for 85 seconds then that is the time the gymnast must spend mentally rehearsing the routine. When a player is mentally rehearsing, visualising or using imagery, it is a good idea to avoid distractions, so a quiet space without any disturbance should be used.

When mental practice is used successfully it can have a positive effect on performance. Studies have measured the performances of athletes who performed an unfamiliar task by (a) mentally practising only, (b) using physical practice only and (c) by doing both physical and mental practice. The best results were achieved by those who did both mental and physical practice. Mental practice reduces anxiety, improves confidence and provides motivation.

Other methods of controlling anxiety can be used specifically during performance. **Positive self-talk** involves athletes reminding themselves what they need to do to succeed. When you watch a rugby union kicker line up an attempt at goal, you will probably see him take a deep breath and you may notice his lips move just before he takes the kick. The player is using positive self-talk to remind himself of the technique needed to make a successful attempt. Positive self-talk can be used to remind a player of tactics and strategies given by the coach before the game; it can be used to break bad habits so that the performer does not keep repeating a poor play; or it can be used to concentrate on weaknesses in the opponent or a

Key term

Positive self-talk: reminding yourself of important information or replacing negative thoughts with positive ones.

strength in the performer's own play. 'Stop that daft shot' or 'Concentrate on the backhand' are comments that players may make to themselves.

Thought stopping is another technique used by players to prevent negative thinking from hindering performance. Thoughts such as 'I can't do that shot' are deliberately put to one side.

Goal setting, as we have already seen, can also be used to control anxiety because it allows players to meet targets and gain confidence when a target is met. Improved confidence is usually a measure of lower anxiety.

Reducing somatic anxiety

Somatic anxiety is physical, so the coach or player can use the following techniques:

Progressive relaxation techniques can be used to relieve muscular tension. The athlete is guided through a series of static tensing exercises that involve holding a particular group of muscles at maximum contraction for a short

Jonny Wilkinson's trademark visualisation and self-talk before attempting a conversion have been much copied

period of time and then gradually releasing the hold. Each part of the body is worked on in turn, starting with the periphery and working towards the body core. The athlete can learn to concentrate on tension reduction, and once the technique is learned, the tension caused by anxiety can be dramatically reduced.

Breathing techniques can also be used to counter physical anxiety. Here the athlete attempts a series of controlled breathing exercises to help them slow their breathing rate and focus on the task. You will often see a football player take a deep breath before attempting a penalty kick.

Biofeedback uses physical measurements to record the reduction in anxiety that can be achieved by the methods mentioned above. For example, a heart monitor could be used to measure the reduction in heart rate achieved by using imagery, visualisation or self-talk. When the results of the different methods are compared, the athlete will know which method works best for them. Biofeedback is therefore a physical way of testing which anxiety counter method — be it somatic or cognitive — is best for them.

Other types of anxiety

Some sports performers tend to worry most of the time, even if there is only a small chance of the things they are concerned about actually happening. Such naturally anxious athletes are said to show **trait anxiety**. Trait anxiety is inherent, consistent and enduring. The athlete will continue to worry in most situations and the coach should use the anxiety control methods outlined above to help reduce both cognitive and somatic anxieties.

> **Key terms**
>
> **Trait anxiety:** an innate characteristic of inherent worry and lack of self-belief.
>
> **State anxiety:** a temporary lack of self-belief in a given situation.

State anxiety is more temporary but equally significant. It occurs in specific situations, such as taking a penalty, or serving for the match in tennis, when a rush of anxious thoughts and physical tension, or loss of concentration, may result in a poor performance. You may have witnessed missed penalties in shoot outs or tennis players who fail to close out the match at match point.

The effects of anxiety are amplified if naturally anxious performers are placed in situations that may cause more anxiety. In other words, players who have the trait are more likely to show state anxiety. The combination of trait and state anxiety can lead to well below par performance. The manager or coach should find out which players are likely to find specific situations stressful by testing them for anxiety before major competitions, so that such players can avoid the threat.

> **Top tip**
>
> The terms 'trait' and 'state' appear more then once in this section of the course, so make sure that you know what these terms mean so that you can use them correctly.

> **Tasks to tackle 10.3**
>
> Make a list of some of the influences that you think could cause anxiety and stress in sport and give an example for each influence that you list.

Measuring anxiety

A number of anxiety tests have been developed that are specifically targeted at sports competition. The **sport competition anxiety test**, or SCAT test, designed by the psychologist Martens, is the best known of these, but you may also see the names SCA1 and CSAI2.

The SCAT test is a questionnaire in which athletes are asked to answer a series of questions by ticking a box and are then given a rating as to their level of anxiety in sporting competition. The test, an example of which is given below, has the same advantages and disadvantages as other personality tests discussed in Chapter 8. In an attempt to avoid the problem of biased answers, some of the questions are unrelated to the subject matter so that the real subject being tested — anxiety — is masked. Have a go at the test and see how you rate. The method of calculating your score is shown at the end of the test.

Statements	Hardly ever	Sometimes	Often
(1) Competing against others is socially enjoyable			
(2) Before I compete I feel uneasy			
(3) Before I compete I worry about not playing well			
(4) I am a good sportsperson when I compete			
(5) When I compete I worry about making mistakes			
(6) Before I compete I am calm			
(7) Setting a goal is important when competing			
(8) Before I compete I get a queasy feeling in my stomach			
(9) Just before competing I notice my heart beats faster than usual			

How to score the test:
- Items 1, 4 and 7 do not count (they are designed to mask the test).
- Score items 2, 3, 5, 8 and 9 as: hardly ever = 1, sometimes = 2, often = 3
- Score item 6 as: hardly ever = 3, sometimes = 2, often = 1

The maximum score is 18. The higher the score, the higher the competitive anxiety. Is this a quick and easy method of assessing personality?

The relationship between arousal and performance

Arousal is defined as the level of readiness to perform. It is an energised state that prepares the body for action and includes:
- an increase in adrenaline levels
- an increase in heart rate
- a muscular anticipation

Key term

Arousal: the degree of activation and readiness to perform a task.

However, too much or too little arousal can have a detrimental effect on performance. Increased arousal can be caused by the approach of a major competition or big game, by others watching the performance (especially if those watching are knowledgeable about the sport, such as a chief scout from a local club, or if they are significant others), by increasingly frustrating circumstances (such as being fouled), or by a fear of failure. When an increase in arousal occurs, the effect on performance is explained by a number of theories.

Drive theory

Drive theory suggests that as the level of arousal increases, so performance improves in a linear or constant fashion. It is explained by the following formula:

$$P = D \times H$$

In other words, performance is the product of drive and habit.

It is suggested that an athlete is initially motivated by the challenge of meeting the task or by the big game, and that the increased effort put in brings success, and the drive to continue performing. The success achieved provides reinforcement and the athlete carries on repeating the successful responses so that the performance becomes habitual. Drive theory is depicted by Figure 10.5, which shows performance improving continuously with increasing arousal.

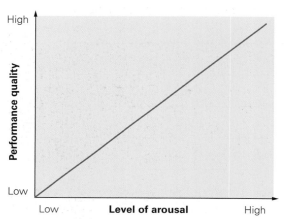

Figure 10.5 Drive theory

However, at high levels of arousal the ability to take in information from the environment is reduced and performers may only focus on the **dominant response**, or the most intense stimulus. Expert performers may be able to continue playing well at high arousal because they can focus on the correct dominant response using their experience, but novices may focus on an incorrect response and their performance could suffer.

Drive reduction theory

This theory suggests that motivation is high at the start of the learning process, when performers are challenged by the need to master the task, but that once success has been achieved that initial drive is lost — the need has been satisfied. The drive to master the task and overcome the challenge is replaced by a sense of satisfaction based on successful completion of the skill. A new challenge or an extension to the skill is needed to provide further motivation.

> **Top tip**
> Exam questions often ask you to describe the relationship between arousal and performance. Make sure that you can sketch the graphs and that you know all the key points that relate to each theory: drive theory, inverted U theory, drive reduction and catastrophe theory. Extra marks can often be gained by giving an explanation of the dominant response and how it affects drive theory and for suggesting that a moderate level of arousal may not always be the most beneficial level of arousal.

The inverted U theory

The inverted U theory states that increases in arousal can improve performance up to an optimum point, which occurs at a moderate level of arousal. Further increases in arousal have a detrimental effect on performance. Therefore, both low and high levels of arousal can produce a performance that is below our best. At low arousal, performers may be under-activated and not sufficiently motivated. At high arousal, performers may begin to suffer from anxiety and tension so that their performance is inhibited. However, a moderate level of arousal may not always be the most productive. The best level of arousal for optimum performance varies according to the task being attempted and the personality and expertise of the performer.

- Experts tend to cope well with high levels of arousal because they are experienced at dealing with the pressures of performance, for example playing in front of a large crowd. Novices may find it hard to cope with the increased pressure and tend to perform best at low levels of arousal.

- **Extroverts** have naturally low levels of adrenaline and are better able to cope with the increases in adrenaline levels associated with arousal than **introverts**, who already have high adrenaline levels.

The amount of stimulation required to provoke increases in arousal and adrenaline is determined by the **reticular activating system**. The reticular activating system (RAS) is the part of the brain believed to be the centre of arousal and motivation in mammals. It brings relevant information to our attention and acts like a filter between the conscious and the subconscious.

- Simple tasks require little decision making and can be performed at higher arousal levels than complex tasks. At high levels of arousal, fewer decisions are attempted because fewer items of information are processed in the brain. Decisions at high arousal are based on limited information. A simple task such as a forward roll can therefore be attempted at high arousal. However, at low arousal we may be more able to make the decisions required for complex skills because more information can be processed.

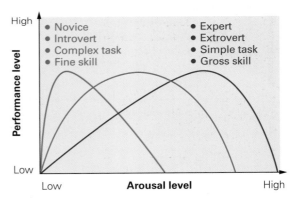

Figure 10.6 The inverted U theory and how it can be adapted to take account of the task and the performer

Top tip

Don't be put off in the exam if you see a graph. The answers to the question can be contained in it!

- Gross skills can be performed at high arousal because they require less control and more muscular involvement. Finer skills require more control and are best performed at low arousal levels. For example, a rugby tackle can be attempted with a higher level of arousal than a badminton drop shot.

Catastrophe theory

This adapted version of the inverted U theory explains why even the best attempts to control arousal levels can suddenly be undermined in sport. Increases in arousal improve performance up to a certain point but then, rather than a gradual decline in performance, a further increase in arousal pushes the performer over the edge and performance falls dramatically. It may only take a small increase in arousal to reach this point of **catastrophe** but this small increase, caused perhaps by a worry about not playing well, by the threat of a difficult opponent or by playing in a major final in front of a big crowd, can have a cumulative effect. When added to existing arousal levels, even experts can experience this kind of disaster.

Changes in the situation can cause a sufficient increase in arousal to invoke a catastrophe. Imagine a tennis player who wins the semi-final of a major tournament. She has been playing her best tennis and knows she has a chance of winning in the final. On the day of the final, she plays great tennis in the first set, taking it to a tie-break. She then begins to feel the pressure of the moment and suddenly her performance plummets.

The catastrophe is caused by a combination of cognitive and somatic anxieties — the internal worries about not playing well are compounded by physical effects such as muscular tension. To get over the catastrophe the performer must return to a level of arousal that was present before the catastrophe occurred — a feat not always possible under extreme pressure.

> **Key terms**
>
> **Catastrophe:** a dramatic and severe deterioration in performance.
> **The zone:** an energised, yet controlled, frame of mind that is focused on the task.

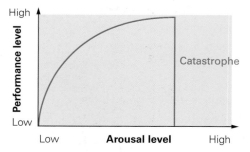

Figure 10.7 Catastrophe theory

The zone

Sometimes, athletes reach a level of performance that is both anxiety free and technically near perfect. They reach what is known as the **zone**, or zone of optimal functioning. The zone is characterised by feelings of calm despite the intense pressure. A sense of supreme confidence exists and the performer is almost totally immersed in the action, with concentration levels at an all-time high. The resultant performance is near perfect, with few errors, lots of energy and correct decision making — the whole event seems to flow in a smooth, efficient manner.

The zone is obviously a state the performer will want to achieve. It is usually associated with top-level athletes who have perfected and practised the anxiety control measures of visualisation, imagery, self-talk and mental rehearsal discussed earlier in this chapter.

The zone of optimal functioning (ZOF), proposed by the psychologist Hanin, is another adaptation of the inverted U theory. Like the inverted U theory, it suggests that the optimum level of arousal varies depending on the type of task being performed and the person performing it. However, the best level of arousal for each situation is depicted by an area — or zone — rather than a point.

The theory suggests that a novice or a person performing a fine task, such as a golf putt, operates best at a low arousal zone (performer A in Figure 10.8). An expert performer or a player performing a gross skill, such as a tackle, requires a higher level of arousal (performer C in Figure 10.8). A moderate level of arousal may be suitable for a player completing a task that requires a degree of control, such as a volleyball block (performer B in Figure 10.8).

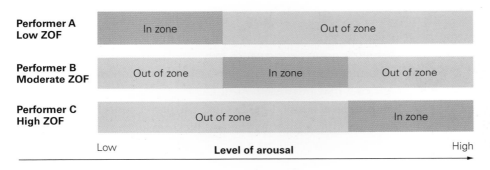

Figure 10.8 Summary showing how the zone of optimal functioning varies for individual performers

Peak flow

The best performance can be achieved when the challenge of the task is appropriate to the performer's skill. According to Figure 10.9, which shows the **peak flow experience**, players who have little skill and are presented with a difficult task will suffer anxiety. For example, novice rock climbers would be nervous if they were asked to ascend a difficult route. Players with little skill who are offered no challenge will be apathetic to the task. Skilled players who are asked to do an easy task that is well below their capability will quickly become bored. For example, a young experienced swimmer who trains five mornings a week would not relish the basic demands of a school swimming lesson for beginners. To produce a top performance and achieve peak flow, skilled players should be set a task that is difficult enough to challenge them and offers a real incentive for success.

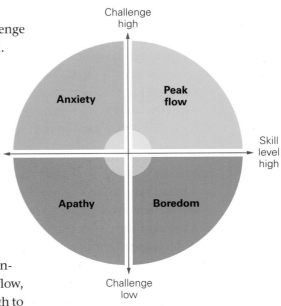

Figure 10.9 Peak flow experience

Attention in sport

Have you ever been in a theory lesson when the teacher has asked you a question to which you were unable to give an answer because you were looking out of the window or thinking about something else? Maybe your attention had begun to wander. In sport it is essential that you pay attention and concentrate on the task to achieve top-level performance. You have to ignore distractions and make sure you pick up the correct cues in order to make the right decisions. Attention is defined as the ability to focus on the relevant environmental cues.

Cue utilisation hypothesis

Easterbrook suggests that the number of environmental cues we can process is related to our level of arousal. In an adaptation of the inverted U theory, he suggests that at low levels of arousal the performer has the capacity to take in a relatively large amount of information but that this wide range of cues may cause confusion and result in a lower level of performance.

> **Key term**
>
> **Cue utilisation:** the degree to which the performer can use information from the environment.

At high arousal performance may also be at a lower level because the performer tends to concentrate on less information and therefore important cues may be missed. At moderate arousal, however, performance tends to be at a high level because the player concentrates on just the right amount of information and picks up all the relevant cues. Since this theory suggests that a moderate level of arousal produces the best performance, it supports the ideas outlined in the inverted U theory.

Attentional style

The psychologist Nideffer suggested that the sports performer should choose the most appropriate style of picking up information from the environment, depending on the situation. There are four possible styles to choose from:

- A broad style is when a wide range of cues is used to make decisions.
- A narrow style is when the player focuses on only one or two cues and makes decisions based on just this information.
- An external style is when the player looks to pick up information from the environment.
- An internal style is when the focus is on information from within.

A matrix of attentional styles is shown in Figure 10.10, indicating that the styles can be combined:

- A broad external style is when the games player, for example, focuses on the entire field to assess the state of play and choose the best option.
- A broad internal style could be the assessment a coach makes of the whole game to then plan for the next game in his or her own mind.
- A narrow external style is when a player has to focus on a specific target, for example a golfer focusing on the hole before making a putt.
- A narrow internal style could be when a player uses mental rehearsal to concentrate on the feel of a shot or a particular tactic.

> **Top tip**
>
> Make sure that you can give a sporting example for each attentional style

Some sports performers can concentrate on two streams of information at once. They often choose the most appropriate style for the situation and can switch from one style to another quite easily. Such players are called effective attenders. An ineffective attender loses concentration easily and fails to cope with distractions. The trick to effective attention is to choose the right style for the right occasion and be able to switch from one to another quickly as the situation demands. A football player might initially use a broad external style to scan the field and choose the best player available to receive a pass. He or she could then switch to a narrow external style and focus on that player prior to delivering the pass.

	External	Internal
Broad	The whole arena e.g. a playmaker reading the game	Analysing and planning e.g. a coach working out tactics
Narrow	Focus on a single cue e.g. a golf putt	Mental rehearsal or feel of task e.g. focus on the grip of the racket

Figure 10.10 A matrix of attentional styles

If attention is lost or the focus is applied to the wrong cues, the performance can be adversely affected. The player might concentrate on the crowd rather than the important stimuli, and such loss of concentration could mean a poor pass or a missed shot. The player could also choose the wrong style, could pick up too much information or could miss important cues. Anxiety could be increased and muscular tension and loss of confidence could occur.

Distraction conflict theory

Have you ever been trying to watch an important game on television and been distracted by a member of your family asking you questions? It is hard to concentrate on two things at the same time. Distraction conflict explains why it is difficult to multi-task.

The theory suggests that the presence of a distraction, which may be from an external source such as the crowd, or from an internal source such as a worry about an injury, while the performer is trying to concentrate on the task will cause an increase in arousal levels. This, in turn, could cause performance to deteriorate, especially if the performer is a beginner. There is conflict between the demands of the task and the draw of the distraction. The effect of distractions is worse if the task is complex. If the distraction is intense, such as a loud shout from the crowd or from the opposition, then the effect can be immediate.

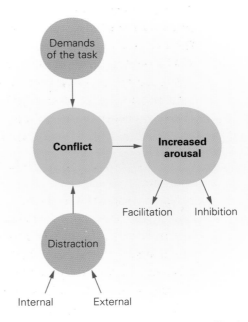

Figure 10.11 A summary of distraction conflict theory

Social facilitation and inhibition

In the last section we noted how being watched can cause a distraction to the performer. The effects of being watched while playing sport can be very different — the performance can either be made better, an effect called **social facilitation**, or it can be made worse, an effect called **social inhibition**.

According to the psychologist Zajonc, there are four types of 'others' who can be present during performance:

- An **audience** simply watches the play. Examples include the silent crowd at a snooker match or the chief scout from a local club making notes during a performance. The audience has no direct part in the performance but applies pressure simply by being there.
- **Supporters**, such as members of the crowd at a football match, are not content with simply watching; they are more interactive and cheer or criticise the performance. They can have a more direct bearing on the player since the encouragement they give can provide motivation.
- A **co-actor** is defined as someone doing the same activity without being in competition, like another jogger in the park when you are out for a run. Their mere presence may be an incentive to perform better.
- A **competitor** is in direct conflict with the performer, for example the other athletes in a 100m race. Competition in sport is a major cause of anxiety.

The main effect of being watched in sport is a rise in the performers' level of arousal. In the same way that arousal levels affect sports performers in different ways according to the inverted U theory, the effect of an audience can vary. An expert performer such as a

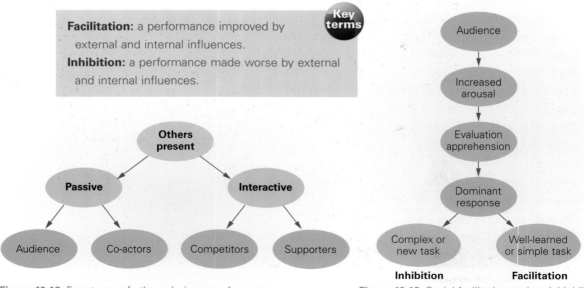

Figure 10.12 Four types of others during a performance

Figure 10.13 Social facilitation and social inhibition

OCR A2 Physical Education

professional football player will be used to playing in front of a crowd and will be able to cope with the pressure of being watched. Sometimes professional players raise their game for the big events and can respond to the crowd — we say their performance is **facilitated**. A novice performer will find the effect more daunting and may be put off by the presence of an audience, resulting in an **inhibited** performance.

The differing effects of an audience also relate to drive theory and the dominant response. At high arousal levels, the performer takes in less information from the environment and tends to focus on the dominant response. For experts who have learned the skill well this response is usually correct and so the performance is facilitated. Novices, however, may not yet have learned the correct response, so under pressure they choose the wrong options.

The type of task being performed is important in determining whether facilitation or inhibition takes place. A simple task requires less decision making and less information, so it can be performed correctly at high arousal levels. A complex task requires more decision making and may not be performed correctly at high levels of arousal when less information is processed by the performer. Therefore, a simple skill may be facilitated if an audience is present and a complex task may be inhibited.

An effect of being watched is a fear of being judged. **Evaluation apprehension** is the term used to describe the fear of being judged. Can you remember what it was like when your

> **Top tip**
>
> Questions on the effects of an audience may ask you to suggest two possible effects of being watched: inhibition or facilitation. Use Figure 10.13 to help you suggest that an audience can either make you perform better or worse. Think about increased arousal, evaluation apprehension and dominant response, then — depending on the performer of the task — how performance can be helped or hindered.

TopFoto

'Henmania' was often considered a contributing factor in Tim Henman's relatively poor showings at Wimbledon despite his high world ranking

parents watched you in your first performance? You felt anxious not only because you were being watched for the first time, but also because you were a beginner. Years later, you might welcome your parents watching you play because as a more proficient player you are more confident. However, if the person watching you is an expert, such as a chief scout from a professional club, then although you know you can play well you still feel anxious about their presence.

The effects of being watched in sport can be influenced by the situation. Most players prefer to play on their home ground, in familiar surroundings, in front of a supportive crowd and such support can enhance performance. Playing away from home can be more distracting, especially when the away crowd is hostile. The preference for playing at home is called the 'home field advantage'. However, the expectation that a team will win at home can put undue pressure on the players and performance might be impaired.

Players who suffer from natural trait anxiety will be even more nervous in front of a big crowd. Remember that those who show trait anxiety are more likely to show state anxiety. Extrovert personalities are more likely to respond positively to the effects of an audience because they prefer to be loud and obvious in front of others. Introvert characters are more likely to suffer in front of an audience because they naturally wish to avoid the limelight. More experienced players are less likely to suffer from inhibition.

There are things that both the player and the coach can do to counter the effects of social inhibition and promote social facilitation. A useful strategy is to allow the players to be watched when they train so that they get used to playing in front of a crowd. Familiarisation with an audience will help the players to develop experience in dealing with being watched. Parents and families could be invited to training and social events at the club. The coach could also attempt to lower the perceived importance of the event. If a big league game is coming up, the coach could suggest that even if the game is lost, there is still an opportunity to win the league.

The players could practise the techniques used to counter both cognitive and somatic anxieties. Relaxation techniques, visualisation and imagery, with special emphasis on games played in front of a big crowd, could be used to help reduce tension and lower levels of arousal.

In summary, playing in front of a crowd can have positive or negative effects depending on the complexity of the task and the experience of the player. Both inhibition and facilitation can be explained by reference to the inverted U and drive theories, since the main effect of being watched is to increase arousal and these theories also explain the relationship between arousal and performance.

Attribution theory

Think of a major game or performance in which you did really well. What reasons can you give for your success? Were those reasons due to your performance or due to things that were out of your control? Now think of a game in which you did not do so well. Were the reasons for that poor performance out of your control? If you listen to a summary of a game by two football managers after the final whistle you might realise that the reasons the winning manager gives for success are often different from those that the losing manager gives for failure.

Attribution theory looks at the reasons sports performers give for winning and losing.

According to Weiner's model, there are four main categories into which the

reasons for winning and losing can be placed. The first two categories define the extent to which the performer has control over the outcome. They are known collectively as the **locus of causality**:

- An **internal reason** is one that is under the control or influence of the performer. Examples include the amount of effort put into the game, the level of ability shown during the performance and the amount of pre-performance practice.
- An **external reason** is one that is said to be outside the control of the performer. Examples include a decision given by a referee, the bounce of the ball or the quality of the opposing team.

The other two categories — collectively known as the **locus of stability** — define how permanent the perceived reasons for winning or losing are.

- A **stable reason** is one that takes time to change. The ability level of the performer is stable. This does not mean that the level of ability will never change, but it will take some time to improve.
- An **unstable reason** is one that is temporary and can change from moment to moment or from week to week. Unstable reasons include psychological factors (such as the impact of missing an open goal), task difficulty (such as playing against difficult opposition), luck (such as a ball hitting the crossbar and either deflecting in or out of the goal) and effort (such as a greater effort put in at the start of the season than at its close when the chances of winning the league have gone).

The attribute of luck can therefore be classed as both unstable and external. The attribute of effort is both unstable and internal. We can sum up the reasons given for winning and losing on a matrix, as shown in Figure 10.14.

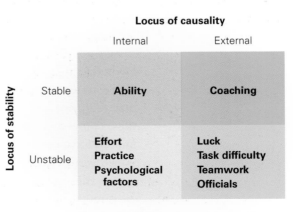

Figure 10.14 Weiner's model of attribution

Tasks to tackle 10.4

Make a copy of the matrix that shows the attributed reasons for success or failure. Consider the following reasons given by athletes for the outcome of a race in which they have just competed and place them in the appropriate area of the matrix:

(a) 'I was feeling good today and my performance reflected that feeling. I had the stamina to push right to the end.'

(b) 'I was given a poor draw in lane 8 and couldn't hear the starter, he just wasn't loud enough.'

(c) 'I gave it my all. I tried to keep up with the pace at the end and I was so nearly in the mix. In a few weeks I will be right up there with that lot, trust me!'

(d) 'We got our plan wrong. The coach suggested I push the pace early but maybe I did not push enough. It's back to the drawing board.'

Self-serving bias

The tendency to blame losing on external and unstable reasons and account for victory using internal and stable reasons is called **self-serving bias**. Coaches can help to motivate players by blaming a loss on external influences beyond the athletes' control, such as bad luck or the decision of the referee. Success should be attributed to internal factors, such as the players' ability and efforts.

Coaches can use factors in the internal part of the attribution model (Figure 10.14) to motivate players, for example by rewarding effort, praising ability and criticising lack of effort.

Learned helplessness and mastery orientation

Learned helplessness is a state of mind that occurs when performers attribute losing to internal and stable reasons. Performers blame themselves and their own ability for losing and think that such failure is inevitable and likely to be repeated. Such learned helplessness can be specific to one sport, such as 'I just can't play tennis', or it can be more general — 'I'm no good at sport'. Causes of learned helplessness can be repeated failure, lack of encouragement from the coach or targets that are simply too high.

To counter learned helplessness the reasons for losing need to be changed from internal and stable ones to external and unstable ones, a process known as attributional retraining. Positive feedback and reinforcement should be offered to encourage more effort and reduce learned helplessness. The goals or targets should be changed, so that they are in line with the ability of the player. Improving the number of drop shots or successful service returns could be a goal that does not just include winning but stresses personal

Top tip

Attributions in sport are important to make sure that players keep motivated. Make sure that you can suggest ways to counter learned helplessness such as setting easy targets at first, being positive and rewarding and using self-serving bias — blaming external and unstable reasons for losing.

improvement. Such targets could be used to redefine failure in the sense that success is not just about winning but includes playing a better game despite the result.

The opposite of learned helplessness is called mastery orientation. Players who show mastery orientation think that success can be repeated, that losing is temporary and can be overcome, and that the reasons for success are internal. Such players tend to show confidence and a real determination to keep on improving. They show the characteristics of a performer with the need to achieve and they are prepared to take risks and to take responsibility for their actions. Such players are just what the coach needs in the team to ensure that the reasons given for winning and losing are used to promote future effort.

Practice makes perfect

1 Goal setting is a strategy used by coaches to improve performance. Why should goal setting lead to improved performance and what principles should the coach consider when setting goals?   *(6 marks)*

2 Name and explain the different forms of anxiety that might be experienced by a sports performer.   *(4 marks)*

3 Some athletes tend to perform well when they are being watched, while others seem to choke under the pressure. Use your knowledge of psychological theories to explain the differing effects an audience can have on a performer.   *(7 marks)*

4 After a competitive match, some players may give reasons for losing that generate feelings of learned helplessness. What is meant by the term learned helplessness and how can a coach prevent learned helplessness from happening?   *(6 marks)*

Chapter *11*
Linear motion in physical activity

What you need to know

By the end of this chapter you should be able to:
- understand Newton's laws as applied to sporting examples
- understand linear motion through definitions, equations, calculations and units of measurement for mass, distance, displacement, speed, velocity and acceleration
- understand graphs of motion through plotting, interpreting and calculating gradients

Newton's laws of motion

Newton's first law of motion (the law of inertia):

A body continues in its state of rest or motion in a straight line, unless compelled to change that state by external forces exerted upon it.

Newton's second law of motion (the law of acceleration):

The rate of change of momentum of a body (or the acceleration for a body of constant mass) is proportional to the force causing it and the change that takes place in the direction in which the force acts.

Newton's second law is often expressed using the equation:

force = mass × acceleration ($F = m \times a$)

Newton's third law of motion:

To every action there is an equal and opposite reaction.

Table 11.1 applies these laws to football.

> **Top tip**
> Make sure you can apply each of Newton's laws of motion to sporting activities.

Table 11.1 The application of Newton's laws to football

Newton's laws	Application
Law of inertia	In a penalty, the ball (body) will remain on the spot (state of rest) until it is kicked by the player (an external force is exerted upon it).
Law of acceleration	When the player kicks (force applied) the ball during the game, the acceleration of the ball (rate of change of momentum) is proportional to the size of the force. So, the harder the ball is kicked the further and faster it will go.
Law of reaction	When a footballer jumps up (action) to win a header, a force is exerted on the ground in order to gain height. At the same time the ground exerts an upward force (equal and opposite reaction) upon the footballer.

Tasks to tackle 11.1

Copy and complete the table below giving an example of how each of the laws can be applied to a sport of your choice.

Newton's laws	Application
Law of inertia	
Law of acceleration	
Law of reaction	

Linear motion

Linear motion is motion in a straight or curved line, when all body parts move the same distance at the same speed in the same direction. In tobogganing, for example, the toboggan moves in a straight line. In the shot put, the shot moves in a curved line.

The measurements used in linear motion are:

- mass
- inertia
- distance
- speed
- acceleration
- displacement
- velocity
- momentum

These measurements can be split into two groups:

- **Scalar quantities** are described in terms of size or magnitude — for example, mass, inertia, distance and speed.
- **Vector quantities** are described in terms of size and direction — for example, acceleration, displacement, velocity and momentum.

Mass

Mass is a physical quantity expressing the amount of matter in a body. Our mass is made up of bone, muscle, fat, tissue and fluid and is measured in kilograms. A sumo wrestler, for example, has a much greater mass than a gymnast. Mass is a scalar quantity because it does not have direction, just size.

Chapter 11 Linear motion in physical activity

Inertia

Inertia is the resistance an object has to a change in its state of motion. If an object is at rest it will remain still. If it is moving in one direction it will continue to do so at the same speed until another force is exerted upon it (see Newton's first law). The bigger the mass, the larger the inertia of the body or object. This means that more force will be needed to change its state of motion. Consider two rugby league players running towards you. One is a prop weighing 100 kg and the other a winger weighing 75 kg; which one would you prefer to stop? The winger will be easier to stop because he has less inertia. Only the very brave would attempt to stop the prop!

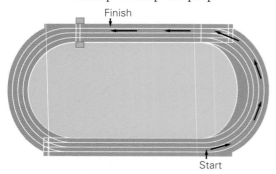

Figure 11.1 The distance of a 200 m race

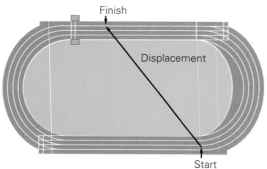

Figure 11.2 The displacement of a 200 m race

Distance versus displacement

Distance and displacement are quantities that are used to describe the extent of a body's motion. **Distance** is the length of the path a body follows when moving from one position to another. For example, a 200 m runner who has just completed a race has run a distance of 200 m as shown in Figure 11.1. This is a scalar quantity because it just measures size.

Displacement is the length of a straight line joining the start and finish points. For example, in a 200 m race on a track the length of the path the athlete follows (distance) is 200 m but his/her displacement will be the number of metres as the crow flies from the start to the finish (Figure 11.2).

Displacement is a vector quantity because it describes both size and direction. Figure 11.3 shows a javelin throw and a basketball free throw to further illustrate the difference between distance and displacement.

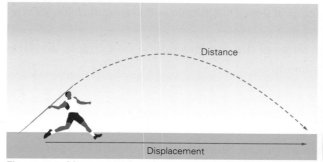
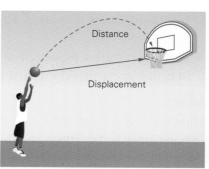

Figure 11.3 More examples of distance and displacement

Speed versus velocity

Speed is the rate of change of position. It is a scalar quantity because it does not consider direction and can be calculated as follows:

$$\text{speed (m s}^{-1}) = \frac{\text{distance covered (m)}}{\text{time taken (s)}}$$

Velocity is the rate of change of position with reference to direction. This means that it is a more precise description of motion and is a vector quantity. It can be calculated as follows:

$$\text{velocity (m s}^{-1}) = \frac{\text{displacement (m)}}{\text{time taken (s)}}$$

Tasks to tackle 11.2

(a) Work out the displacement of the following components of a triathlon:

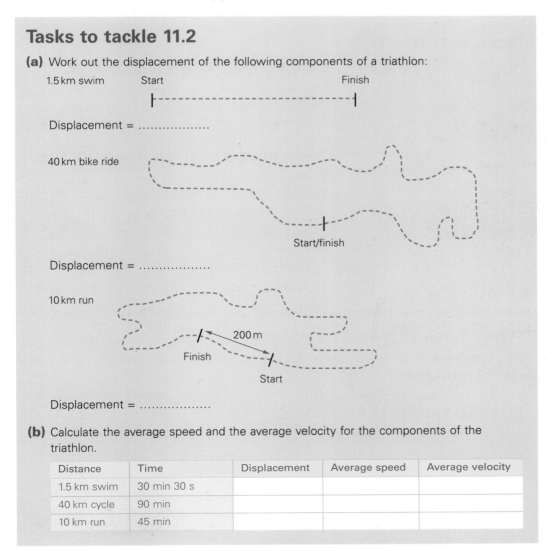

1.5 km swim   Start   Finish

Displacement = ...

40 km bike ride

Start/finish

Displacement = ...

10 km run

200 m

Finish

Start

Displacement = ...

(b) Calculate the average speed and the average velocity for the components of the triathlon.

Distance	Time	Displacement	Average speed	Average velocity
1.5 km swim	30 min 30 s			
40 km cycle	90 min			
10 km run	45 min			

Acceleration

Acceleration can be defined as the rate of change of velocity. It occurs when velocity increases (positive acceleration) or decreases (negative acceleration). Acceleration is a vector quantity because direction is important. It is measured in metres per second per second (ms^{-2}).

Acceleration can be calculated as follows:

$$\text{acceleration} = \frac{\text{change in velocity (ms}^{-1})}{\text{time (s)}}$$

To calculate the change in velocity the following equation is used:

$$\text{change in velocity} = \frac{V_f - V_i}{t} = \frac{\text{final velocity} - \text{initial velocity}}{\text{time}}$$

Tasks to tackle 11.3

(a) Think of three examples in any team game where acceleration and/or deceleration are important quantities.

1 ....

2 ....

3 ....

(b) In the table below, calculate the average acceleration of a 100 m runner over 20-metre intervals (no change of direction).

Distance (m)	0	20	40	60	80	100
Velocity (ms⁻¹)	0.00	8.5	11.1	11.5	11.5	9.5
Time (s)	0.0	2.9	5.6	7.6	9.4	11.4
Acceleration (ms⁻²)	N/A					

Momentum

Momentum is the product of the mass and velocity of an object. It can be calculated as follows:

$$\text{momentum (kg m s}^{-1}) = \text{mass (kg)} \times \text{velocity (m s}^{-1})$$

Since momentum is calculated using velocity, it has magnitude and direction and is therefore a vector quantity.

Tasks to tackle 11.4

Complete the blanks in the table below.

Performer	Mass (kg)	Velocity (ms⁻¹)	Momentum (kgms⁻¹)
100 m sprinter	80	10	
Prop	105		893
Centre forward	70	9.5	
Middle-distance runner	65		585

From the table in task 11.4 it can be seen that a large mass, coupled with the ability to run at a high velocity, results in a high momentum. If you had to stop any of the performers listed, the prop would be the most difficult as his momentum is the greatest.

In a closed system, total momentum is conserved. So when two objects collide, for example, the total momentum stays the same, although some may transfer from one object to the other. Most sporting situations, however, are not closed systems. For example, when a cricket bat hits the ball, the ball is squashed to a degree. After a few milliseconds, it rebounds back. This contraction and rebound action causes the release of heat energy, and some momentum is lost.

Graphs of motion

For the purposes of your exam you need to be able to plot, interpret and make calculations from three types of graph:

- distance/time
- speed/time
- velocity/time

Graphs are one method of presenting information on motion from which changes and patterns in motion can be interpreted. Graphs of motion are often used to analyse running activities such as sprinting. In the 100 m, for example, Usain Bolt set a world record at the 2008 Beijing Olympics of 9.69 seconds. This means his average speed throughout the race was $10.32\,\text{m s}^{-1}$. However, this speed would not have remained constant throughout the race. At the start, when he was accelerating, it would have been slower, which means that at some point in the race he must have been running faster than $10.32\,\text{m s}^{-1}$. Graphs would help Usain Bolt to analyse his performance and see his speed at various stages of the race.

Top tip

Remember to always label the axes when plotting a graph, as marks are awarded for this.

Distance/time graphs

This type of graph shows the distance travelled over a period of time.

- In Figure 11.4(a) the line does not go up or down so no distance is travelled. This means the performer must be stationary. It could represent a netball player taking a shot or a goalkeeper in football before a penalty is taken.
- In Figure 11.4(b) the line goes up in a constant diagonal direction. This indicates that the performer is running the same distance over the same amount of time so his/her speed must be constant. This could occur in the middle of a long-distance race.

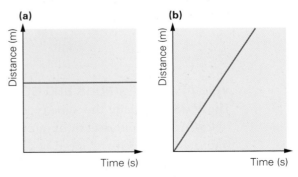

Figure 11.4 Distance/time graphs

(c)

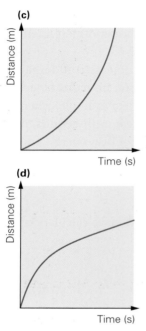

(d)

Figure 11.4 (continued)
Distance/time graphs

- In Figure 11.4(c) the line is curved and gradually gets steeper. This indicates that more distance is being covered in a certain amount of time so the performer must be accelerating, for example at the start of a race.
- In Figure 11.4(d) the curve starts to level off and less distance is travelled in a certain amount of time. This means that deceleration is occurring, which would happen once the performer has crossed the finishing line.

The gradient of a graph

When asked to look at the gradient of a graph, all this requires you to do is to look at its slope. This is determined by:

$$\frac{\text{changes in the } y \text{ axis}}{\text{changes in the } x \text{ axis}}$$

In Figure 11.4:
- (a) There is no gradient, so there is no movement.
- (b) The gradient is constant, so speed is constant.
- (c) The gradient is increasing, so speed is increasing.
- (d) The gradient is decreasing so speed is decreasing.

Tasks to tackle 11.5

Explain what is happening at each stage in this distance/time graph.

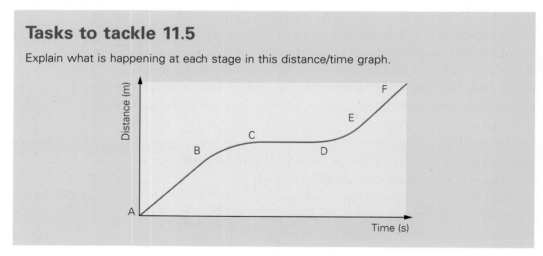

Velocity/time graphs and speed/time graphs

These are essentially the same type of graph. The shape of the velocity/time graph will represent the same pattern of motion as the shape of a speed/time graph. These graphs indicate the velocity or speed of a performer or object per unit of time. The gradient of the graph will help you to decide whether the performer is travelling at a constant velocity, accelerating or decelerating.

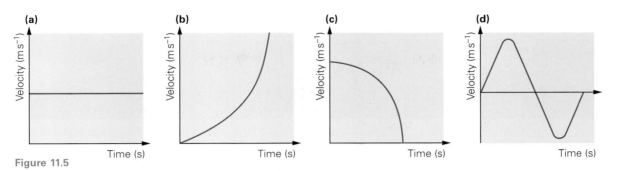

Figure 11.5

- In Figure 11.5(a) the gradient remains constant, which indicates that the performer is travelling at a constant velocity.
- In Figure 11.5(b) the gradient gets steeper (increases). This indicates that the performer is moving with increasing velocity, or accelerating.

$$\text{gradient of graph} = \frac{\text{change in velocity}}{\text{time}}$$

- In Figure 11.5(c) the gradient decreases. This shows that the performer is moving with decreasing velocity, or decelerating.
- In Figure 11.5(d) the curve appears below the *x*–axis. This means that there has been a change in direction.

Practice makes perfect

1 The table below gives Asafa Powell's 100 m split times and velocity when he equalled the world record at the 2006 Golden League meeting in Zurich.

10 m splits	Time (s)	Time for each split (s)	Velocity (m s^{-1})
10	1.87	1.72 (reaction time was 0.15)	0.58
20	2.89	1.02	9.8
30	3.81	0.92	10.9
40	4.68	0.87	11.5
50	5.52	0.84	11.9
60	6.36	0.84	11.9
70	7.20	0.84	11.9
80	8.05	0.85	11.8
90	8.91	0.86	11.6
100	9.77	0.86	11.6

From this table, calculate Powell's acceleration in:
(a) the first 10 m
(b) from 10 m to 20 m   (4 marks)

2 Use Newton's laws of motion to explain how a high jumper takes off from the ground.   (6 marks)

What you need to know

By the end of this chapter you should be able to:
- give definitions and units of measurement of force and be able to identify the effects of a force
- understand the types of force: weight, reaction, friction and air resistance, and be able to apply these to running, jumping, throwing, hitting and kicking
- understand how to sketch free body diagrams, showing all the vertical and horizontal forces acting on a performer
- understand net forces through definitions and application of balanced and unbalanced forces
- understand impulse and the relationship it has with increasing and decreasing momentum
- understand graphical representation of impulse

What is a force?

A **force** can be described as a 'push' or 'pull'. It can cause a body at rest to move or cause a moving body to stop, slow down, speed up or change direction. Forces can be either internal or external. Internal forces are generated through the contraction of skeletal muscle, whereas external forces come from outside the body, for example air resistance, friction, weight and reaction. Force can be calculated using the following equation (refer to Newton's second law of motion):

$$\text{force} = \text{mass} \times \text{acceleration} \ (F = m \times a)$$

Note that as force is a vector quantity, an arrow can be used to represent it.

It is important to consider the following when describing a force:

- The size or magnitude of the force — this is dependent on the size and number of muscle fibres used.
- The direction of the force — if a force is applied through the middle of an object it will move in the same direction as the force, as shown in Figure 12.1.

Figure 12.1 A central force gives movement in the same direction as the force

- The position of application of the force — this is an important factor in sport. Applying a force straight through the centre will result in movement in a straight line (linear motion), as shown in Figure 12.2. Applying a force off-centre will result in spin (angular momentum), as shown in Figure 12.3.

Applying a force straight through the centre will result in movement in a straight line

Applying a force off-centre will result in spin (angular momentum)

Figure 12.2 A central force gives straight-line movement

Figure 12.3 An off-centre force gives spin

Tasks to tackle 12.1

(a) Look at the following pictures and decide where the force is being applied (point of application). Mark this position with a cross.

(b) Now label the direction in which the force is acting. Use an arrow starting at the point of application and then draw it in the direction you think the force is acting.

(c) Finally decide how big this force is. The larger the force, the bigger the arrow.

Chapter 12 Force

Types of force acting on a sports performer

Both vertical and horizontal forces act upon a sports performer. Vertical forces are weight and reaction and horizontal forces are friction and air resistance.

Vertical forces

Weight

Remember, weight is a gravitational force that the earth exerts on a body, pulling it towards the centre of the earth (or, effectively, downwards).

Figure 12.4 Weight

Reaction force

Remember Newton's third law of motion: 'For every action there is an equal and opposite reaction'. This means that there is always a reaction force whenever two bodies are in contact with one another. When the feet are in contact with the ground, there is a ground reaction force.

Figure 12.5 Reaction force

Horizontal forces

Friction

Friction occurs whenever there are two bodies in contact with each other that may have a tendency to slip or slide over each other. Friction acts in opposition to motion. Try to remember that friction resists the slipping or sliding motion of two surfaces. Therefore, in diagrams, a friction arrow is drawn in the opposite direction from this slipping. Usually, this means that a friction arrow points in the same direction as motion, as in Figure 12.6(a). However, in skiing, where the slipping occurs in a forward direction, the friction arrow is reversed as in Figure 12.6(b).

Figure 12.6
Friction opposes the slippage between objects. For a runner (a), the slippage is backwards so the friction arrow points forwards. For a skier (b), the slippage is forwards so the friction arrow points backwards.

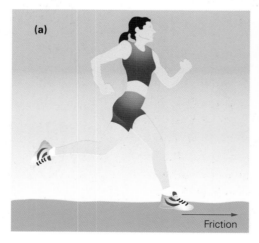
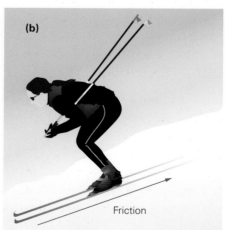

(a)

Friction

(b)

Friction

OCR A2 Physical Education

The footwear worn by a sports performer can increase or decrease friction. Athletes wear spikes so that they can increase friction with the ground and therefore increase forward acceleration. The same is true in rugby or football where studs or blades are worn to increase friction on a soft, slippery ground where players need to be able to swerve round opponents in an attempt to break away from them. Other performers need to decrease friction to meet the demands of their activity. Skiers, for example, will wax their skis to ensure there is as little friction with the surface of the snow as possible. In addition, different surfaces can increase or decrease friction. Try playing hockey on grass as opposed to an all-weather pitch, or think of a ball travelling along the grass as opposed to a puck travelling along the ice.

Air resistance

Air resistance opposes the motion of a body travelling through the air. Imagine trying to run into a strong head wind — this is not an easy task as the force of the wind is trying to push you backwards in the opposite direction. Air resistance depends upon:

- the velocity of the moving body — a greater velocity results in a greater resistance
- the cross-sectional area of the moving body — the larger the cross-sectional area, the greater the air resistance. For example, think of how Tour de France competitors reduce their cross-sectional area by crouching low over the handlebars, rather than sitting upright.
- the shape and the surface characteristics of the moving body — a streamlined shape results in less resistance, as does a smooth surface

Air resistance is sometimes referred to as **drag**. Drag is more commonly used to describe the force opposing motion in water as opposed to air. Drag will depend on the factors listed above and in addition the type of fluid environment through which the body is travelling. Compare running in water with running on land. There is a much greater drag force in water due to its greater density.

Most elite swimmers shave off all body hair to create a smooth surface; many wear a swimming cap for the same reason. More recently, swimmers have started to wear 'shark suits', or full-body swimsuits, to streamline their surface.

Top tip

Questions often refer to the fluid environment of a travelling body. This fluid is either air or water. For the purpose of your exam try to remember that air resistance is the force opposing motion in air and drag is the force opposing motion in water.

Free body diagrams

For your exam, you need to know how forces are applied in sporting activities. By using free body diagrams you can show the forces acting on a body in the form of an arrow. The longer the arrow, the bigger the size of the force. If the reaction force is the same size as the weight force then the net force is 0. Free body diagrams are summarised in Table 12.1.

Table 12.1 Summary of free body diagrams

The weight force is always drawn down from the centre of mass.	The reaction force starts from where two bodies are in contact with one another. This contact can be the foot with the ground, which is therefore drawn in an upward direction, or can be the contact between sports equipment and a ball such as a tennis racket and a tennis ball.	The friction force starts from where the two bodies are in contact and is opposite to the direction of any potential slipping. It is usually drawn in the same direction as motion.	Air resistance is drawn from the centre of mass opposing the direction of motion of the body.
W	R	F	AR

Net force

This is the resultant force acting on a body when all other forces have been considered. Net force is often discussed in terms of balanced versus unbalanced forces.

A **balanced force** is when there are two or more forces acting on a body that are equal in size but opposite in direction. In this case there is zero net force, and therefore no change in the state of motion. This is illustrated in Figure 12.7.

An **unbalanced force** is when a force acting in one direction on a body is larger than the force acting in the opposite direction. This is illustrated in Figure 12.8.

Figure 12.7 When standing, the weight force and reaction force are equal in size but opposite in direction

Figure 12.8 When jumping in the air, the performer accelerates upwards because the reaction force is bigger than the weight force

OCR A2 Physical Education

Similarly, if the friction force arrow is equal in length to the air resistance arrow then the net result is zero, as shown in Figure 12.9(a). If the friction arrow is longer than the air resistance arrow the body will accelerate, as shown in Figure 12.9(b). If the friction arrow is shorter than the air resistance arrow the body will decelerate, as shown in Figure 12.9(c).

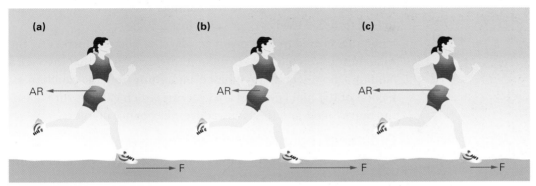

Figure 12.9 (a) $F = AR$ so the net force is 0 (b) $F > AR$ = acceleration (c) $F < AR$ = deceleration

Tasks to tackle 12.2

Draw the relevant forces on the following diagrams:

Impulse

Impulse is the product of the average magnitude of a force acting on a body and the time for which that force acts. It is equivalent to the change in momentum of a body as a result of a force acting on it. Impulse can be calculated as follows:

impulse (newton seconds/ NS) = force × time

In a sporting environment, impulse can be used to add speed to a body or object, or to slow it down on impact. Speeding up a body or object can be achieved by increasing the amount of

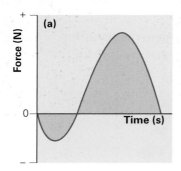

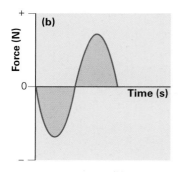

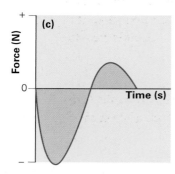

muscular force that is applied. In basketball, for example, a large force is generated when jumping for a rebound in order to get as much height as quickly as possible to catch the ball. Speeding up a body or object can also be achieved by increasing the amount of time for which the force is applied. In the hammer throw, for example, three to four turns are used as opposed to just a single swing.

Impulse is used to slow down an object or body by increasing the time during which forces act upon it. In any activity that involves a landing action, such as a gymnast dismounting from the parallel bars, flexion of the hip, knee and ankle occurs which extends the time of the impact force and therefore reduces the chance of injury.

Graphical representation of impulse

Impulse is represented by a force/time graph. The graphs in Figure 12.10 show various stages of a 100 m sprint.

It is important to note that in running/sprinting, positive impulse occurs for acceleration at take-off, whereas negative impulse occurs when the foot lands to provide a braking action.

Key term

Net impulse: a combination of positive and negative impulses.

Figure 12.10
(a) Start of the race — the net impulse is positive, which shows that the sprinter is accelerating
(b) Middle of the race — positive and negative impulses are equal (net impulse zero), which means that there is no acceleration or deceleration, so the sprinter is running at a constant velocity
(c) End of the race — the net impulse is negative, which shows that the sprinter is decelerating

Practice makes perfect

1 What is meant by the term 'impulse', and how can an athlete use impulse during sprinting or take-off? *(4 marks)*

2 A sprinter with a mass of 75 kg accelerates during the first 20 m of a 100 m sprint at 6.9 m s^{-2}. Calculate the force that is needed to achieve this. *(2 marks)*

3 Identify the forces acting on a 200 m sprinter at the start of the race through the use of a free body diagram. *(4 marks)*

Chapter *13*

Projectiles

What you need to know

By the end of this chapter you should have an understanding of:
- parabolas, flight paths and forces acting during flight
- how to resolve the forces acting during flight through the use of a parallelogram of forces to explain variations in flight path
- description, explanation and application of the Bernoulli principle
- the types of spin in sport (top, back and side), and how spin is imparted on projectiles
- the Magnus effect and how it causes deviations in flight

Projectile motion

This is the motion of either an object or the human body being 'projected' into the air at an angle. We do this all the time in sport, for example with the ball as a projectile when it is kicked, hit or thrown, and with the human body as a projectile when it is propelled into the air during the long jump or gymnastic vault.

Flight path

The flight path of a projectile is influenced by its release. Three factors determine the horizontal distance that a projectile can travel: angle of release, velocity of release and height of release.

Angle of release

To achieve maximum horizontal distance, the angle of release of the projectile is important. The optimum angle of release is dependent upon release height and landing height. When both the release height and the landing height are equal then the optimum angle of release is 45°. This would be the case for a long jumper, as in Figure 13.1.

Figure 13.1 An equal release height and landing height gives an optimum angle of release of 45°

If the release height is greater than the landing height, the optimum angle of release is less than 45°. This can be seen in the shot put, as in Figure 13.2.

Figure 13.2 A release height above the landing height gives an optimum angle of release of less than 45°

If the release height is below the landing height then the optimum angle of release is greater than 45°. Shooting in basketball highlights this (assuming the ring is the landing height) as shown in Figure 13.3.

Figure 13.3 A release height below the landing height gives an optimum angle of release of more than 45°

Velocity of release

The greater the release velocity of a projectile, the greater the horizontal distance travelled. In the throwing events in athletics, the rotational speed across the circle ensures greater horizontal distance.

Height of release

A greater release height results in an increase in horizontal distance. This means that when fielding a ball in cricket, the taller the fielder the further the distance he can throw the ball, providing the angle of release and velocity of release are the same. In order for a smaller fielder to achieve the same distance, he will have to change the angle or velocity of release.

Tasks to tackle 13.1

Work out the optimum angle of release of the following:

Activity	Is the optimum angle of release: 45°, more than 45°, or less than 45°?
A lofted football pass to the foot of a team-mate	
A lofted football pass to the head of a team-mate	
High jump take-off	
Tennis smash	

Forces affecting projectiles during flight

Weight and air resistance are two forces that affect projectiles while they are in the air. These two factors are crucial in deciding whether a projectile has a flight path that is a true parabola (see Figure 13.4) or a distorted parabola.

Projectiles with a large weight force have a small air resistance force and follow a true parabolic flight path, as shown in Figure 13.5.

As the effects of air resistance increase, the flight path of the projectile will deviate from a true parabola to a distorted parabola. This can be seen in projectiles with a lighter mass, such as a shuttlecock, as shown in Figure 13.6.

Figure 13.4 A true parabola is a uniform curve that is symmetrical at its highest point

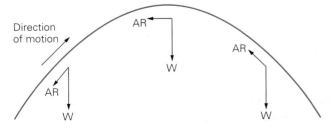

Figure 13.5 The forces acting on the flight path of a shot put

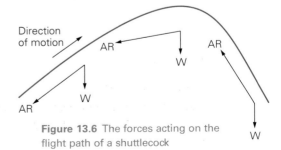

Figure 13.6 The forces acting on the flight path of a shuttlecock

Table 13.1 lists other objects that follow a true or distorted parabola.

Table 13.1 Parabolic flight paths of various sporting objects

Object	Flight path	Why?
Golf ball	Distorted	The ball travels at high speed so is affected by air resistance. However, if both a golf ball and a table tennis ball (both are a similar size) were projected into the air at the same height, angle and velocity, then the golf ball would follow more of a true parabola because it is heavier and has less air resistance
Football	Slightly distorted	Relatively large cross-sectional area so more air resistance
Javelin	True	Little weight and low air resistance

Parallelogram of forces

We now know that weight and air resistance are the two forces that act on a projectile. The effect of these two forces can be represented by a single resultant force. To work out the size and direction of this resultant force a parallelogram of forces is used. Look at Figure 13.7, which shows a parallelogram of forces at the start of the flight path of a shot put.

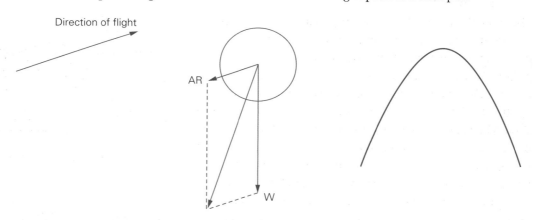

Figure 13.7 A parallelogram of forces for the start of a shot put's flight path

The resultant force has been worked out as follows:
- The two force arrows of weight and air resistance, including direction, are drawn. The length of the arrows is determined by considering the mass, velocity and cross-sectional area of the projectile.
- The missing sides of the parallelogram are added geometrically (dotted lines).
- A diagonal arrow is drawn from the origin of the forces to the opposite corner of the parallelogram (red arrow). This is the resultant force and is in a similar direction to the weight arrow of the shot put. This means that air resistance is negligible and the shot put will follow a flight path close to a true parabola.

OCR A2 Physical Education

If we consider a table tennis ball and construct a parallelogram of forces, the resultant arrow ends up in a different position, as shown in Figure 13.8. This is because the weight arrow is shorter than that of the shot put, because the table tennis ball is lighter. This means that there will be more air resistance, so this arrow needs to be longer. Now the resultant force (red arrow) is in a similar direction to air resistance, which will result in the table tennis ball's flight path deviating from a true parabola.

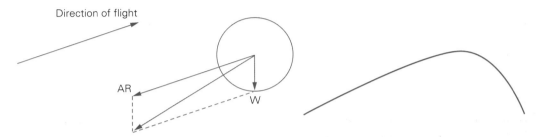

Figure 13.8 A parallelogram of forces for the start of a table tennis ball's flight path

Projectiles and lift

The more lift a projectile has during flight, the longer it will stay in the air and the further the horizontal distance it will travel. Lift is achieved when different air pressures act on an object. Air that travels faster has a lower pressure than air that travels slower. This is the **Bernoulli principle**. If this is applied to the discus (see Figure 13.9), the point of release should be at an angle where the air that travels over the top of the discus has to travel a longer distance than the air underneath. This results in the air above the discus travelling at a faster velocity which therefore creates a lower pressure. This lower pressure above the discus creates an upward lift force and allows the discus to stay in the air for longer, resulting in a greater horizontal distance.

The Bernoulli principle can also be used to describe a downward lift force, such as that required by speed skiers, cyclists and racing cars. The car, bike and skis need to be pushed down into the ground so that a greater frictional force is created. In a racing car, for example, the spoiler is angled so the lift force can act in a downward direction.

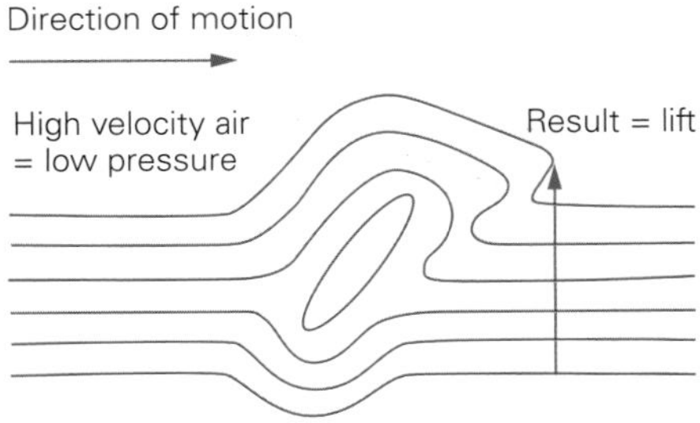

Figure 13.9 The Bernoulli principle during a discus flight

Bernoulli principle: where air molecules exert less pressure the faster they travel and more pressure when they travel slower.

Projectiles and spin

Remember that spin is imparted onto a projectile by applying a force outside the centre of mass of the object. This is often referred to as an eccentric force. For the purposes of your exam you need to be aware of three types of spin.

Chapter *13* Projectiles

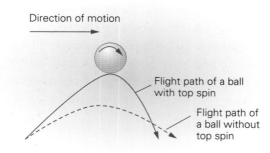

Figure 13.10 Side view of top spin

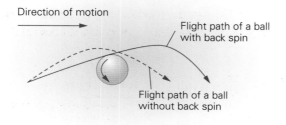

Figure 13.11 Side view of back spin

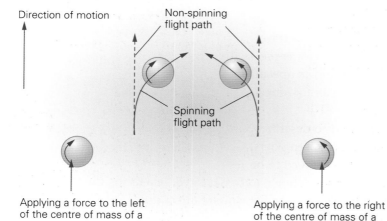

Applying a force to the left of the centre of mass of a ball makes it spin to the right and as a result it travels to the right

Applying a force to the right of the centre of mass of a ball makes it spin to the left and as a result it travels to the left

Figure 13.12 Top view of side spin

Top spin

In tennis, for example, this is created when a force is applied over the top of the centre of mass of a ball. It causes the ball to rotate forwards resulting in it dipping and a reduction in the distance travelled. However, when the ball hits the ground it bounces forward quickly at a low angle from the ground. This increase in speed is used to try to beat the opponent.

Back spin

This is created in golf when the force is applied underneath the centre of mass. It causes the golf ball to rotate backwards resulting in it floating and travelling further in the air. When the ball lands, it bounces up at a large angle from the ground, its speed decreases and it stops quickly or travels backwards. This allows the golfer to have control over the landing of the ball. Back spin is also often used in tennis for the drop shot.

Side spin

Whether a ball goes to the left or the right depends upon the position of application of the eccentric force. Figure 13.12 shows a top view of side spin both to the left and to the right.

Table 13.2 summarises the impact of different types of spin on flight path and bounce.

Table 13.2 Summary of the effects of spin

Types of spin	Flight path	Bounce
Top spin	Shortens flight path	Leaves the ground quickly at a low angle
Back spin	Lengthens flight path	Leaves the ground at a large angle and slows down or travels backwards depending on degree of spin
Side spin	Ball deviates left or right depending on where the force has been applied	The ball leaves the ground in the opposite direction to the spin, i.e. spin causing the ball to deviate left results in the ball bouncing to the right

The Magnus effect

The Magnus effect is named after a German scientist called Gustav Magnus. It is concerned with the deviation of the flight path of a spinning projectile towards the direction of the spin. The Magnus effect is crucial in lots of sports. In golf it is important to control the landing of a ball, in tennis it is used to outwit an opponent, in football it is used to bend a free kick around the wall of defenders, or in basketball it is used to increase the chances of a successful shot.

Top spin

When top spin is applied to a ball, the surface at the top of the ball is travelling in the opposite direction to airflow. This means the air slows down and a high pressure is created. At the bottom of the ball the surface is travelling in the same direction as the airflow so the air accelerates and a lower pressure is created (Bernoulli effect). The result of this difference in pressure between the top and the bottom surface causes the ball to move towards the area of low pressure (bottom surface). This means the ball dips and the distance travelled decreases.

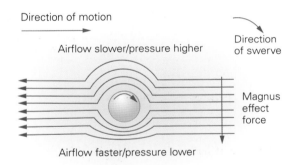

Figure 13.13 Impact of the Magnus effect on top spin (side view)

Back spin

During back spin, the surface at the top of the ball is travelling in the same direction as airflow. This means the air accelerates and the pressure drops. The surface at the bottom of the ball now travels in the opposite direction to airflow so the air slows down and pressure increases (Bernoulli effect). This means the ball moves to the area of low pressure which is now at the top of the ball. This results in the ball floating and the distance travelled increasing.

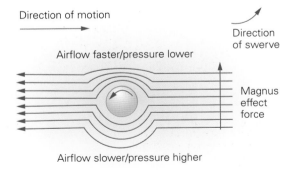

Figure 13.14 Impact of the Magnus effect on back spin (side view)

Chapter *13* Projectiles

Practice makes perfect

1 When a performer hits or kicks the ball into the air in hockey, golf and rugby, it becomes a projectile. Explain how the various forces involved act to affect a projectile during its flight.

(3 marks)

2 The diagrams below show the effects of two types of spin on the bounce of a ball. Identify the types of spin used in diagram A and diagram B.

(2 marks)

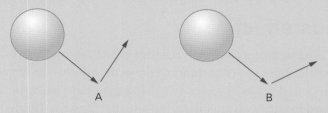

A   B

3 A rugby player needs to make a very long kick to win the game. What factors does he need to consider at the point of release to gain maximum horizontal distance.

(4 marks)

Chapter 14

Angular motion

What you need to know:

By the end of this chapter you should be able to understand:

* centre of mass — its definition, how it relates to stability and rotation, and the relationship between centre of mass and different sporting positions
* levers — the definition of the three lever systems, examples in the body of where these types of levers can be found, advantages and disadvantages of different types of levers
* the definition of moment of force, or torque, and calculation using appropriate units of measurement
* the three major axes of rotation — longitudinal, transverse, frontal
* the definition and units of measurement for angular distance, angular displacement, angular speed, angular velocity and angular acceleration
* the application of Newton's laws to rotating bodies
* the moment of inertia — definition and explanation, and the effects of increasing or decreasing moment of inertia on efficiency and ease of movement
* angular momentum — definition, control and the formulation of equations in relation to the law of conservation of angular momentum
* how to sketch graphs of angular motion

Centre of mass

The **centre of mass** is the point of concentration of mass or, more simply, the point of balance. In the human body, the position of the centre of mass cannot be easily defined due to the body's irregular shape. In addition, because the body is constantly moving, the centre of mass changes. For example, raising your arms in the air raises your centre of mass in order to keep the body balanced. In general, the centre of mass for someone adopting a standing position is in the lower abdomen and differs according to gender. Males have more weight concentrated in their shoulders and upper body, so their centre of mass is slightly higher than in females who have more body weight concentrated at their hips.

> **Key term**
>
> **Centre of mass:** the point of balance.

Figure 14.1 The centre of mass

A balanced stable position depends on:

- the centre of mass being over the base of support
- the line of gravity running through the middle of the base of support
- the number of contact points — the more contact points, the more stable the person is — for example, a headstand has more contact points than a handstand, so is a more balanced position
- the mass of the performer — the greater the mass, the more stability there is

Line of gravity: **Key term**

the line extending vertically downwards from the centre of mass.

To be in a balanced position, the centre of mass needs to be in line with the base of support. If you lower your centre of mass, your stability increases but if your centre of mass starts to move near the edge of the base of support, then you will start to overbalance. Sprinters in the 'set' position will have their centre of mass right at the edge of the area of support. As they move on hearing the starting pistol, they lift their hands off the ground and become off-balanced. This will allow the athletes to fall forward and help to create the speed required to leave the blocks as quickly as possible.

When performing the Fosbury flop in the high jump, the centre of mass of the performer passes under the bar while the body goes over. Compare this with a scissor kick, where the centre of mass remains in the body and therefore has to be lifted over the bar. The Fosbury flop is therefore an effective technique for the athlete.

Figure 14.2 The centre of mass during the Fosbury flop passes under the bar

Levers

A lever consists of three main components, namely a pivot (fulcrum), the weight to be moved (load) and a source of energy (effort). Our skeleton forms a system of levers that allows us to move. The bones act as the levers, the joints are the fulcrums, the load (resistance) is the weight of the arms and legs (and the object that needs to be moved), and the effort is provided by the agonist muscle.

A lever has two main functions:

- to increase the speed at which a body can move
- to increase the resistance a given effort can move

Classification of levers

Levers can be classified into three types according to the arrangement of the fulcrum, load and the effort:

- **First-order levers** — here, the fulcrum is between the effort and the resistance (Figure 14.2). This type of lever can increase the effects of the effort and the speed of a body. Examples of first-order levers can be seen in the movement of the head and neck during flexion and extension, and in the action of extending the limbs, for example the arm or the lower leg.
- **Second-order levers** — here, the resistance lies between the fulcrum and the effort (Figure 14.3). This type of lever is generally thought to increase only the effect of the effort force (i.e. it can be used to overcome heavy loads). Plantarflexion of the ankle in the standing position involves the use of a second-order lever.
- **Third-order levers** — these are responsible for the majority of movements in the human body and are where the effort lies between the fulcrum and the resistance (Figure 14.4). Third-order levers can increase the body's ability to move quickly but in terms of applying force they are very inefficient. An example can be seen in the forearm during flexion of the elbow.

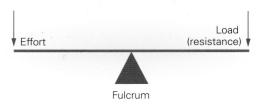

Figure 14.2 First-order lever

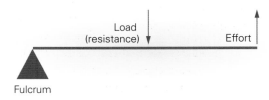

Figure 14.3 Second-order lever

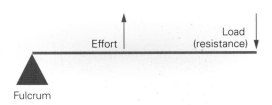

Figure 14.4 Third-order lever

> **Top tip**
>
> When trying to remember where different levers are located in the body, remember that they are all third-order levers except for plantarflexion of the ankle, which is a second-order lever, and the neck and extension of the elbow and knee joints, which are first-order levers.

Tasks to tackle 14.1

Label the fulcrum, effort and resistance on this diagram.

The **effort arm** is the shortest perpendicular distance between the fulcrum and the application of force (effort). The **resistance arm** is the shortest perpendicular distance between the fulcrum and the load. The force arm and the load arm are shown in a third-order lever in Figure 14.5.

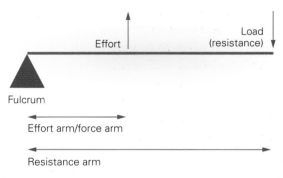

Figure 14.5 The effort arm and the resistance arm

When the resistance arm is longer than the effort arm, the lever system is at a **mechanical disadvantage**. This means that it cannot move as heavy a load but it can move the load faster. **Mechanical advantage** is when the effort arm is longer than the resistance arm. This means that the lever system can move a large load over a short distance and requires little effort.

Key terms

Mechanical advantage: when the effort arm is longer than the resistance arm.

Mechanical disadvantage: when the resistance arm is longer than the effort arm.

Length of lever

Most levers in the body are third-order levers where the resistance arm is always longer than the effort arm (mechanical disadvantage). The longer the resistance arm of the lever, the greater the speed will be at the end of it. This means that if the arm is fully extended when bowling or passing, for example, the ball will travel with most force and therefore at greatest speed. The use of a cricket bat, tennis racket or golf club effectively extends the arm and allows more force to be exerted.

Moment of force, or torque

Torque (often called the moment) can be described as a rotational force. It causes an object to turn about its axis of rotation. Increasing the size of the force and the perpendicular distance of the force from the pivotal point (axis of rotation) will increase the moment of the force. Moment of a force or torque can be calculated as follows:

$$\text{moment of force or torque (newton metres)} = \text{force (newtons)} \times \text{perpendicular distance from the fulcrum (metres)}$$

This is highlighted in Figure 14.6.

Principle of moments

When a lever system is balanced, the moment of force acting in a clockwise direction is equal to the moment of force acting in an anti-clockwise direction. The principle of moments is applied to any lever system that is balanced. An example of a balanced lever system is one that is stationary with no rotation about the fulcrum. This can be seen in Figure 14.7 of a gymnast holding a pike position on the rings.

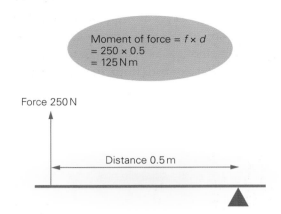

Moment of force = $f \times d$
= 250×0.5
= $125\,\text{N}\,\text{m}$

Force 250 N

Distance 0.5 m

Figure 14.6 Moment of force

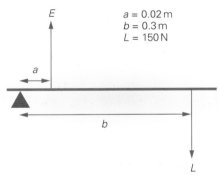

E

$a = 0.02\,\text{m}$
$b = 0.3\,\text{m}$
$L = 150\,\text{N}$

a

b

L

Figure 14.7 A balanced lever system

The principle of moments can be used to calculate the effort required by the hip flexors to hold the gymnast in this position. The following calculation would be used:

clockwise moment of force =
anticlockwise moment of force

$L \times b$	$=$	$E \times a$
150×0.5	$=$	$E \times 0.02$
75	$=$	$E \times 0.02$
$75 \div 0.02$	$=$	E
3750	$=$	E

So the effort required is 3750 N

Principle axes of rotation

There are three axes of rotation, which all pass through the centre of mass, as shown in Figure 14.8:

- the longitudinal axis runs from top to bottom
- the frontal axis runs from front to back
- the transverse axis runs from side to side across the body

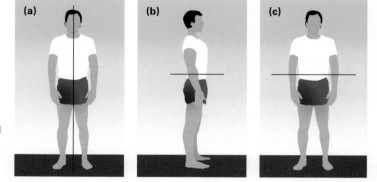

Figure 14.8 (a) The longitudinal axis, (b) the frontal axis and (c) the transverse axis of the human body

Angular motion

Angular motion is movement around a fixed point or axis — for example, a somersault. Remember, angular motion occurs when a force is applied outside the centre of mass. An off-centre force is referred to as an eccentric force.

Tasks to tackle 14.2

List three sporting examples when a force is applied outside the centre of mass of an object or body to cause rotation.

1 ....

2 ....

3 ....

Quantities used in angular motion

Knowledge of the following measurements will be useful in your study of the mechanics of movement:

- **Angular distance** is the angle rotated about an axis when moving from one position to another. Angular distance is measured in radians (1 radian = 57.3 degrees).
- **Angular displacement** is the smallest change in angle between the starting and finishing point. Angular displacement is also measured in radians.

- **Angular speed** is the time it takes to turn through an angle and is measured in radians per second. It is calculated as follows:

$$\text{angular speed (rad s}^{-1}) = \frac{\text{angular distance (rad)}}{\text{time taken (s)}}$$

- **Angular velocity** is a vector quantity as it makes reference to direction. Angular velocity refers to the angular displacement that is covered in a certain time and is calculated as follows:

$$\text{angular velocity (rad s}^{-1}) = \frac{\text{angular displacement (rad)}}{\text{time taken (s)}}$$

- **Angular acceleration** is the rate of change of angular velocity over time. It is calculated as follows:

$$\text{angular acceleration (rad s}^{-2}) = \frac{\text{change in velocity (rad s}^{-1})}{\text{time taken (s)}}$$

Let us look at the example of a gymnast spinning on a bar (Figure 14.9).

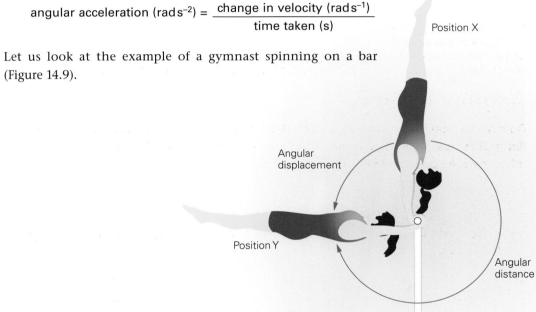

Figure 14.9 Calculating the quantities used in angular motion

Angular distance	Angular displacement	Angular speed	Angular velocity	Angular acceleration
= 270°	= 90°	$= \dfrac{\text{angular distance (rad)}}{\text{time taken (s)}}$	$= \dfrac{\text{angular displacement (rad)}}{\text{time taken (s)}}$	$= \dfrac{\text{change in angular velocity (rad s}^{-1})}{\text{time taken (s)}}$
= 4.7 radians	= 1.5 radians	If time taken from position X to position Y = 0.5 s	$= \dfrac{1.5}{0.5}$	position X = 0 rad s^{-1}
		$= \dfrac{4.7}{0.5}$	= 3 rad s^{-1}	position Y = 3 rad s^{-1}
		= 9.4 rad s^{-1}		$= \dfrac{3}{0.5}$
				= 6 rad s^{-2}

Newton's laws of motion related to angular motion

Newton's laws of motion also apply to angular motion (we looked at Newton's laws in relation to linear motion in Chapter 11). We only need to amend the terminology.

Newton's first law means that this skater will continue to spin until he lands

Newton's first law:

A rotating body will continue in its state of angular motion unless an external force (torque) is exerted upon it.

Think of an ice-skater completing a spinning jump. He will continue to spin until he lands. The ground exerts an external force (torque), which changes his state of angular momentum.

Newton's second law:

The rate of change of angular momentum of a body is proportional to the force (torque) causing it and the change that takes place in the direction in which the force (torque) acts.

For example, leaning forwards from a diving board will create more angular momentum than standing straight.

Newton's third law:

When a force (torque) is applied by one body to another, the second body will exert an equal and opposite force (torque) on the other body.

For example, in a dive, when changing position from a tight tuck to a layout position, the diver rotates the trunk back (extends the trunk). The reaction is for the lower body to rotate in the opposite direction (extension at the hips).

Moment of inertia

Inertia is a resistance to change in motion, so moment of inertia is the resistance of a body to angular motion (rotation). This depends upon the mass of the body and the distribution of mass around the axis.

Mass of the body/object

The greater the mass, the greater the resistance to change and therefore the greater the moment of inertia. For example, a medicine ball is more difficult to roll along the ground than a tennis ball.

Distribution of mass from the axis of rotation

The closer the mass is to the axis of rotation, the easier it is to turn — so the moment of inertia is low. Increasing the distance of the distribution of mass from the axis of rotation will increase the moment of inertia. In the example illustrated in the photos below, a somersault in a straight position has a higher moment of inertia than the tucked somersault. This is because in the straight position the distribution of the diver's mass is further away from the axis of rotation.

Bending (flexion) of the arms and legs reduces the moment of inertia. A pole-vaulter, for example, will flex the knees on the way up to make rotation easier and give him/her more chance of clearing the bar. It is the same in sprinting. When the knee is flexed in the recovery phase of the run, the moment of inertia is reduced as the mass of the leg moves closer to the hip joint. This will make rotation faster as well as easier and the leg can be brought through quickly in readiness for the drive phase. Hence the emphasis on a high knee lift.

Gouhier-Hahn-Nebinger/ABACA/PA Photos

(a) High moment of inertia
(b) Low moment of inertia

Angular momentum

In its simplest form, angular momentum is spin. It involves an object or body in motion around an axis. It depends upon the moment of inertia and angular velocity. These two are inversely proportional — if moment of inertia increases, angular velocity decreases, and vice versa.

Conservation of angular momentum

Angular momentum is a conserved quantity — it stays constant unless an external torque (force) acts upon it (Newton's first law). When an ice-skater executes a spin, for example, there is no change in his angular momentum until he uses his blades to slow the spin down.

    The conservation of angular momentum can be highlighted when a figure-skater performs a spin, turning on a longitudinal (vertical) axis. Ice is a friction-free surface so there is no resistance to movement. Only the figure-skater, therefore, can manipulate his moment of inertia to increase or decrease the speed of the spin. At the start of the spin, the arms and leg are stretched out as shown in Figure 14.10. This increases their distance from the axis of rotation, resulting in a large moment of inertia and a large angular momentum in order to start the spin (rotation is slow).

Figure 14.10 The start of a spin

Figure 14.11 Increasing angular momentum during a spin

    When the figure-skater brings his arms and legs back in line with the rest of his body (as in Figure 14.11), the distance of these body parts to the axis of rotation decreases significantly. This reduces the moment of inertia, meaning that angular momentum has to increase. The result is a very fast spin.

OCR A2 Physical Education

Practice makes perfect

1 Explain how a spinning ice-skater is able to alter her speed of rotation by changing her body shape. *(6 marks)*

2 Coaches use biomechanical analysis to help optimise performance. The diagram below shows three lines representing aspects of angular motion during a backward tucked somersault. Label all three curves, giving reasons for your answers. *(3 marks)*

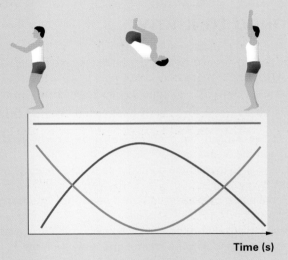

Time (s)

3 In a biceps curl, identify and sketch the type of lever in the arm as the dumb-bell is lowered to the downward position. *(3 marks)*

Energy

What you need to know

By the end of this chapter you should be able to:

- define energy, work and power and identify the units they are expressed in
- explain the role of ATP
- understand the principle of coupled, endothermic and exothermic reactions
- explain the three energy systems: ATP-PC, lactic acid and the aerobic system, making sure that you have knowledge of the type of reaction (aerobic or anaerobic), the chemical or food fuel used, the site of the reaction, the controlling enzyme, energy yield, specific stages within each system and the by-products
- use duration and intensity to explain the contribution of each energy system and to identify the predominant energy system
- explain the energy continuum by describing how a performer interchanges between thresholds during activity
- explain how the following impact on the energy continuum: OBLA, availability of oxygen and food fuels, fitness level and enzyme control of energy systems

Energy concepts

We need a constant supply of energy so that we can perform everyday tasks such as tissue repair and body growth. When we exercise we need energy for muscle contraction in order to produce movements such as running, jumping, catching and throwing. The more exercise we do, the more energy is required. This chapter looks at how this energy is provided and how the body caters for different types of exercise, from the 100 metres where energy is required very quickly,

Table 15.1 Energy concepts

Energy	• the ability to perform work • measured in joules • chemical energy = food • kinetic energy = movement • potential energy = stored
Work	• force × distance • measured in joules
Power	• work performed over a unit of time • a combination of strength and speed • measured in watts

to the marathon where energy needs to be provided for a long period of time. The *intensity* and *duration* of an activity play an important role in the way in which energy is provided.

Adenosine triphosphate (ATP)

Adenosine triphosphate, more commonly referred to as ATP, is the only usable form of energy in the body. The energy we derive from the foods that we eat, such as carbohydrates, has to be converted into ATP before the potential energy in them can be used. As its name suggests, an ATP molecule consists of adenosine and three (tri) phosphates (Figure 15.1).

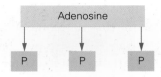

Figure 15.1 An ATP molecule

The release of ATP

Energy is released from ATP by breaking down the bonds that hold this compound together (Figure 15.2).

Enzymes are used to break down compounds, and in this instance ATP-ase is the enzyme used to break down ATP into ADP (adenosine diphosphate) + **Pi** (Figure 15.3).

> **Key terms**
>
> **Adenosine triphosphate (ATP):** the only usable form of energy in the body.
> **Pi:** a free phosphate.

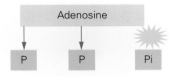

Figure 15.2 Energy is released when the molecule is broken down

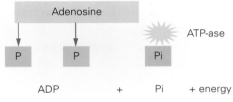

Figure 15.3 ATP → ADP + Pi + energy

This type of reaction is an **exothermic reaction** because energy is released. A reaction that needs energy to work is called an **endothermic reaction**. Regenerating or resynthesising ATP from ADP + Pi is an endothermic reaction.

The resynthesis of ATP

As there is only a limited store of ATP within the muscle fibres, it is used up very quickly (in about 2–3 seconds) and therefore needs to be replenished immediately. There are three energy systems that regenerate ATP:

- the ATP-PC system
- the lactic acid system
- the aerobic system

Each energy system is suited to a particular type of exercise depending on the intensity and duration and whether oxygen is present. The higher the intensity of the activity the more the individual will rely on anaerobic energy production from either the ATP-PC or lactic acid systems. The lower the intensity and the longer the duration of the activity, the more the individual will use the aerobic system.

Sources of energy to replenish ATP

Each of the above energy systems uses fuels for ATP regeneration. These fuels can be derived from either a chemical or a food source.

Phosphocreatine is a chemical produced naturally by the body and used to regenerate ATP in the first 10 seconds of intense exercise. It is easy to break down and is stored within the muscle cells but its stores are limited. This is the fuel for the ATP-PC system.

Carbohydrates are stored as **glycogen** in the muscles and the liver, and converted into glucose during exercise. During high-intensity anaerobic exercise, glycogen can be broken down without the presence of oxygen (in the lactic acid system), but it is broken down much more effectively during aerobic work when oxygen is present (in the aerobic system).

Fats are stored as triglycerides and converted to free fatty acids when required. At rest, two-thirds of our energy requirements can be achieved through the breakdown of fatty acids. This is because fat can produce more energy per gram than glycogen. Fat contains a lot of carbon, which is why it gives us so much energy. It is the secondary energy fuel for low-intensity, aerobic work such as jogging, but has to be used in combination with glycogen due to its hydrophobic quality (low water solubility), which inhibits fat metabolism.

Protein, in the form of amino acids, provides the source of approximately 5–10% of energy used during exercise. It tends to be oxidised when stores of glycogen are low.

Carbohydrates and fats are the main energy providers and the intensity and duration of exercise plays a major role in determining which of these are used. The breakdown of fats to free fatty acids requires around 15% more oxygen than is required to break down glycogen, so during high-intensity exercise when oxygen is in limited supply, glycogen will be the preferred source of energy. Fats, therefore, are the favoured fuel at rest and during long, endurance-based activities.

Stores of glycogen are much smaller than stores of fat and it is important during prolonged periods of exercise not to deplete glycogen stores. Some glycogen needs to be conserved for later when the intensity could increase, for example during the last kilometre of a marathon.

Anaerobic energy systems: the ATP-PC system

Phosphocreatine (PC) is an energy-rich phosphate compound found in the sarcoplasm of the muscles, and is readily available. Its rapid availability is important for providing contractions of high power, such as in the 100 m or in a short burst of intense activity during a longer game (for example, a serve followed by a sprint to reach the return and perform a winning volley in tennis, or a fast break in basketball). However, there is only enough PC to last for up to 10 seconds and it can only be replenished when the intensity of the activity is sub-maximal.

> **Key term**
>
> **Phosphocreatine (PC):** an energy-rich phosphate compound found in the sarcoplasm of the muscles.

The ATP-PC system regenerates ATP when the enzyme creatine kinase detects high levels of ADP. It breaks down the phosphocreatine to phosphate and creatine, releasing energy:

phosphocreatine (PC) → phosphate (Pi) + creatine (C) + energy

OCR A2 Physical Education

This energy is then used to convert ADP to ATP (Figure 15.4). This breaking down of PC to release energy which is then used to convert ADP into ATP is a **coupled reaction** — for every molecule of PC broken down there is enough energy released to create one molecule of ATP. This means that the system is not very efficient but it does have the advantage of not producing fatiguing by-products and its use is important in delaying the onset of the lactic acid system.

Table 15.2 Advantages and disadvantages of the ATP-PC system

Advantages of the ATP-PC system	Disadvantages of the ATP-PC system
• ATP can be regenerated rapidly using the ATP-PC system. • Phosphocreatine stores can be regenerated quickly (30 s = 50% replenishment and 3 min = 100%). • There are no fatiguing by-products. • It is possible to extend the time the ATP-PC system can be utilised through use of creatine supplementation.	• There is only a limited supply of phosphocreatine in the muscle cell, i.e. it can only last for 10 s • Only one molecule of ATP can be regenerated for every molecule of PC. • PC regeneration can only take place in the presence of oxygen (i.e. when the intensity of the exercise is reduced).

Figure 15.4 The ATP-PC system

Tasks to tackle 15.1

Give three sporting examples in which the ATP-PC system would be the predominant method of regenerating ATP.

Anaerobic energy systems: the lactic acid system

Once PC is depleted (at around 10 seconds) the lactic acid system takes over and regenerates ATP from the breakdown of glucose. Glucose is stored in the muscles and liver as glycogen. Before glycogen can be used to provide energy to make ATP it has to be converted to glucose. This process is called **glycolysis** and the lactic acid system is sometimes referred to as **anaerobic glycolysis**, due to the absence of oxygen.

In a series of reactions, the glucose molecule is broken down into two molecules of pyruvic acid, which is then converted to lactic acid by the enzyme lactate dehydrogenase, because oxygen is not available. The main enzyme responsible for the anaerobic breakdown of glucose is phosphofructokinase (PFK), activated by low levels of phosphocreatine. The energy released from the breakdown of each molecule of glucose is used to make two molecules of ATP.

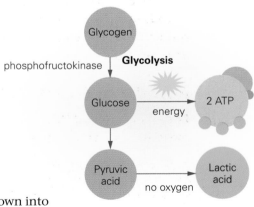

Figure 15.5 The lactic acid system

Glycolysis: the breakdown of glucose into pyruvic acid.

Key term

The lactic acid system provides energy for high-intensity activities lasting up to 3 minutes but peaking at 1 minute, for example running 400 m.

Table 15.3 Advantages and disadvantages of the lactic acid system

Advantages of the lactic acid system	Disadvantages of the lactic acid system
• ATP can be regenerated quite quickly due to very few chemical reactions being required. • In the presence of oxygen, lactic acid can be converted back into liver glycogen or used as a fuel through oxidation into carbon dioxide and water. • The process comes into use for a sprint finish (i.e. to produce an extra burst of energy).	• Lactic acid is the by-product of this system. The accumulation of lactic acid in the body denatures enzymes and prevents them increasing the rate at which chemical reactions take place. • Only a small amount of energy can be released from glycogen under anaerobic conditions (5% as opposed to 95% under aerobic conditions).

The aerobic system

This system breaks down glucose into carbon dioxide and water which, in the presence of oxygen, is much more efficient. The complete oxidation of glucose can produce up to 38 molecules of ATP and has three stages:

1 **Glycolysis**. This process is the same as anaerobic glycolysis (see above) but occurs in the presence of oxygen. Lactic acid is not produced and the pyruvic acid is converted into a compound called acetyl-coenzyme-A (acetyl-CoA).

2 **Krebs cycle**. Once the pyruvic acid diffuses into the matrix of the mitochondria (the powerhouses of muscle cells) forming acetyl-CoA, a complex cycle of reactions occurs in a process known as the Krebs cycle. Here, acetyl-CoA combines with oxaloacetic acid, forming citric acid. The reactions that occur result in the production of two molecules of ATP, as well as carbon dioxide, which is breathed out, and hydrogen, which is taken to the electron transport chain.

Key term

Krebs cycle: a series of cyclical chemical reactions that use oxygen and take place in the matrix of the mitochondria.

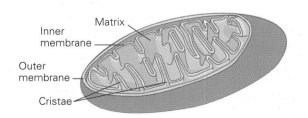

Figure 15.6 A cross-section through a mitochondrion

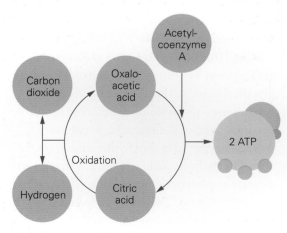

Figure 15.7 The Krebs cycle

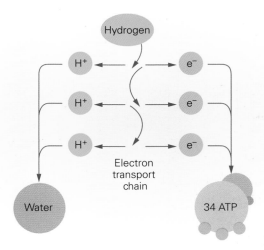

Figure 15.8 The electron transport chain

3 **Electron transport chain**. Hydrogen is carried to the electron transport chain by hydrogen carriers. This occurs in the cristae of the mitochondria. The hydrogen splits into hydrogen ions and electrons and these are charged with potential energy. The hydrogen ions are oxidised to form water, while the electrons provide the energy to resynthesise ATP. Throughout this process, 34 ATP molecules are formed.

Beta oxidation

Fats can also be used as an energy source in the aerobic system. The Krebs cycle and the electron transport chain can metabolise fat as well as carbohydrate to produce ATP. First, the fat is broken down into glycerol and free fatty acids. These fatty acids then undergo a process called beta oxidation whereby they are broken down in the mitochondria to generate acetyl-CoA, which is the entry molecule for the Krebs cycle. From this point on, fat metabolism follows the same path as carbohydrate (glycogen) metabolism. More ATP can be made from one molecule of fatty acids than from one molecule of glycogen, which is why in long-duration exercise fatty acids will be the predominant energy source.

Top tip

Make sure you have a basic overview of each energy system and can identify when each system is used. If the question asks for the main energy system used, then just give the relevant one — if you name all the systems no marks will be awarded.

Table 15.4 Advantages and disadvantages of the aerobic system

Advantages of the aerobic system	Disadvantages of the aerobic system
• More ATP can be produced than by anaerobic systems — 38 ATP molecules from the complete breakdown of each glucose molecule. • There are no fatiguing by-products (only carbon dioxide and water). • There are lots of glycogen and triglyceride stores, so exercise can last for a long time.	• This is a complicated system so cannot be used straightaway. It takes a while for enough oxygen to become available to meet the demands of the activity and ensure glycogen and fatty acids are completely broken down. • Fatty acid transportation to muscles is low and fatty acids require 15% more oxygen to break them down than glycogen.

Figure 15.9 shows a summary of ATP regeneration from the complete breakdown of glycogen.

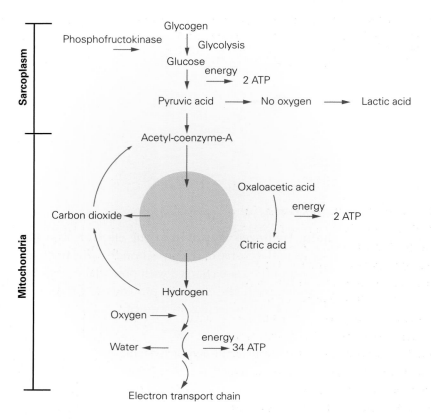

Figure 15.9 Summary of the aerobic system

The energy continuum

When we start any exercise the demand for energy will rise rapidly. All the energy systems contribute during all types of activity but one of them will be the predominant energy provider. The intensity and duration of the activity are the factors that decide which will be the main energy system in use. For example, jogging is a long-duration, sub-maximal exercise so the aerobic system will be the predominant energy system. An explosive, short-duration activity such as the 100 m will use the ATP-PC system. However, in a game there will be a mix of all three energy systems and the performer will move from one energy system to another. This continual movement between the thresholds of each energy system is known as the energy continuum.

> **Key term**
>
> **Energy continuum:** the continual movement between the threshold of each energy system depending on the intensity and duration of the exercise.

OCR A2 Physical Education

Tasks to tackle 15.2

Copy and complete the table below by giving examples from a game of your choice to show when each of the three energy systems will be used.

Name of game	ATP-PC system	Lactic acid system	Aerobic system

The energy continuum is often explained in terms of thresholds. The ATP-PC/lactic acid threshold is the point at which the ATP-PC energy system is exhausted and the lactic acid system takes over. This is shown on Figure 15.10 at 10 seconds, with lactic acid production then peaking at 1 minute. The lactic acid/aerobic threshold, shown in Figure 15.10 at 3 minutes, is the point at which the lactic acid system is exhausted and the aerobic system takes over.

The aerobic threshold is the point at which energy can no longer be supplied aerobically and instead there is a switch to the use of the anaerobic systems. OBLA, the onset of blood lactate accumulation, is a good indicator of this.

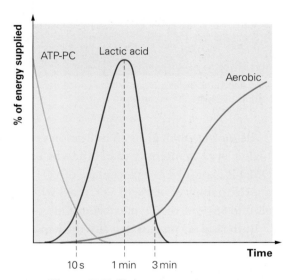

Figure 15.10 The energy continuum

Onset of blood lactate accumulation (OBLA)

Lactate is produced when hydrogen is removed from the lactic acid molecule. **Onset of blood lactate accumulation**

> **Key term**
>
> **Onset of blood lactate accumulation (OBLA):** the point at which lactate starts to accumulate in the blood.

(OBLA) is the point at which lactate starts to accumulate in the blood. At rest, approximately 1–2 millimoles per litre (mmol l^{-1}) of lactic acid can be found in the blood. However, during intense exercise, levels of lactic acid rise dramatically. Lactate levels in the blood start to accumulate when the concentration of lactic acid is around 4 mmol l^{-1}.

Runners finish a 400 m race with a blood lactate concentration that is 20–25 times higher than resting level

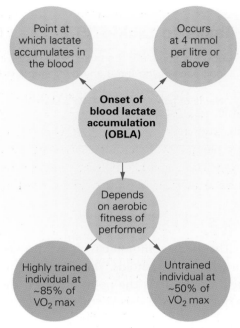

Figure 15.11 Summary of OBLA

Measuring OBLA gives an indication of endurance capacity. Some individuals can work at higher levels of intensity than others before OBLA and can delay when the threshold occurs. OBLA is expressed as a percentage of VO_2 max. An average untrained individual will work at approximately 50–60% of VO_2 max, whereas a trained endurance performer can work at around 85–90% of VO_2 max before OBLA occurs.

Buffering is a process that aids the removal of lactic acid and maintains acidity levels in the blood and muscle. A trained performer can cope with higher levels of blood lactate and can speed up its removal.

The multistage fitness test is a good example to illustrate OBLA. The performer reaches a point, due to the increasing intensity of this test, where energy cannot be provided aerobically. This means that the performer has to use the anaerobic systems to regenerate ATP. Blood lactate levels start to increase until eventually muscle fatigue occurs and the performer slows down and is no longer able to keep up with the bleep.

Enzyme control of energy systems

Enzymes are responsible for the activation of each energy system. Creatine kinase is the controlling enzyme for the ATP-PC system and is activated when levels of ADP are high. PFK (phosphofructokinase) is the controlling enzyme for the lactic acid system and is activated when there is a decrease in phosphocreatine stores. PFK is also one of the controlling enzymes for

Key term

Enzymes: biological catalysts, i.e. they increase the rate of chemical reactions.

the aerobic system. It is the most important regulatory enzyme for glycolysis and is activated when there are high levels of ADP and AMP (adenosine monophosphate), and a low level of free phosphate (Pi).

The availability of oxygen and food fuels

The availability of oxygen is an important factor in determining which energy system is used. It is also an important factor in deciding which food fuel can be broken down. The breakdown of fats to free fatty acids requires more oxygen than is required to break down glycogen. It is also a much slower process. Therefore, during high-intensity exercise when oxygen is in limited supply, glycogen will be the preferred source of energy. Fats, consequently, are the favoured fuel at rest and during long endurance-based activities.

Practice makes perfect

1 Name the main energy system being used in the 100 m and explain how this system provides energy for the working muscles.   *(4 marks)*

2 During exercise all three energy systems are used for ATP resynthesis but at certain times one system is predominant. Sketch a graph to show the relationship between the predominant energy system and the duration of the exercise.   *(4 marks)*

3 Identify the missing information for the aerobic system in the table below.   *(4 marks)*

Site of reaction	Fuel used	Active enzyme	Molecules of ATP produced

The recovery process

What you need to know:

By the end of this chapter you should be able to:

- explain EPOC/oxygen debt
- describe the alactacid and lactacid components of oxygen debt
- explain the replenishment of myoglobin and fuel stores
- describe how carbon dioxide is removed from the body
- explain the implications of the recovery process for planning training sessions

The recovery process involves returning the body to the state it was in before exercise. The reactions that occur and how long the process takes depend on the duration and intensity of the exercise undertaken and the individual's level of fitness. During recovery, heart and breathing rates remain high in order to continue taking in large amounts of oxygen. This oxygen is then used to return the body to its pre-exercise state.

Tasks to tackle 16.1

Copy and complete the table below to show the changes that take place during exercise.

Factor	Change
Temperature	
ATP stores	
Phosphocreatine stores	
Glycogen stores	
Triglyceride stores	
Carbon dioxide levels	
Oxygen/myoglobin stores	
Lactic acid levels	

Excess post-exercise oxygen consumption (EPOC)

After strenuous exercise there are four main tasks that need to be completed before the exhausted muscle can operate at full efficiency again:

- replacement of ATP and phosphocreatine (the fast replenishment stage)
- replenishment of myoglobin with oxygen
- removal of lactic acid (the slow replenishment stage)
- replacement of glycogen

The first three of these tasks require a large amount of oxygen. Therefore, during recovery the body takes in elevated amounts of oxygen and transports it to the working muscles to maintain elevated rates of aerobic respiration. This surplus energy is then used to help return the body to its pre-exercise state. This process is known as **excess post-exercise oxygen consumption (EPOC)**. The processes that take place during EPOC are summarised in Figure 16.1.

When we start to exercise, insufficient oxygen is distributed to the tissues for all the energy production to be met aerobically, so the two anaerobic systems have to be used. The amount of oxygen that the subject was short of during the exercise is known as the **oxygen deficit**. This is compensated for by the surplus amount of oxygen — or **oxygen debt** — that results from EPOC. However, oxygen debt does not always equal oxygen deficit because oxygen is used during recovery to provide energy to maintain elevated heart and breathing rates.

Let's look at the four tasks involved in EPOC in more detail.

The alactacid component (fast replenishment stage)

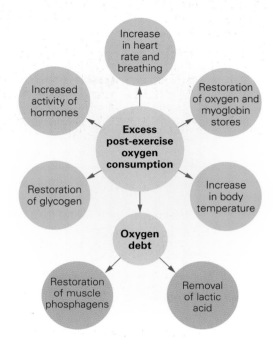

Figure 16.1 The processes involved in EPOC

During the **alactacid component** (also known as the **fast replenishment stage**), elevated rates of respiration continue to supply oxygen to provide the energy for ATP production and phosphocreatine replenishment. Complete restoration of phosphocreatine takes up to 3 minutes, but 50% of stores can be replenished after only 30 seconds, during which time approximately 3 litres of oxygen are consumed. Figure 16.2 shows the relationship between recovery time and the replenishment of muscle phosphagens (ATP and phosphocreatine) after exercise.

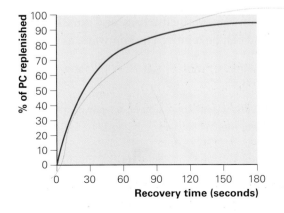

Figure 16.2 Recovery time and PC regeneration

EPOC (excess post-exercise oxygen consumption): the process by which more oxygen is consumed during recovery from exercise than would have been consumed at rest during the same time.

Alactacid component: the restoration of ATP and phosphocreatine stores and the resaturation of myoglobin with oxygen.

Chapter *16* The recovery process

This knowledge is useful for a coach or performer, who will want to prevent the use of the lactic acid system with its fatiguing by-product. A time-out in basketball will allow for significant restoration of PC stores.

Key terms

Myoglobin: a protein that stores oxygen in the muscle.

Lactacid component: the removal of lactic acid.

Myoglobin and replenishment of oxygen stores

Myoglobin has a high affinity for oxygen. It stores oxygen in the muscle and transports it from the capillaries to the mitochondria for energy provision. After exercise, oxygen stores in the myoglobin are limited. The surplus of oxygen supplied through EPOC helps replenish these stores, taking up to 2 minutes and using approximately 0.5 litres of oxygen.

Top tip

Questions on EPOC often involve a description of the alactacid and lactacid components.

The lactacid component (slow replenishment stage)

This stage is concerned with the removal of lactic acid and is also known as the **slow replenishment stage**. It is the slower of the two replenishment processes and full recovery may take up to an hour, depending on the intensity and duration of the exercise. Lactic acid can be removed in four ways, as shown in Table 16.1.

Table 16.1 Component stages of lactic acid removal

Destination	Approximate % lactic acid involved
Oxidation into carbon dioxide and water in the inactive muscles and organs	65
Conversion into glycogen — then stored in muscles/liver	20
Conversion into protein	10
Conversion into glucose	5

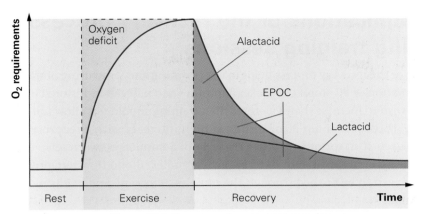

Figure 16.3 Recovery after maximal exercise

The majority of lactic acid can be oxidised, so performing a cool-down accelerates its removal because exercise keeps the metabolic rate of muscles high and keeps capillaries dilated. This means that oxygen can be flushed through, removing the accumulated lactic acid. The lactacid oxygen recovery begins as soon as lactic acid appears in the muscle cell and continues, using breathed oxygen, until recovery is complete. This can take up to 5–6 litres of oxygen in the first half hour of recovery, removing up to 50% of the lactic acid.

Glycogen replenishment

Glycogen, as the main fuel for the aerobic system and lactic acid system, is depleted during exercise. The stores of glycogen in relation to the stores of fat are relatively small, so it is important to conserve glycogen in order not to cross the lactate threshold. The replacement of glycogen stores depends on the type of exercise undertaken and when and how much carbohydrate is consumed following exercise. It may take several days to complete the restoration of glycogen after a marathon, but a significant amount of glycogen can be restored in less than an hour after long-duration, low-intensity exercise. Eating a high-carbohydrate meal will accelerate glycogen restoration, as will eating within 1 hour following exercise.

Increase in breathing and heart rates

The continuation of sub-maximal exercise (such as a cool down) will keep hormone levels elevated and this will keep breathing and metabolic levels high so that extra oxygen can be taken in. This also means that more carbon dioxide can be expelled from the lungs. Carbon dioxide is a by-product of aerobic respiration (see the Krebs cycle). Most of the carbon dioxide is removed in the plasma of the blood by forming carbonic acid. This high acidity is detected by chemoreceptors which then stimulate the cardiac centre and the respiratory centre located in the medulla oblongata. As a result, cardiac output remains high, so more carbon dioxide can be transported to the lungs, and the higher breathing rate means that more carbon dioxide can be expelled.

The implications of the recovery process for planning training sessions

Knowledge of the recovery process helps in the planning and structuring of training sessions:

- Full restoration of PC stores only takes 3 minutes and half can be restored in 30 seconds. If athletes wish to increase their PC stores then training should not allow full recovery — for example, three sets of ten 30 m sprints at high intensity with a recovery of 30 seconds between each 30 m sprint and with a recovery of 5 minutes between sets.
- Performing a cool down will increase recovery rates. Blood flow remains high and this allows oxygen to be flushed through the muscles, removing and oxidising any lactic acid that remains.
- Heart rate can be monitored to highlight when thresholds are reached. This could prevent the occurrence of OBLA.
- A thorough warm-up ensures that myoglobin stores are full, which will reduce the oxygen deficit at the start of exercise.

Practice makes perfect

1 State what the letters A and B represent on the graph below. Describe the processes that take place during these times. *(6 marks)*

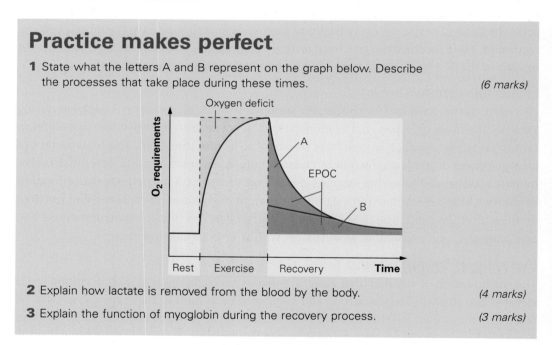

2 Explain how lactate is removed from the blood by the body. *(4 marks)*

3 Explain the function of myoglobin during the recovery process. *(3 marks)*

Chapter *17*

Health-related components of physical fitness

What you need to know

By the end of this chapter you should be able to:

- give definitions of aerobic capacity, different types of strength, flexibility and body composition
- explain the factors affecting VO_2 max, strength and flexibility
- describe and explain tests that can be used to evaluate aerobic capacity, strength, flexibility and body composition
- explain the different types of training that can be used to develop aerobic capacity, strength and flexibility
- describe which energy system and food/chemical fuels are used during aerobic activity, strength training and flexibility training
- describe the adaptations that take place after a period of aerobic training, strength training and flexibility training
- identify how target heart rates can be used as an intensity guide
- be able to calculate an individual's BMI (body mass index)
- understand the term BMR (basal metabolic rate) and the different energy requirements of various physical activities
- calculate your daily calorific requirements based on your BMR and your average additional energy consumption
- critically evaluate your personal diet and calorie consumption
- understand the health implications of being overweight or obese and how this can affect involvement in physical activity

Aerobic capacity

A good endurance performer can utilise the aerobic system efficiently through both the effective transportation of oxygen and the effective use of oxygen to break down glycogen, fats and proteins to release energy. This section looks at aerobic capacity and discusses the factors that affect it, how it can be measured, what types of training can be used to improve aerobic capacity and what adaptations will take place in the body as a result of this training.

Aerobic capacity is often referred to as **VO_2 max**. It is the maximum volume of oxygen that can be taken in

> **Key term**
>
> **Aerobic capacity/**
> **VO_2 max:** the maximum volume of oxygen that can be taken in and used by the muscles per minute.

Paula Radcliffe's VO_2 max is around $80\,ml\,kg^{-1}\,min^{-1}$. This means she has more oxygen going to the muscles and can use this oxygen to provide energy to enable a high rate of exercise.

and used by the muscles per minute. A person's VO_2 max will determine endurance performance in sport. Average VO_2 max for an A-level student is around 45–55 ml kg^{-1} min^{-1} for males and 35–44 ml kg^{-1} min^{-1} for females.

VO_2 max depends on:

- how effectively an individual can inspire and expire
- once he/she has inspired, how effective the transportation of the oxygen is from the lungs to where it is needed
- how well that oxygen is then used

Factors affecting aerobic capacity

VO_2 max is affected by a number of factors:

Lifestyle

Smoking, a sedentary lifestyle and poor diet can all reduce VO_2 max values.

Training

VO_2 max can be improved by up to 10–20% following a period of aerobic training (continuous, fartlek and aerobic interval).

Body composition

Research has shown that VO_2 max decreases as the percentage of body fat increases.

Gender

A male endurance athlete will have a VO_2 max of around 70 ml kg^{-1} min^{-1}, whereas a female endurance athlete will have a VO_2 max of around $60\,ml\,kg^{-1}\,min^{-1}$. This is because the average female is smaller than the average male. Females have:

- a smaller left ventricle and therefore a lower stroke volume
- a lower maximum cardiac output
- a lower blood volume, which results in a lower haemoglobin level
- lower tidal and ventilatory volumes

Age

As we get older our VO_2 max declines as our body systems become less efficient:

- Maximum heart rate drops by around 5–7 beats per minute per decade.
- An increase in peripheral resistance results in a decrease of maximal stroke volume.
- Blood pressure increases both at rest and during exercise.

- Less air is exchanged in the lungs due to a decline in vital capacity and an increase in residual air.

Physiological factors

The following physiological factors will lead to an improved VO_2 max:

- increased maximum cardiac output
- increased stroke volume/ejection fraction/cardiac hypertrophy
- greater heart rate range
- less oxygen being used for heart muscle, so more available to muscles
- increased arterio-venous oxygen difference (A-VO_2 diff) — the difference in oxygen content between the arteries and the veins
- increased blood volume and haemoglobin/red blood cells/blood count
- increased stores of glycogen and triglycerides
- increased myoglobin (content of muscle)
- increased capillarisation (of muscle)
- increased number and size of mitochondria
- increased concentrations of oxidative enzymes
- increased lactate tolerance
- reduced body fat
- slow twitch hypertrophy

Evaluation of VO_2 max

There are various methods of evaluating VO_2 max.

The **Douglas bag** is one very accurate method carried out under laboratory conditions. The athlete runs on a treadmill, to the point of exhaustion — i.e. it is a maximal test. The air that is expired is collected in a Douglas bag. The concentration of oxygen in the expired air is then measured and compared with the percentage of oxygen that is in atmospheric air to see how much oxygen has been used during the task. This test requires access to expensive hi-tech equipment, so less expensive predictive tests (indirect tests) have been developed to estimate the performer's VO_2 max.

One such test is the **multistage fitness test** developed by the National Coaching Foundation. The athlete performs a 20 m progressive shuttle run in time with a bleep, to the point of exhaustion. The level reached depends on the number of shuttle runs completed and is ascertained from a standard results table.

This test gives only an estimate of VO_2 max and is nowhere near as accurate as the Douglas bag test. However, it does provide a guide from which progress can be monitored, and is easy to set up. The equipment required is limited, making it a cheap alternative. It is also possible to test large numbers of people simultaneously, so it is not as time consuming as the Douglas bag test.

The **Harvard step test** involves the athlete stepping up and down rhythmically on a bench for 5 minutes. The recovery heart rate is then measured and used to predict VO_2 max.

The **PWC170 cycle ergometer test** involves three consecutive 4-minute workloads on a cycle ergometer. The heart rate for each workload is plotted on a graph and a line of best fit is drawn. Both this test and the Harvard step test are sub-maximal. The **Cooper 12-minute run** requires the athlete to run as far as he/she can in 12 minutes and the distance covered is recorded and compared to a standardised table. In this test the performer runs to exhaustion.

Training to develop aerobic capacity

There are four main types of training that can be used to develop aerobic capacity.

Continuous running

This involves exercise without rest intervals and concentrates on developing endurance, therefore placing stress on the aerobic energy system. Continuous training is done at a steady pace over a long period of time. The emphasis is on distance rather than speed. The duration of the run should be approximately 30–45 minutes at a training intensity of 60–75% of maximum heart rate.

Repetition running

Repetition running is used to develop speed, speed endurance and local muscular endurance. A set distance is run a specific number of times. The running is set at a faster pace than continuous training and unlike interval training there is complete rest between runs. The speed of the repetition should be the same if not faster than racing pace. A long-distance runner, for example, may do repeated runs of 1000 m, 1500 m, 2000 m and 3000 m.

Fartlek training

This is a slightly different method of continuous training where the word 'fartlek' means speed-play. Here the performer varies the pace of the run to stress both the aerobic and anaerobic energy systems. This is a much more demanding type of training and will improve an individual's VO_2 max and recovery process. A typical session will last for approximately 40 minutes with the intensity ranging from low to high. For example:

- 10-minute jog
- 6 × (20 seconds fast running with 80 seconds recovery)
- 5-minute walk
- 5-minute jog
- 2 × run uphill for 1 minute, jog down
- 3-minute jog
- 2-minute walk

Interval training

Interval training can be used for both aerobic and anaerobic training. It is a form of training in which periods of work are interspersed with recovery periods. Four main variables are used to ensure the training is specific:

OCR A2 Physical Education

- the duration of the work interval
- the intensity or speed of the work interval
- the duration of the recovery period
- the number of work intervals and recovery periods

It is possible to adapt interval training to overload each of the three energy systems. Anaerobic intervals would be short-distance, high-intensity and aerobic intervals would be long-distance, sub-maximal intensity. This is summarised in Table 17.1.

Table 17.1 Adaptations of interval training for the different energy systems

Energy system	Duration/ distance of work interval	Intensity of work interval	Duration of recovery	Number of work intervals/ recovery periods
ATP-PC	60 m	High intensity — 90% max heart rate (10 s)	30 s	10
Lactic acid	200 m	High intensity — 80–90% max heart rate (35 s)	110 s	8
Aerobic	1500 m	Sub-maximal — 60–75% max heart rate (6 min)	5 min	3

The use of target heart rates as an intensity guide

Heart rate training zones can be used to gauge how hard a performer is working. Most training zones are calculated from the maximum heart rate. Remember that this is estimated as:

220 – age

So, if you are 17, your maximum rate is assumed to be:

220 – 17 = 203

You then need to work at a certain percentage of this maximum heart rate. One way of doing this is by using the **Karvonen principle**. This is more accurate than other methods because it uses resting heart rates (i.e. it takes into account individual fitness levels) to work out an individual's training zone. Karvonen suggests a training intensity of 60–75% of maximum heart rate, using the following calculation:

60% = resting heart rate + 0.6(max heart rate – resting heart rate)
75% = resting heart rate + 0.75(max heart rate – resting heart rate)

For a 17-year-old with a resting heart rate of 60 beats per minute, the calculation would be:

60% = 60 + 0.6 (203 – 60)
= 60 + (0.6 × 143)
= 60 + 86 (85.8)
= 146

75% = 70 + 0.75 (203 – 60)
= 70 + (0.75 × 143)
= 70 + 107 (107.25)
= 177

Therefore, a 17-year-old with a resting heart rate of 60 beats per minute working at an intensity of 60–75% of maximum heart rate should be working at 146–177 beats per minute.

Table 17.2 The relationship between aerobic intensity and fuel used

Intensity of continuous running (% max heart rate)	Fuel
50–60%	Fats
60–70%	Glycogen and fat
70–80%	Glycogen

Energy system and food/chemical used

In order to improve aerobic capacity, the aerobic system needs to be used. It is possible to work at different levels of intensity and still use the aerobic system. The more training an individual does, the higher the level of intensity he/she can work at before using anaerobic energy systems. The intensity and duration of the activity will be the deciding factor in fuel usage, as shown in Table 17.2.

Adaptations to aerobic training

Physiological adaptations are long-lasting changes that occur in the body as a result of following a training programme. These changes take place to allow improvement in fitness. The type of training you choose to do will result in specific adaptations, as outlined in Table 17.3.

If you perform continuous, repetition running, fartlek or aerobic interval training over a period of time, physiological adaptations take place that would make the initial training sessions appear very easy. This is because your aerobic capacity/VO_2 max improves as the adaptations take place.

Table 17.3 Adaptations to aerobic training

Site	Adaptations
Heart	Hypertrophy of the myocardium (heart gets bigger and stronger), which means more blood can be pumped around the body
	Increase in stroke volume and maximum cardiac output
	Decrease in resting heart rate (bradycardia) because stroke volume has increased, so the heart can beat less often
Lungs	Maximum minute ventilation increases due to an increase in tidal volume and respiratory rate
	Respiratory muscles become stronger, making breathing more efficient
	Small increases in resting lung volume, which result in a greater area for diffusion to take place
	Diffusion rates improve
Vascular system	An increase in the elasticity of the arterial walls, making it easier to cope with fluctuations in blood pressure
	Increase in the density of the capillary networks surrounding the lungs and skeletal muscle, allowing more gaseous exchange to take place
Blood	Blood volume increases, due mainly to an increase in blood plasma, which will decrease blood viscosity and allow a greater flow through capillaries, and a small increase in red blood cells, which enhances oxygen transport
	Blood less acidic at rest but more acidic during exercise due to a greater tolerance of lactic acid
Muscle	Increase in myoglobin levels, which means more oxygen can be stored in the muscle
	Increase in mitochondria, which raises aerobic metabolism
	Increase in activity of the respiratory enzymes, which increases the efficiency of the aerobic system
	Increase in energy stores (glycogen and triglycerides) in the muscle cells

Tasks to tackle 17.1

(a) Define aerobic capacity and identify the factors that affect a performer's VO$_2$ max.

(b) Plan a training programme to improve your aerobic capacity (based on the requirements of your own physical activity).

Strength

A common definition of strength is the maximum force that can be exerted by a muscle or group of muscles during a single contraction. In sport we use various types of strength:

- **Maximum strength** is the maximum force a muscle is capable of exerting in a single maximal voluntary contraction, and is used during weightlifting. Due to higher levels of testosterone, men have a larger muscle mass and so can exert greater maximum strength than women. In addition, fast glycolytic fibres are important for maximum strength, as they can produce more force than slow-twitch fibres.

- **Elastic strength (power)** is the ability to overcome resistance with a high speed of contraction. It can be seen in explosive events such as sprinting, throwing and hitting, where a high percentage of fast glycolytic fibres is needed for a good performance.

- **Strength endurance** is the ability of a muscle to perform repeated contractions and withstand fatigue, and is important for a rower or swimmer. In addition, when a team game goes into extra time, players with better strength endurance will be in a stronger position to maintain a high level of performance.

- **Static strength** is the ability to apply a force where the length of the muscle does not change and there is no visible movement at a joint — for example, the 'Pillars of Hercules' in the 2008 World's Strongest Man competition..

- **Dynamic strength** is the ability to apply a force repeatedly over a period of time. It is essential for explosive activities such as sprinting and is similar to elastic strength.

Dynamic strength comes into play in many team sports, with rugby being a prime example

Factors affecting strength

Strength is dependent on two main factors.

Fibre type

There are three types of muscle fibre:

- slow oxidative (type I)
- fast oxidative glycolytic (type IIa)
- fast glycolytic (type IIb)

Fast-twitch fibres contract more quickly and produce more power and maximum strength. They are also designed to grow larger as a result of training. Muscle fibre percentage is mostly genetically determined.

Cross-sectional area of the muscle

The cross-sectional area of the muscle can affect how much strength is produced. The greater the cross-sectional area, the greater the strength produced. However, two individuals with an equal cross-sectional area of muscle may produce different amounts of strength. This is due to the lever system of the body, which in itself is determined by the position of the muscle attachment. Muscles with the largest cross-sectional area tend to be found in the legs. An individual can, on average, produce 4–8 kg of force per cm^2 of muscle cross section.

Evaluating strength

Ways of evaluating each type of strength are described in Table 17.4.

Table 17.4 Methods of strength evaluation

Maximum strength	Hand grip dynamometer	The performer squeezes the dynamometer while lowering it from shoulder height to his/her side. The highest reading from three attempts is recorded.
	1 rep max test	The performer lifts the maximum weight he/she can just once. It may take a bit of trial and error to find this maximum, so there should be ample rest between attempts.
Elastic strength (also dynamic strength)	Wingate test	The performer pedals as fast as he/she can for 30 seconds. The resistance on the bike is related to body weight (75 g per kg of body weight). The number of revolutions is then recorded for every 5 seconds of the test.
	Vertical jump	The performer's standing reach is measured against a wall. From a squatting position he/she then jumps up as high as possible, marking the wall at the top of the jump.
Muscular endurance	NCF abdominal curl	The performer does as many sit-ups as he/she can, keeping in time with a bleep. The test finishes when the performer can no longer keep up with the bleep and the stage reached is recorded.
Static strength	Isometric mid-thigh pull exercise	The performer pulls on an immovable bar (performed in a power rack with pins) and maintains the effort for 5 seconds.

Training to develop strength

Some individuals do a form of strength training to improve performance in their chosen activity. Improvements in strength result from working against some form of resistance. In this instance, it is important to make any strength training programme specific to the needs of the activity. To do this, the following factors must be considered:

- the type of strength to be developed — maximum, elastic or strength endurance
- the muscle groups to be improved
- the type of muscle contraction performed in the activity — concentric, eccentric or isometric

Other individuals do strength training for muscle growth and need to ensure that any exercises they perform will overload the anaerobic energy systems, which will result in hypertrophy of fast-twitch fibres.

Strength can be improved by doing the following types of training.

Weights

Weight training is usually described in terms of sets and repetitions. The number of sets and repetitions completed and the quantity of weight lifted will depend on the type of strength that the performer wishes to improve. Before designing a training programme, it is important to determine the maximum amount of weight that a performer can lift with one repetition. Then, if maximum strength is the goal it will be necessary to lift heavy weights with low repetitions, for example three sets of two to six repetitions at 80–100% of maximum load. However, if strength endurance is the goal it will be necessary to perform more repetitions of lighter weights, for example three sets of ten repetitions at approximately 50% of maximum load.

The choice of exercise should relate to the muscle groups used in sport — both the agonists and antagonists. The exercises are usually classed into four groups:

- shoulders and arms, such as bench presses, curls and pull downs
- trunk and back, such as sit-ups and back hyper-extensions
- legs, such as squats, calf raises and leg presses
- all-body exercises, such as power clean, snatches and dead lifts, which use various muscles throughout the body, such as the arms, legs and trunk

Circuit/interval training

Circuit training for strength can also be referred to as interval training for strength, although the two methods are slightly different. Interval strength training involves completing an exercise on one muscle group, then resting for 1 to 2 minutes before moving on to the next exercise and muscle group. In circuit training, the athlete performs a series of exercises in succession, with no rests. These exercises include press-ups, sit-ups and squat thrusts to name a few. The resistance used is the athlete's body weight and each exercise concentrates on a different muscle group to allow for recovery. A circuit is usually designed for general

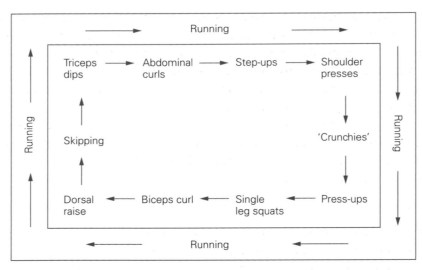

Figure 17.1 Circuit training

body conditioning and it is easily adapted to meet the needs of an activity. An example of a circuit can be seen in Figure 17.1.

Most circuits are completed in pairs. For example, A runs while B completes the exercises. After two complete running circuits, the partners change activity so that A now completes the exercises and B runs.

Plyometrics

Plyometrics is a method of strength training that improves power or elastic strength. It is used if leg power is crucial to successful performance, for example in the long jump and 100 m sprint in athletics or rebounding in basketball. It works on the idea that muscles can

Figure 17.2 Plyometric training

       OCR A2 Physical Education

generate more force if they have previously been stretched. This occurs in plyometrics when, on landing, the muscle performs an eccentric contraction (lengthens under tension). This stimulates the muscle spindle apparatus as it detects the rapid lengthening of the muscle and then sends nerve impulses to the central nervous system (CNS). If the CNS believes the muscle is lengthening too quickly it will initiate a stretch reflex, causing a powerful concentric contraction as the performer jumps up.

To develop leg strength a line of benches, boxes or hurdles is made and the performer has to jump, hop or leap from one to the other. Recovery occurs as the performer walks back to the start line to repeat the exercise. To develop arm strength, press-ups with mid-air claps or throwing and catching a medicine ball are good exercises.

Energy system and food/chemical used

You need to be able to state the energy system and the food/chemical fuel used during each type of strength training as shown in Table 17.5.

Table 17.5 Energy system and fuel used during strength training

Type of strength	Energy system	Food/chemical
Maximum	ATP-PC	Phosphocreatine
Elastic strength	ATP-PC and lactic acid system	Phosphocreatine and glycogen
Muscular endurance	Lactic acid system/ aerobic system	Glycogen and fats
Static/dynamic strength	ATP-PC and lactic acid system	Phosphocreatine and glycogen

Adaptations to strength training

Neural adaptations to strength training

- More strength can be generated by the recruitment of more motor units.
- The inhibitory effect of the Golgi tendon organs is reduced, which allows the muscle to stretch further and generate more force.

Adaptations to muscle fibres

The type of strength training undertaken will result in specific adaptations. With weight training, for example, light weights and high repetitions allow adaptations to occur in slow oxidative fibres, whereas heavy weights and low repetitions allow adaptations in fast glycolytic fibres.

Aerobic adaptations in slow oxidative fibres include:
- hypertrophy of slow-twitch fibres. This is where the myofibrils become thicker due to increased muscle synthesis. However, hypertrophy in slow-twitch muscle fibres is not as great as in fast-twitch fibres.
- an increase in mitochondria and myoglobin
- an increase in glycogen and triglyceride stores
- an increase in capillaries

Anaerobic adaptations to fast-twitch fibres include:
- hypertrophy of fast oxidative glycolytic and fast glycolytic fibres. In addition, hyperplasia (a relatively new term) may occur, whereby the splitting of muscle fibres leads to the

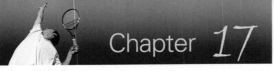

creation of new ones. This has yet to be proven in humans but it is thought that, together with muscle hypertrophy, it contributes to an increase in size.
- an increase in ATP and PC stores
- an increase in glycogen stores
- greater tolerance of lactic acid

Tasks to tackle 17.2

(a) Following a period of strength training, what adaptations would occur in the skeletal muscle of a performer?

(b) Identify one test that can be used to evaluate maximum strength and one test for muscular endurance.

Flexibility

There are two main types of flexibility:
- **Static** flexibility is the range of movement around a joint, for example doing the splits.
- **Dynamic** flexibility is the resistance of a joint to movement, for example kicking a football without hamstring and hip joint resistance.

Factors affecting flexibility

Flexibility is affected by a range of factors:
- the elasticity of ligaments and tendons
- the amount of stretch allowed by surrounding muscles
- the type of joint — for example, the knee is a hinge joint allowing movement in only one plane (flexion and extension); the shoulder is a ball-and-socket joint and allows movement in many planes (flexion, extension, abduction, adduction, medial and lateral rotation, circumduction)
- the structure of a joint — the hip and shoulder are both ball-and-socket joints, but the hip joint has a deeper joint cavity and tighter ligaments to keep it more stable but less mobile than the shoulder
- the temperature of surrounding muscle and connective tissue
- training — flexibility can decrease during periods of inactivity
- age — the older you are, the less flexible you tend to be
- gender — females tend to be more flexible than males due to hormonal differences

Evaluation of flexibility

Sit-and-reach test

The sit-and-reach test gives an indication of flexibility of the hamstrings and lower back. To complete this test, a sit-and-reach box is required. Participants have to sit on the floor with

An Olympic rhythmic gymnast demonstrates her extreme flexibility

their feet flat against the box and legs straight. They then reach forward as far as possible, pushing the marker with their fingertips, holding for 3 seconds and reading off the score. Tables are used to compare results and obtain a rating.

Goniometer

A goniometer can also be used to measure flexibility. This is an instrument that measures angles at various joints.

Figure 17.3 The sit-and-reach test

Training to develop flexibility
Static stretching

- Active — the performer works on one joint, pushing it beyond its point of resistance, lengthening the muscles and connective tissue surrounding it.
- Passive — this is when a stretch occurs with the help of an external force, such as a partner, gravity or a wall.

Figure 17.4 A static active stretch

Figure 17.5 Dynamic stretching

Ballistic stretching

This involves performing a stretch with swinging or bouncing movements to push a body part beyond its normal range of motion. It is important that this type of stretching should only be performed by an individual who is extremely flexible, such as a gymnast or a dancer.

Dynamic stretching

This involves controlled leg and arm swings that take a body part gently to the limit of its range of motion.

Proprioceptive neuromuscular facilitation (PNF)

First the muscle is passively stretched. It is then contracted isometrically against a resistance while in a stretched position for a period of at least 10 seconds. When it is passively stretched again there is an increase in the range of motion.

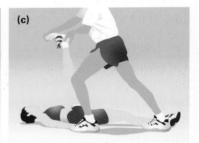

Figure 17.6 (a) The individual performs a passive stretch with the help of a partner and extends the leg until tension is felt. This stretch is detected by the muscle spindle apparatus.
(b) The individual then isometrically contracts the muscle for at least 10 seconds by pushing his/her leg against the partner who supplies just enough resistance to hold the leg in a stationary position.
(c) There is further relaxation of the target muscle as a result and it can be stretched further during the next passive stretch.

Adaptations to flexibility training

Adaptations occur after a period of flexibility training. The tendons, ligaments and muscles surrounding a joint have elastic properties, which allow a change in length. There is more of a change to muscle tissue than to tendons or ligaments. A permanent change is known as a plastic change.

> **Tasks to tackle 17.3**
>
> What factors can affect the flexibility of a performer?

Body composition

Body composition is the physiological make-up of an individual in terms of the distribution of lean body mass and body fat. On average, men have less body fat than women: around 15% compared with 25%. Obviously, body composition has an important role in sport. Excess body fat can lead to health problems such as cardiovascular disease, and any exercise will require greater energy expenditure as more weight has to be moved around. It is generally agreed that the less body fat there is, the better the performance, but there are some sports with specific requirements for larger amounts of fat, such as the defensive linesman in American football or, if we take it to the extreme, a sumo wrestler! In most team games, however, excess body fat would affect a performer's ability to move freely around the court/field and would increase the onset of fatigue during the game.

Evaluation of body composition

Skin fold test

The skin fold test involves taking measurements from one side of the body, from the biceps, triceps, sub-scapular (below the shoulder blade) and supra iliac (hip region). Each skin fold is held and the callipers placed over it, taking care not to pinch the skin fold too hard. The callipers are slowly released until the entire force is on the skin fold. The callipers will move a little at this stage, so the reading is allowed to settle for a few seconds, and then the skin fold measurement is taken (in mm). The measurements are added together and the total compared with standardised tables.

Bioelectric impedence

Electrodes are attached at the ankles and wrists and a small electrical current is passed through them. As fat offers greater resistance to the flow of the electrical current, the amount of impedance gives an estimate of the percentage of body fat.

Figure 17.7 The skin fold test

Hydrostatic weighing

The body is immersed in water. Body mass is divided by the volume of water displaced when immersed. This calculates body density, which can be used to predict the percentage of body fat.

Body mass index (BMI)

This test is looked at in more detail in the next section.

Body mass index (BMI)

Body mass index (BMI) is a measurement of body fat that is based on height and weight and applies to both men and women. To calculate your BMI, divide your weight in kilograms by your height in metres squared. For example, someone who weighs 75 kg and is 1.81 m tall can calculate their BMI as follows:

Table 17.6 BMI values

BMI	Classification
<19	Underweight
19–25	Normal
26–30	Overweight
30–40	Obese
>40	Morbidly obese

$$BMI = \frac{weight\ (kg)}{height\ (m) \times height\ (m)}$$

$$= \frac{75}{1.81 \times 1.81}$$

$$= 22.89$$

BMI values vary but Table 17.6 is representative of most literature.

Basal metabolic rate (BMR)

Basal metabolic rate (BMR) refers to the amount of energy needed by the body to sustain life while at rest. BMR decreases with age as the body's ability to burn energy gradually slows. However, regular aerobic exercise will increase BMR. Once you are aware of your BMR it is possible to calculate your daily calorific needs.

A rough estimation of BMR can be achieved using an equation based on weight, sex, age and height. A more accurate evaluation requires gas analysis and calorimetry.

> ## Tasks to tackle 17.4
>
> Describe and explain two methods of measuring body composition.

> **Key term**
>
> **Basal metabolic rate (BMR):** the amount of energy needed by the body to sustain life while at rest.

Energy balance of food (calories)

When we take part in physical activity, the body requires energy and the amount of energy we need is dependent on the duration and type of activity. Energy is measured in calories and is obtained from the body's stores or the food we eat. A calorie (cal) is the amount of heat energy required to raise the temperature of 1 g of water by 1°C. A kilocalorie (kcal) is the amount of heat required to raise the temperature of 1000 g of water by 1°C.

The basic energy requirements of the average individual are 1.3 kcal per hour for every kg of body weight. Therefore if you weigh 60 kg you will require:

1.3 × 24 (hours in a day) × 60

= 1872 kcal day^{-1}

This energy requirement increases during exercise to up to 8.5 kcal per hour for each kg of body weight. Therefore in a 1-hour training session the performer would require an extra $8.5 \times 1 \times 60 = 510$ kcal.

From these calculations it is possible to calculate the energy requirements of this performer by adding his/her basic energy requirements (1872 kcal) to the extra energy needed for that 1 hour training session (510 kcal):

$$1872 + 510 = 2382$$

Diet

Nutrition and diet can contribute to a successful performance. A balanced diet is essential for optimum performance in all sporting activities. What you eat can have an effect on your health, your weight and your energy levels. Top performers place huge demands on their bodies during both training and competition. Their diet must meet those energy require-ments as well as providing nutrients for tissue growth and repair. An average diet should contain around 15% protein, 30% fat and 55% carbohydrate. During exercise, this percentage needs to change in favour of carbohydrates. Sports nutritionists recommend the following:

- Proteins: 10–15%
- Fats: 20–25%
- Carbohydrates: 60–75%

Tasks to tackle 17.5

Copy and complete the table below with suggestions for the diet of an 18-year-old long-distance runner weighing 60 kg who trains five times per week, each session lasting 2 hours.

Energy requirements without exercise	
Energy requirements including exercise	
% carbohydrates	
% fats	
% proteins	

Obesity and exercise

Definitions of obesity vary from one textbook to another. In general, obesity is an excess of total body fat, usually due to energy intake being greater than energy output. As well as the psychological problems of dealing with being obese, obesity carries an increased risk of heart disease, hypertension, high blood cholesterol, stroke and diabetes, caused by a diet high in sugar and fat. It can also increase stress on joints and limit flexibility.

TopFoto

The increase in childhood obesity is a cause for concern

Obesity occurs when an individual's body weight is 20% or more above normal weight or when his/her percentage body fat is over 40%. The body mass index or BMI is also a common measure of obesity. This takes into account body composition. An individual is considered obese when his or her BMI is over 30.

Obese children will not have many of the medical problems listed above but their high sugar and fat diet can lead to these conditions very quickly if the problem is not addressed. However, they will have a lot of weight-related issues such as lower back pain, poor posture, low mobility and flexibility, and an increase in the stress placed on joints.

Practice makes perfect

1 (a) Identify and describe two methods of training used to develop aerobic capacity. *(4 marks)*

(b) What physiological adaptations occur in the cardiovascular system to allow a performer to work at a higher intensity of his/her VO_2 max? *(4 marks)*

2 Strength is an important component of fitness in power events and varies from one person to another. Identify the factors that can affect strength. *(4 marks)*

3 (a) Identify and describe what is meant by the term PNF. *(3 marks)*

(b) What adaptations occur following a period of flexibility training? *(4 marks)*

4 (a) What is meant by the term body composition? *(1 mark)*

(b) What are the health implications of being obese? *(3 marks)*

Chapter 18

Application of the principles of training

What you need to know

By the end of this chapter you should be able to:
- give a definition of periodisation to include the macrocycle, mesocycle and microcycle
- plan a personal health and fitness programme that takes into account the principles of training

Principles of training

You should already be aware of the principles of training from your GCSE PE course — they are listed below to remind you. In order to improve fitness, it is important to follow an effective training programme that includes the principles necessary for improvement and applies the principles to the training year.

Overload (FITT)

This is achieved by increasing or applying one or more of the following.

Frequency

The number of times per week that an individual trains depends on the amount of time that he/she can devote to training. It may be more practical or convenient to increase the intensity or duration of each session.

Intensity

This refers to how hard the performer works. For example, it is possible to increase the intensity of a run through an increase in the pace or by the addition of some uphill runs.

If you wish to increase aerobic fitness it is important to increase the intensity of the exercise by training above the aerobic threshold but below the anaerobic threshold. Training zones help us to do this and one of the most recognised methods follows the **Karvonen principle**. Karvonen suggested a training intensity of between 60% and 75% of maximum heart rate, using the following calculation:

60% = resting heart rate + 0.6(max heart rate − resting heart rate)
75% = resting heart rate + 0.75(max heart rate − resting heart rate)

Time

This is the length of the session. For example, a 30-minute run could be increased to a 40-minute run. A session should last a minimum of 20 minutes.

Type

This refers to the type of training that is most suitable. For example, if the aim of the training session is to improve aerobic capacity, then continuous training would be a suitable method.

Progression

This involves the application of overload. It is important to overload the body in order to improve fitness but this should be done gradually.

Specificity

The training should be relevant to the sport for which the individual is training. For example, a sprinter will do strength training on the muscles required for his/her event and will do speed training to improve the efficiency of the energy system used when competing.

Reversibility

This is often referred to as detraining. If you stop training, the adaptations that have occurred as a result of training will deteriorate, although it is suggested that the aerobic adaptations are lost more quickly than strength adaptations.

Moderation

Don't overdo it! Over training can lead to injury.

Variance

A training programme needs to have variety in order to maintain interest and motivation.

Periodisation: dividing the training year into sections for a specific purpose.

Periodisation

Periodisation is a key factor when planning a training programme. It involves dividing the year into periods when specific training occurs.

The seasonal approach is now commonly adapted to macrocycles, mesocycles and microcycles, which describe periods of time that are more prescriptive for individual needs.

Macrocycle

The macrocycle — the 'big' period — involves a long-term performance goal. For a footballer this may be the length of the season or for an athlete it could be 4 years as he/she builds up to the Olympic Games. The macrocycle is made up of three distinct periods.

Tasks to tackle 18.1

Using your own sport, list the activities that you would do during the following periods:

(a) off season

(b) pre-season

(c) competitive season

The preparation period

This is often referred to as pre-season training and is divided into:

- Phase 1 — general conditioning training. This should consist of a lot of low-intensity work with the aim of developing aerobic and muscular endurance, general strength and mobility.

- Phase 2 — competition-specific training. This involves an increase in the intensity of training. During this time, strength and speed work should be done. This phase also introduces technique and tactical work, so that the performer is prepared for the start of the competitive season.

The competition period

The main aim of this period is to optimise competition performance. Levels of fitness and conditioning should be maintained, as should the competition-specific aspects of training. Volume of training is decreased but intensity is increased. The competition period can be divided into the following phases:

- Phase 3 (6–8 weeks). This is the typical competition period, with a reduction in the volume of training and an increase in competition-specific training. Trials and qualifying competitions fall within this phase.
- Phase 4 (4–6 weeks). During a long competitive season it is a good idea to have a mini period where competitions are kept to a minimum or eliminated altogether and the level of competition-specific training is reduced. This allows the body to recover and prepare for phase 5.
- Phase 5 (3–4 weeks). This is the end of the training year when all the major events and competitions fall, for example a football Cup Final or the Commonwealth Games. Competition-specific training is maintained and tapering should occur.

Tapering is a reduction in the volume of training prior to major competition. This allows the athlete to reach peak performance. It is important for the coach to ensure that peak performance occurs in a certain time span so that the performer can benefit from the removal of training-induced fatigue but reversibility has not yet come into effect. A typical taper will last between 10 days and 21 days but can vary between different sports and performers.

The transition or recovery period

This is phase 6, the final phase of the year, and involves recovery. This phase allows the athlete to recharge physically and mentally and ensures an injury-free start to the season. General, fun exercise should be carried out during this phase.

Mesocycle

This describes a short-term goal within the macrocycle that may last for 2–8 weeks. This cycle may have a component of fitness as the focus, for example a sprinter will focus on power, reaction time and speed, whereas an endurance performer will focus more on strength endurance and cardio-respiratory endurance.

Microcycle

This is normally just a description of 1 week of training that is repeated throughout the length of the mesocycle. It could set out what the performer is going to do on each day from Monday to Sunday, including rest days (usually in a 3:1 ratio).

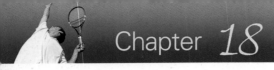
The training unit

This is a description of one training session, which will be following a key training objective.

Tasks to tackle 18.2

Copy and complete the table below to describe what activities you might do to satisfy the aims of the session.

Training aim	Details of training session
A session to improve lactate tolerance	
A session to improve strength in the upper body	

Double periodisation

Some sports require an athlete to peak more than once in a season. A long-distance athlete, for example, may want to peak in winter during the cross-country season and then again in the summer on the track. An international footballer may want to peak for an important Cup Final for his club and for a cup competition later in the year for his country. In this case, these performers have to follow a double periodised year.

Planning a personal health and fitness programme

When planning a training programme it is important to take note of the following:

- What is the aim of the training programme?
- What are the associated macro, meso and microcycles?
- Which energy systems need training?
- Which fitness components need improving? Test these first and then at the end you can re-test to see if there is any improvement.
- What are the main muscle groups used?
- What type of contractions are needed?
- Decide on the most suitable method(s) of training.
- Apply the principles of training — progression, overload, specificity, moderation, variance and reversibility.

Practice makes perfect

1 Many coaches plan the year using a technique called periodisation. Explain what is meant by periodisation. *(4 marks)*

2 When planning an aerobic training programme, what factors do you need to take into account? *(4 marks)*

Chapter 19

Ergogenic aids

What you need to know

By the end of this chapter you should be able to:

- explain the positive and negative effects of each of the aids listed
- identify which type of performer would benefit from each aid
- explain whether the aid is legal or illegal

Dietary manipulation

It is possible to adapt or change a performer's diet according to the demands of his/her activity in order to maximise performance.

Diet composition of an endurance athlete versus a power athlete

The body's preferred fuel for any endurance sport is muscle glycogen. If muscle glycogen breakdown exceeds its replacement, then glycogen stores become depleted. This results in fatigue and the inability to maintain the duration and intensity of training. In order to replenish and maintain glycogen stores, an endurance athlete needs a diet rich in carbohydrates. Most research suggests that endurance athletes need to consume at least 6–10 grams of carbohydrate per kilogram of their body weight per day.

Water is also essential to avoid dehydration.

Some endurance athletes manipulate their diet to maximise aerobic energy production. One method of achieving this is glycogen loading, often called carbo-loading (see page 222).

In general, endurance athletes require more carbohydrates than power athletes because they exercise for longer periods and need more energy. By contrast, proteins are very important for power athletes. The building blocks of protein are amino acids and although the body can make non-essential amino acids, essential amino acids must be supplied by the diet. Too little protein in the diet will lead to muscle breakdown. Proteins are also important for tissue growth and repair and can be a minor source of energy.

Pre- and post-competition meals

What should you eat before a competition?

In order to achieve optimal performance in sport, it is essential to be well fuelled and well hydrated. This means that the importance of a pre-competition meal should not be

Pre-competition food

- Chicken breast without skin (preferably poached)
- Vegetable-based sauce
- Two carbohydrate sources such as brown rice or wholemeal pasta
- Unglazed vegetables
- Salad, without a dressing
- Selection of fresh fruit (lots of bananas)
- Fresh fruit salad and yoghurt
- Scrambled eggs, bacon, baked beans and fresh wholemeal toast
- Porridge, Special K, muesli

Drinks

- Still water, orange and apple juice

understated. It should be eaten about 3–4 hours before competing, as the food consumed needs to be digested and absorbed in order to be useful. The meal needs to be high in carbohydrate, low in fat and moderate in fibre in order to aid digestion (foods high in fat, protein and fibre tend to take longer to digest). High levels of carbohydrate will keep the blood glucose levels high throughout the duration of the competition/performance. Suggestions for foods for pre-competition meals are provided in the box on the left.

What should you eat after a competition?

Most exercise will deplete stores of glycogen so it is important to replenish these stores. Eating a high-carbohydrate meal will accelerate glycogen restoration, as will eating within 1 hour following exercise.

Fluid intake

Water constitutes up to 60% of a person's body weight and is essential for good health. It carries nutrients to cells in the body and removes waste products. It also helps to control body temperature. When athletes start to exercise, their production of water increases (water is a by-product of the aerobic system). We also lose a lot of water through sweat. The volume of water we lose depends on the external temperature, the intensity and duration of the exercise, and the volume of water consumed before, during and after exercise. Water is important in order to maintain optimal performance. Make sure you take on fluids regularly. Sports drinks, such as Lucozade Sport and Gatorade, can boost glucose levels before competition, while water will re-hydrate during competition.

Glycogen loading

Glycogen loading is a form of dietary manipulation involving maximising glycogen stores. It is often used by long-distance runners and other endurance athletes and is popularly known as carbo-loading. Before an important competition the performer eats a diet high in protein and fats for 3 days and exercises at a relatively high intensity so that glycogen stores are depleted. This is followed by 3 days of a diet high in carbohydrates and some very light training. Studies show that this will greatly increase the stores of glycogen in the muscle and can prevent a performer from 'hitting the wall'.

Table 19.1 The advantages and disadvantages of glycogen loading

Advantages of glycogen loading	Disadvantages of glycogen loading
<ul><li>Increases glycogen synthesis</li><li>Increases glycogen stores in the muscle</li><li>Delays fatigue</li><li>Increases endurance capacity</li></ul>	<ul><li>Water retention, which results in bloating</li><li>Heavy legs</li><li>Affects digestion</li><li>Weight increase</li><li>Irritability during the depletion phase</li><li>Alters the training programme</li></ul>

OCR A2 Physical Education

Pharmaceutical aids

Creatine

Creatine is a legal supplement used to increase the amount of phosphocreatine stored in the muscles. It extends the duration of use of the ATP-PC system and can help to improve recovery times. Possible side effects include dehydration, bloating, muscle cramps and slight liver damage. However, studies suggest that a daily intake of 5 grams or over usually ends up in the urine rather than in the muscle! Creatine is used by athletes in explosive sprinting, jumping and throwing events.

HGH

Artificially produced human growth hormones (HGH) are illegal in sport. Benefits of HGH use are increased muscle mass and a decrease in fat. The potential side effects, however, include heart and nerve diseases, glucose intolerance and high levels of blood fats. HGH is known to be used across a range of sports, from sprinting to explosive activities such as rugby, and even to enhance endurance performance. It is not known how widespread the use of this drug is as it is difficult to test for.

Gene doping

The use of synthetic genes is illegal in sport. They can last for long periods of time and their detection is difficult as they do not enter the bloodstream. Some genes, such as IGF-I, are taken to produce large amounts of naturally occurring muscle-building hormones. Others, such as repoxygen, which was first recorded in use in the 2006 Winter Olympics, are used to increase the number of red blood cells. The associated side effects depend on the gene used, but there have been reported problems with the heart and the liver. Although users vary depending on the gene used, synthetic genes are most commonly used by endurance athletes who wish to improve oxygen uptake.

Blood doping

Blood doping is illegal. It involves removing and storing a performer's blood. The body compensates for this loss and makes more red blood cells. The stored blood is then injected back into the performer allowing him/her to have a higher red blood cell count. This improves aerobic capacity by increasing the oxygen-carrying capacity of the body, allowing the performer to work for longer. A potential side effect is an increase in the viscosity of the blood, which could lead to clotting and a risk of death. Blood doping is used by endurance performers, such as cyclists and cross-country skiers.

Rh-EPO

Erythropoietin (EPO) is a natural hormone produced by the kidneys to increase red blood cells. Now it can be artificially manufactured as recombinant EPO (Rh-EPO) to cause an increase in haemoglobin levels. Its use in sport is illegal. As with blood doping, the benefits are that an increase in the oxygen-carrying capacity of the body can lead to an

Tasks to tackle 19.1

Below are pictures of an endurance performer and a power athlete. List the pharmaceutical aids that could benefit each type of performer.

increase in the amount of work performed. However, this can result in blood clotting, stroke and in a few cases death. Rh-EPO is used by endurance performers such as long-distance runners.

Cooling aids

Water

Water plays an important part in regulating body temperature. When a performer takes part in exercise, energy is required and some of that energy is released as heat. Water keeps the performer from overheating. Both sweating and evaporation cool the body down, but this means that water is lost during the cooling process. Once the body starts to lose water during exercise, this can lead to a drop in blood volume. When this occurs, the heart works harder in order to move blood through the vascular system and the amount of oxygen available to the working muscles is reduced, which will affect performance. It is therefore important when exercising to drink early and often.

Sports clothing

Many manufactures advertise clothing such as vests, caps, neck wraps and wrist bands that are designed to keep performers cool. These contain a special gel that has the ability to keep temperature constant for long periods. The vests, for example, are made from 'sportwool' and microfibre and weigh less than a kilogram. However, such clothing that is designed to cool the body down has its sceptics and is not, as yet, widely used.

Ice baths

An ice bath is used for cooling body tissue down after exercise and is a popular recovery method. After a gruelling training session or match, sports performers get into an ice bath for 5–10 minutes. The cold water causes the blood vessels to tighten and drains the blood out of the legs. On leaving the bath, the legs fill up with new blood that invigorates the muscles with oxygen to help the cells function better. The blood that leaves the legs takes away with it the lactic acid that has built up during the activity. Ice baths are now used by most professional sportsmen and women who train and play regularly. Most rugby Super League teams do 'hot and cold' sessions, where players spend 2 minutes in the steam room followed by

A post-training ice bath

1 minute in the cold plunge pool. The purpose is to flush lactic acid from the muscles, reducing soreness for the week ahead. Despite its unpleasantness, the benefits can be felt immediately, especially in the legs. Some players include 'hot and colds' in their pre-match routine on game day.

Training aids

Many training aids are used to increase resistance.

Pulleys

These are rope or bungee-type harnesses that allow an athlete to train against a resistance. Swimmers are attached to an elastic-type harness. They swim until the elastic is tense and try to maintain this position. If they stop or slow down, the elastic will drag them backwards. The advantage of this method of strength training is that the exact movement pattern of the given sport can be performed while the resistance is being applied.

Parachutes

Parachutes are used to develop speed, power and strength in the leg muscles. This will lead to a more powerful performance. Performers run with a small parachute billowing out behind them. The parachute is attached to a simple harness. The advantage of this type of resistance training is that it replicates the athlete's running action using the muscles in the same way.

Practice makes perfect

1 Ice baths are increasingly used by sports performers as a cooling/recovery aid. How does an ice bath help a performer to recover? *(3 marks)*

2 Name two illegal ergogenic aids that would be of benefit to an endurance performer and explain how they can help performance. *(6 marks)*

3 Glycogen loading is often used by endurance performers. What is glycogen loading and what are the advantages and disadvantages to the performer? *(6 marks)*

Unit G454

The improvement of effective performance and the critical evaluation of practical activities in physical education

Chapter 20

Practical skills

Performance

The A2 coursework follows a similar pathway to the AS coursework in that you can be assessed in three roles: that of a performer, a coach/leader or an official. However, at A2 you are assessed in only *one* activity and this activity must be one of the activities for which you were assessed in the AS course (Unit G452). The assessment is set and organised by your centre, marked by your teachers and then moderated externally by the exam board.

You are also required to demonstrate your knowledge of sporting principles by observing a performance in your chosen activity and giving a verbal analysis of that performance called an 'Evaluation and appreciation' of the activity. The observation will take place regardless of whether you have been assessed as a coach/leader, performer or official.

Your chosen activity and your appreciation and evaluation are each marked out of 30. The activity profiles from which you choose to be assessed are the same as the AS course and are outlined below.

- **Athletic activities** (e.g. athletics). The performance and refinement of a range of dynamic skills with the intention of improving personal and collective bests in relation to speed, height, distance and accuracy.
- **Combat activities** (e.g. boxing and tae kwon do). Performers select, develop, apply and adapt skills, strategies and tactics with the intention of outwitting their opponent in a range of combats.
- **Dance activities**. Performers use their imagination and ideas to create, perform, appreciate and develop dances with an awareness of historical and cultural contexts. The artistic intention makes use of rhythm, space and relationships, expressing and communicating ideas, moods and feelings.
- **Game activities**. Performers select, apply and adapt skills, strategies and tactics, on their own and in teams, with the intention of outwitting the opposition in a range of different game types. The game activity context is subdivided into:
  - **invasion game activities** such as football, rugby, netball, hockey and basketball
  - **net/wall game activities** such as tennis, badminton, volleyball and squash
  - **striking/fielding game activities** such as cricket and rounders
  - **target game activities** such as golf

OCR A2 Physical Education

- **Gymnastic activities** (e.g. gymnastics and trampolining). Performers devise aesthetically pleasing sequences using combinations of skill and agility, which they repeat and perform with increasing control, precision and fluency
- **Outdoor and adventurous activities** (e.g. canoeing). Performers develop, individually and in teams, the ability to analyse, plan and then respond effectively and safely to physical challenges and problems they encounter in familiar, changing and unfamiliar environments.
- **Swimming activities and water safety**. Performers develop the confidence and ability to stay afloat and to swim unaided for sustained periods of time, selecting, adapting and refining their skills so that they can swim safely and engage in a variety of different activities in and around water.
- **Safe and effective exercise activities** (e.g. weight training). Performers exercise safely and effectively for the benefit of health and well-being.

Performing an activity

Your performance mark will be based on how well you apply the skills of your chosen sport in a real competitive situation. You will be judged on how well you select the right skill at the right time in the right situation and then on how well you perform it. For example, in a team game, did you make the correct choice of pass to the best available player and was it executed skilfully? You will be assessed in an authentic situation — a situation that is challenging enough to allow you to show how well you can perform the skills of the sport consistently when faced with different choices to make.

In the performance in which you are assessed you will be expected to show effort and endeavour. To gain the highest marks, a degree of creativity and an ability to adapt (especially when under pressure) are essential.

Displaying a sense of sportsmanship and fair play will impress the examiners and you will benefit from an understanding of the rules, regulations and codes of practice of your chosen activity. Good tactical awareness or the ability to show choreographic or compositional awareness in appropriate activities will gain the highest marks.

Coaching/leading an activity

This role will again be assessed in an authentic environment (one in which the activity normally takes place) and you will be judged on your ability to deliver an organised coaching session with confidence that motivates others. You will be expected to show an understanding of coaching method. In other words, your coaching sessions should:
- be well planned and prepared
- show progression to develop skills
- show that you are able to analyse and correct faults and therefore help in improving skills

Don't just pick a drill and run it without giving some advice to the people you are coaching.

Unit G454 The improvement of effective performance and the critical evaluation
of practical activities in physical education

229

After your coaching sessions you will need to evaluate your performance so that you can make adjustments to future coaching sessions, pointing out what aspects of your coaching went well and what did not meet with your expectations. You should make sure that you include all types of abilities and specific needs within your coaching — so your sessions need to be adaptable and pitched at the correct level. Safety is an important aspect of coaching and you should be aware of the health and fitness requirements of the chosen activity. Be aware of any required need to wear appropriate clothing and carry out a risk assessment prior to starting your session. Good communication skills are an essential part of good coaching, so make sure you develop this ability. Be organised and well prepared and you will gain high marks.

To provide evidence that you can meet the demands of the coaching/leading aspect of the course you will be required to keep a log that records your coaching/leading activities over a 6-month period. The log should contain:

- a scheme of work detailing at least 10 hours of session plans that show progression, a risk assessment and an evaluation of each session
- a video record of at least 40 minutes of actual coaching/leading
- details of health and safety requirements
- details of child protection issues, especially when working with young children
- first aid qualifications
- evidence to show how the coaching/leading you have done improves fitness and health

This log *will* be required by the examiner so make sure you keep it up to date and start it early.

Note that when you are being assessed in coaching/leading you will still need to adhere to the requirements of the OCR specification even if you have already gained, or are working towards, a governing body level 3 qualification in your chosen activity.

Officiating an activity

To ensure parity with the other two roles, you will be assessed when you are officiating in an authentic environment. You will be expected to show control and facilitate enjoyment in sporting or recreational activities that are challenging and realistic. Perhaps the most essential requirement of good officiating is a detailed knowledge of the rules and regulations of your chosen activity, but you will also be expected to display personal qualities such as excellent communication skills and the ability to show fairness and consistency in your decisions. You should be aware of the health and safety requirements of the activity (a first aid qualification might help here) and show an understanding of the fitness and health benefits of the activity. You should undertake a risk assessment before you attempt to officiate, since part of your role is to ensure that activities are carried out in a safe environment. You should be able to evaluate your performance, detailing the positive and negative aspects of it and showing how you could improve in future.

To show evidence that you meet these demands you will have to keep a detailed log of your officiating activities that contains the following information:

- *at least four* evaluations of sessions officiated by qualified assessors
- any risk assessments
- a video record of at least 40 minutes officiating in a real live situation
- details of health and safety issues related to the activity
- child protection procedures
- evidence of how your officiating improves health and fitness

Note that when you are being assessed in officiating you will still need to adhere to the requirements of the OCR specification even if you have already gained or are working towards a governing body level 3 qualification in your chosen activity.

Evaluation and appreciation

The second part of your A2 coursework assessment is when you are required to observe a live performance by another candidate in the activity for which you are being assessed and recommend a strategy to make improvements to that performance based on the observations you have made. Your observations can then be verbally communicated to your teacher or examiner who will award marks based on your comments. There are 30 marks available for this part of the course.

You will have to make evaluative comments to judge the quality of the performance you have just seen, so you need to use technical language to help you make such judgements and impress the examiner. In your verbal response you should prioritise the areas of the performance that most need improving, so the most significant weakness should be addressed first. When such weaknesses are identified you should come up with a technical model or strategy that is aimed at addressing that particular weakness and it would be a good idea to set some goals that will help to improve that aspect of the performance — use the principles of goal setting discussed in Chapter 10 to help you.

In effect, you will be required to design an 'action plan' aimed at addressing the weaknesses you have identified as part of your observation, and you will have to describe this action plan to your assessor. Make sure the action plan includes detailed coaching points, progressive practices to remedy any weaknesses, and comments on skills, tactics and strategies/compositional aspects of the activity. Your action plan should have a clear timescale to indicate how long it will take to make the improvements you suggest. When you identify a weakness or suggest an improvement strategy you should try as much as possible to relate your comments to the theories and principles you have learned in your A-level PE course. Comments from the physiological, psychological and sociocultural parts of the course should form an integral part of your action plan. A framework to help with your appreciation and evaluation is given below.

Evaluation and appreciation: a framework for assessment

When you start to conduct your written interview you might be asked something along the lines of: 'Take a look at a performance related to your chosen activity. Identify any strengths

Unit G454 The improvement of effective performance and the critical evaluation
of practical activities in physical education

231

and weaknesses in that performance and use your knowledge of physical education gained throughout the course to suggest an action plan designed to address one of the weaknesses you have identified.' In order to answer this question you need to:
- evaluate the performance, highlighting the strengths and weaknesses
- concentrate on one weakness and devise an action plan to improve/correct it
- apply theory to back up your evaluation and action plan

The following information will help you.

Identification of strengths and weaknesses

What is good and/or bad about the performance? Look at the skills, tactics and fitness components of the activity.

Watch the skill closely and list the coaching points of the skill under the phases relevant to your activity. Then use these coaching points to state the strengths and weaknesses you can see in the performance. You should have at least two or three coaching points under each heading so you will then have about nine strengths and weaknesses to comment on.

Phases:
- **games** — preparation, execution, result and recovery, overall efficiency
- **competitive swimming** — arm action, leg action, body position, breathing, overall efficiency
- **athletics**
  - *track* — posture, leg action, arm action, head carriage, overall efficiency
  - *jumps* — approach, take-off, flight, landing, overall efficiency
  - *throwing* — initial stance, grip and preparation, travel and trunk position, throwing action, release, overall efficiency

Table 20.1 might help you if you are evaluating a game. If you write down what you see, you can refer to your notes in the interview.

Table 20.1 Evaluating performance during a game

Phase	Coaching points	Strengths/weakness
Preparation	1	1
	2	2
	3	3
Execution	1	1
	2	2
	3	3
Result and recovery	1	1
	2	2
Overall efficiency	1	1
	2	2

Tactics

Look at any tactics relevant to your activity. Be aware of some before the interview so that you can comment on them. Knowledge of tactics will come from participating in your activity and from coaching manuals and your own coach/teacher.

Fitness

Make sure the fitness components are relevant to your sport. The fitness components you comment on could include strength, stamina, speed and suppleness.

Action plan

Once you have given a full account of strengths and weaknesses you must then suggest an 'action plan' designed to rectify one of the weaknesses you have noticed. Your action plan should contain the following points:

- **goals** — state what you are aiming to achieve
- **time scale** — state how long your action plan will take. It may also be useful to suggest how long it might take to perfect each part of a skill and how long you might spend on each practice.
- **method of achieving goals** — list progressive practices. You should give a detailed description of the drills you would use to help the performer improve his/her level of skill, starting from the easiest to the more difficult. Make sure that your practices start at the level that is appropriate to the performer you are observing.
- **method for evaluating achievement of goals** — here you need to say how you are going to check how successful you have been in achieving your goal. A specific test will help determine this — for example, Cooper's 12 minute run if you have looked at stamina, or a 'stats sheet' before and after your action plan if you are looking at a skill in a game.

Application of theory

You must ensure that you apply your knowledge from the physiological, psychological and sociocultural areas of study to support your answers throughout your evaluation and action plan. The following notes are suggestions to help you to do this.

Physiology

- EPOC — the importance of recovery rates within your training programme.
- Health-related fitness components used in the activity — definitions, and what training methods you could use to improve them.
- Energy systems — give an example of when each of the three energy systems could be used.

Psychology

- The factors affecting team dynamics such as leadership or cohesion.
- Motivation/arousal — does the performer need any motivation? What methods could be used to provide this motivation, for example a reward?

Unit G454 The improvement of effective performance and the critical evaluation
of practical activities in physical education

233

- Is the performer's level of arousal appropriate to the task? If the performer's arousal level is too high, performance will suffer. How could you lower arousal levels (for example, using mental rehearsal)?

Sociocultural

- Sports excellence — how is talent being developed?
- How does your activity relate to National Curriculum PE.
- Look at the key historical developments of your sport (if you have covered Historical studies).
- Compare the status of your activity to its importance in other countries (if you have covered Comparative studies).

Answers

Tasks to tackle

1.1 (page 3)

1700s	*Eighteenth* century	Pre-industrial
1800s	*Nineteenth* century	Industrial
1900s	Twentieth century	Post industrial

1.2 (page 6)

Social and cultural factors that influenced the playing of mob games in the era of popular recreation activities.

1 Local	1 Because of limited communications/free time
2 Rural	2 Most people lived in villages/small towns
3 Simple/unwritten rules	3 Low literacy levels; no NGBs of sport
4 Occasional	4 Limited free time; legal and religious constraints
5 Violent and cruel	5 Harsh society; relatively uncivilised life
6 Ritual/festival	6 Held on religious days; games had festival origins (Shrove Tuesday)
7 Wagering	7 Part of occasion along with drink; wagering was 'fashionable'
8 Natural and simple	8 Used existing facilities (e.g. spare land) and equipment (e.g. pig's bladder)

1.3 (page 8)

Pedestrianism was a popular recreation sport because it was part of a 'festival' occasion, often associated with prize fighting. It provided fame/status/ occupation/ prize money for competitors. It was a cheap and simple activity to participate in.

1.4 (page 12)

Comparison of mob football and real tennis as recreation games. Note that you must give both 'sides' of a comparison to receive a mark.

Characteristics of mob football	Characteristics of real tennis
Played by lower classes	Played by gentry/upper classes
Few/simple rules	Complex rules
Violent/unruly	Civilised/etiquette
Irregular	Played regularly
Local	Geographically widespread
Occupational	For 'leisured' classes
Natural	Purpose-built/specialist facilities

2.1 (page 14)

Characteristics of rational recreation:

- played regionally
- played respectably
- played regularly
- played to set rules
- played in purpose-built facilities
- played as amateurs/professionals
- played as a result of revolutions — urban and industrial
- played under gambling controls

2.2 (page 15)

Summary of the key differences between popular recreation in pre-industrial Britain and rational recreation in post-industrial Britain.

Popular recreation	Rational recreation
1 Local	1 *Regional/national*
2 *Uncodified*	2 Codified
3 *Cruel and violent*	3 Respectable
4 Occasional	4 *Regular*
5 Rurally based	5 *Urban*
6 Natural resources	6 *Purpose-built facilities*

2.3 (page 17)

Saturday half day meant early closing for shops on Saturdays. It gave increased time to the working classes for playing and watching sport. This particularly influenced the development and popularity of football (played on Saturday afternoons).

2.4 (page 19)

Sociocultural factors that influenced the development of rationalised sports and pastimes. Note that each factor needs to be listed and explained in order to receive a mark.

- travel/communications — improved accessibility of sport for spectators and participants (e.g. railways — took less time to go longer distances) led to the spread of fixtures across the country
- emergence of an urban middle class — led to the increased respectability of sport; public school influence; benevolence and support from middle class factory owners (e.g. excursions, facilities, teams)
- urbanisation — greater numbers were potentially available to play/watch sport; led to the development of purpose-built facilities due to lack of space
- religion — the church accepted the more rational game of football
- time — time available for sport initially decreased (industrialisation) but then gradually increased (e.g. Saturday half day)
- literacy — increased literacy led to the formation of NGBs and development of rules

2.5 (page 22)

The emergence of amateur athletics during the late nineteenth century:

- middle classes keen to stay exclusive; AAC formed by ex-university amateurs
- middle classes keen to dissociate themselves from corrupt professional form (i.e. pedestrianism)
- exclusion clause imposed and enforced by AAC
- working classes competed to earn money (NB: smaller amounts than in pre-industrial races)
- middle classes competed for intrinsic rewards (as a test of 'self')
- gentlemen amateurs formed own clubs and NGBs (AAC — 1866; AAA — 1880)

3.1 (page 28)

Characteristics of public schools in the early 1800s linked to their effects on sporting development:

Characteristic	Contribution to development of school sport
Fee paying and endowed	Provided finance for facilities
Boys only	Similar motivation and high energy levels
Boarding	Lengthy periods of time available
Gentry	Had organisational experience
Non-local	Regional variations in games brought to schools
Control by trustees	Had to give approval to sporting activities
Spartan	Reflected in the violent nature of games
Rural	Lots of space/land available to play games on

Answers

3.2 (page 31)

Stage 1 — boy culture; bullying; brutality	
1 Regular opportunity due to	→ *Lots of free time available*
	→ *Boarding school nature of public schools*
2 Variations of activities due to	→ *Non-local nature of schools meant activities brought from home were adopted*
	→ *Different versions played based on a school's unique features*
3 Violence/cruelty due to	→ *Schools based on bullying/brutality*
	→ *Sports reflecting harshness of wider society*

3.3 (page 34)

Athleticism means the combination of physical endeavour and moral integrity.
Physical benefits from team games:

- energetic/strong/endeavour/manliness
- bravery/physical contact
- break from study
- catharsis/stress relief

Social benefits from team games:

- teamwork/cooperation
- fair play/sportsmanship
- respect for opponents/rules/leaders
- test of temperament/cope under pressure
- learn leadership qualities

3.4 (page 35)

How public school old boys helped the spread of rational sport to wider society:

- as teachers — old boys coached and played sport as masters in their former schools
- as industrial leaders/factory owners — improved sporting opportunities for workers
- as curates, parsons, social Christians — set up parish teams
- as army officers — spread games to the lower ranks and colonies around the world
- entered universities — the 'melting pot' at Oxford and Cambridge led to modification of the rules
- as parents — when bringing up their own children

3.5 (page 37)

Reasons for the decline of hare and hounds in public schools:

- damage to property, crops, fences
- illegal trespass onto private property
- harmed relationships with local communities
- danger of boys getting lost or injured

4.1 (page 43)

The main aims of the 1902 Model Course:

- fitness for war (following poor Boer War performance)
- develop discipline/obedience
- improve health of working classes
- weapons training

4.2 (page 45)

Key features of the 1933 PT syllabus:

- physical fitness development/exercise
- holistic aims (mind and body)
- skills taught — games, gymnastics, athletics
- command style (mostly led by the teacher)
- some freedom of movement
- some group work/minor games
- syllabus set out in tables for teacher to select from
- age differentiated
- special clothing and equipment

4.3 (page 47)

(a) The aims of a lesson based on *Moving and Growing* (1952) or *Planning the Programme* (1954):

- learn physical skills in a variety of activities (e.g. gym, dance, games, swimming)
- learn social skills (e.g. group work)
- learn cognitive skills
- enjoyment/fun
- all involved

(b) Development of state PE summary table

	1902 The Model Course	1919 physical training (PT)	1933 physical training (PT)	1950 physical education (PE)
What was the point of the activities? (objectives)	Increase fitness to fight Instil obedience and discipline	Raise health standards	Improve health appropriate to age Improve physique/posture	Increase involvement for all Variety/enjoyment Develop skills
What did a typical lesson involve? (content)	Exercises at desks Marching to command with staves	Table of exercises Folk dance Play, e.g. 'Oranges and Lemons', 'In and Out the Dusty Bluebells'	Table of Exercises Play for under-7s Gymnastic skills Small sided games	Gym Games Swimming Dance

continued overleaf

continued	1902 The Model Course	1919 physical training (PT)	1933 physical training (PT)	1950 physical education (PE)
Who was it taught by? In what style? (teaching method)	NCO led Direct command Rank Unison	Teachers — still in rank/unison but kinder approach	Teachers Direct and group work	Specialist PE teachers Child centred Educational (post war emphasis on problem solving)
Where was it carried out?	At desks/in classrooms In school clothes	Outdoor yard School hall Playground	School hall apparatus (gymnasium) Outdoor lessons	Playing fields Gymnasium (with climbing frames/ apparatus)
What cultural factors influenced it?	Poor performance in Boer War 1870 compulsory schooling (primary) Colonel Fox (government appointed)	End of First World War (1914–18) Women/girls' increased interest Dr Newman: Schools Medical Service	Following 1920s Depression no benefits for masses; therefore, important to raise levels of health/spirits of the nation	1944 secondary schooling (11+) Compulsory to 15 yrs Extensive post-Second World War (1939–45) rebuilding Laban influence

4.4 (page 51)

Similarities:

- Both were centralised/government run.
- Both aimed to improve health and fitness.
- Both were compulsory — you had to do them.

Differences:

- National Curriculum PE has a lot more activities; it is broader.
- National Curriculum PE has lots of key stages at different ages, with different aims.
- National Curriculum PE uses lots of different teaching styles, not just command.

5.1 (page 56)

(a) Historical factors affecting sports development:

- Britain was the first industrialised country
- modern sport evolved in the UK (e.g. codification/structure)
- British Empire resulted in export and import of cultural activities

(b) Climate

- temperate climate
- lots of precipitation throughout the year
- PE/sports traditionally linked to main seasons

(c) Transport

- extensive road/railway network
- all areas can be accessed in a day

(d) Population
- high density of population
- urban-industrial conurbations surrounded by greenbelts

5.2 (page 61)
Reasons why schools might have difficulty meeting the minimum 2 hour NC PE entitlement:
- 2 hours is a guideline, not compulsory
- PE is traditionally low status in comparison to subjects such as science and maths
- timetable restrictions
- lack of specialist teachers
- lack of finance/facilities
- lack of support from senior management

5.3 (page 62)
(a) Sporting Champions:
- organises face to face meetings between young people and sporting heroes
- arranges about 450 visits each year
- each visit must be linked into plans to raise participation in schools or the wider community

(b) Its main aims are to:
- show young people that sport can and should be fun and sow the seeds of lifelong enjoyment of physical activity
- raise awareness of sport and the benefits of physical activity
- increase the profile of a variety of sports/local sports clubs

6.1 (page 72)
Examples of violence in American football:
- very physical game
- tackling off the ball
- padding takes away the physical inhibition
- helmet renders a player 'anonymous'

Links to American culture:
- sensation-seeking society; demand for action and entertainment
- players perceived as 'gladiators'
- Lombardian ethic
- incentive of the American Dream
- tradition/acceptability of violence
- frontier legacy, sport as 'last frontier'
- media influence
- influence of successful role models performing in an aggressive manner

6.2 (page 78)

(a) How high schools develop talent:
- give time to practice
- provide high-quality facilities to train and perform in
- employment of specialist coaches
- strong emphasis from an early age on the Lombardian ethic/elitist approach
- provision of scholarships
- use of media to highlight successes and raise revenue

(b) Reasons for lower status of PE:
- many states are replacing PE with other subjects
- school boards are voting PE off the curriculum
- PE is unpopular with many students
- PE is becoming an option in senior school/is no longer compulsory in senior school
- withdrawing PE saves money

(c) Reasons for increase in female participation in high schools:
- Title IX
- legalised equal entitlement to funds, facilities, coaching
- increased sponsorship opportunities/recognition of their efforts and successes
- more positive role models and media coverage
- lawsuits in favour of women giving more serious consideration of equality issues
- change in society's perception of women (more positive image/awareness of their capabilities)

(d) Benefits to children from summer camp attendance:
- self-discovery/awareness of limitations
- gain independence as you get the chance to live away from home
- development of various skills (depending on the type of camp)
- development of leadership skills/working as a team
- learn to respect the natural environment
- gain knowledge/awareness of American ideologies (e.g. the frontier spirit)

6.3 (page 79)

(a) Reasons for the establishment of Midnight Basketball Leagues:
- attempt to control poor behaviour
- allow a chance to experience success/gain self esteem
- integration/increase belief that mainstream American society is accessible to all

(b) Reasons for lack of mass participation:
- limited sports club provision
- membership of clubs and sports participation in general is expensive
- limited selection for scholarships causes large drop out
- high media coverage encourages passive spectatorism/greater inclination to watch rather than play

6.4 (page 81)

(a) Benefits from Little League participation:
- grass roots development of motor skills
- participation in organised competition/leagues
- chance of specialist coaching
- opportunities for social development
- preparation for progression in sport
- preparation for competitive lifestyle in USA
- chance to gain media attention

(b) Reasons for high school students accepting a scholarship:
- opportunity to improve as a result of high-level coaching
- perform in top-class sports facilities
- talent identification for pro-draft system
- chance to play at a higher level
- chance to fulfil the American Dream/upward social mobility
- media attention/big crowds at college sports events
- it pays for a college education
- it is the accepted route to high-level sport

(c) Ways in which the American college system develops sports excellence:
- awards sports scholarship to outstanding high school players
- scholarship is a binding contract
- students devote more time to developing sports talent than to study
- special admit programmes allow for scholarships to outstanding players who are academically under-qualified
- colleges are recognised as centres of excellence for sport
- the Lombardian ethic is instilled
- specialist coaches are employed
- college sport is organised as a commercial business
- high-quality facilities are provided to train and perform in
- matches replicate professional standards
- outstanding college players progress through the pro-draft system

7.1 (page 88)

(a) How Australia's colonial history is reflected in its sports:
- tending to play sports that originated in the UK (e.g. cricket and rugby)
- Australia has only really 'adapted' one sport — Aussie Rules (from rugby)
- more recent European immigration has increased the popularity of association football

(b) Cultural factors influencing the development of sport in Australia:
- it has an almost obsessive interest in sport
- its colonial influence means it takes great satisfaction in defeating the motherland
- sport is used to publicise/promote a positive image of Australia on the world stage
- it is a 'young culture' using sport as a way of establishing a positive international identity
- sport is being used to shed the 'bush culture' image
- nationalism in sport has played an important role in unifying Australia
- it has a highly favourable climate for participation in outdoor activities
- it has a relatively small population with a high level of participation

7.2 (page 91)

(a) Key features of SEPEP:
- loose framework as a teaching guide (retains teacher autonomy)
- large framework of intra-school and inter-school sports
- broad range of options to cater for all interests/prepare for active leisure
- basic skills/fundamental skills programme in primary schools as a means of developing confidence in performance and encouraging continued participation

(b) Examples of PE/sport strategies in Australia:
- PASE — professional development programme for teachers
- Sports Linkage — links between schools and clubs (e.g. sharing facilities, passing on talented children to clubs)
- exemplary schools — schools with excellent programmes are funded to share good practice
- Sports Search — students select sports which suit them best by accessing a database/use of sport/talent search
- awards — state awards, de Coubertin award
- top-level performers are used as role models; support career development of performers

7.3 (page 92)

(a) The main aims of More Active Australia:

- increase participation
- promote social, health and economic benefits of participation
- ensure/increase equality of opportunity to participate
- increase numbers of officials and administrators in sport
- improve the relationship between national, state and local sports organisations
- develop school–club links
- assist clubs to achieve high performance outcomes

(b) Reasons for More Active Australia achieving national importance:

- helps improve overall fitness of nation
- provides a wide base of mass participation which helps in the future production of champions (i.e. provides a wide talent base to draw from)
- success improves the national pride and morale of a nation

7.4 (page 94)

(a) Structure of the AIS:

- based in Canberra
- decentralised — each state has a replica AIS
- each AIS has specialisms
- each AIS is becoming multi-sport based

Functions of the AIS:

- provide top-level facilities to train in
- top coaches for top performers
- sports science research to further improve elite levels of performance
- gives sports medicine support to elite performers
- provides educational/lifestyle support to performers
- coordinates AIS Connect and the Sports Person in Schools Project (role models inspire participation/raise performance standards)

(b) Ways Australia has attempted to improve its chances of winning medals:

- set up AIS/network of sports institutes
- provided elite athletes with top-level facilities, coaches, sports science, medical support
- state grants to allow full time training/financial rewards or success
- talent identification schemes help to identify potential talent from an early age
- widening participation/increasing equality creates a larger potential pool of talent to choose from and develop

7.5 (page 101)

How Aussie Rules developed as a 'game of the people':

- players from all social backgrounds
- all levels of society as spectators (social class mix, as well as gender mix)
- reflection of 'frontierism', spirit of working together
- now adopted as a game of cosmopolitan Australia and has spread beyond Victoria into all states
- wide media appeal for all of society

8.1 (page 105)

Methods of collecting information on personality. At least one point in each category.

Method	Advantages	Disadvantages
Questionnaire	Quick Deals with lots of information Cheap Objective	Biased answers Socially acceptable answers Misunderstand question
Observation	True to life	Subjective Observer needs training
Physiological	Factual Can make comparisons	May cause stress Restrictive to players, therefore not used in real game

8.2 (page 109)

Three components of attitude:

Cognitive. Beliefs — any example showing a belief in exercise or training to improve health, well-being or fitness, e.g. you believe in the health benefits of going to the gym.

Affective. Feelings — any example to show enjoyment of physical activity, e.g. you enjoy a football training session.

Behavioural — any example to show physical actions and participation, e.g. you go to football training twice a week.

8.3 (page 113)

Features of aggression. Freedom of expression is allowed here to show any aspect of aggression similar to the one shown.

9.1 (page 118)

Stages of group formation.

Forming — meeting up and getting to know the others in the team and their roles and personalities

Storming — conflict and tension as rivalries are encountered

Norming — settling down as differences are resolved

Performing — working together to try to achieve goals and results

9.2 (page 119)

Factors that affect team cohesion. The important thing is that you can recognise the difference between task and social cohesion. Some suggestions:

- type of sport — task cohesion
- leadership — task and social cohesion
- past/future success — task cohesion
- coordination — task cohesion
- social loafing — task and social cohesion

9.3 (page 125)

Leadership styles for differing situations:

- autocratic — danger or team that is unsure of themselves
- democratic — with a small group
- rewarding — with beginners
- social support — with an individual after a defeat
- training and instruction — leading up to a major game to improve performance
- laissez faire — with experts

10.1 (page 129)

Self-efficacy theory:

Performance accomplishments — set easy goals, allow early success, point out past success

Vicarious experience — show role models of same age and ability successfully doing the task, give accurate demonstrations

Verbal persuasion — use positive feedback, positive reinforcement, give encouragement

Emotional arousal — control anxiety with relaxation techniques and imagery, use positive self talk

10.2 (page 131)

Any goals that show steps towards success, including both process and performance goals that are short term, before the long-term objectives are met. For example, a tennis player might improve her service technique (process), then make a greater percentage of successful first serves in each game (performance) to improve her ranking (long term).

10.3 (page 136)

Causes of anxiety include being watched, increased competition such as a big game, frustration, conflict, evaluation apprehension. For example, being watched by a county selector during a trial game.

10.4 (page 148)

Locus of causality

	Internal	External
Stable	a	d
Unstable	c	b

Locus of stability (vertical axis label)

11.1 (page 151)

Newton's laws	Application
Law of inertia	Any sporting example where the state of motion of either the ball or the body changes, e.g. a rally in tennis when the ball changes direction
Law of acceleration	Any sporting example where the force applied is proportional to the rate of change of momentum, e.g. the more force applied to a football, the faster and further it will go.
Law of reaction	Any sporting example where the action force is equal to the reaction force, e.g. when jumping for a rebound in basketball, the more force applied to the ground, the bigger the reaction force from the ground and the higher the resulting jump

11.2 (page 153)

(a) Displacement: swim = 1.5 km, bike ride = 0 km, run = 200 m

(b) The average speed and the average velocities for the components of the triathlon:

Distance	Time	Displacement	Average speed	Average velocity
1.5 km swim	30 min 30 s	1.5 km	0.82 m s^{-1}	0.82 m s^{-1}
40 km cycle	90 min	0.0 km	7.41 m s^{-1}	0.0 m s^{-1}
10 km run	45 min	0.2 km	3.7 m s^{-1}	0.07 m s^{-1}

11.3 (page 154)

(a) Any three examples when acceleration or deceleration may be important: to lose a player, to beat an opponent, to get to the ball first, to create momentum.

(b)

Distance (m)	0	20	40	60	80	100
Velocity (m s^{-1})	0.0	8.5	11.1	11.5	11.5	9.5
Time (s)	0.0	2.9	5.6	7.6	9.4	11.4
Acceleration (m s^{-2})	N/A	2.93	0.96	0.20	0.00	−1.00

11.4 (page 154)

Performer	Mass (kg)	Velocity (m s^{-1})	Momentum (kg m s^{-1})
100 m sprinter	80	10.0	800
Prop	105	8.5	893
Centre forward	70	9.5	665
Middle-distance runner	65	9.0	585

11.5 (page 156)

A–B = constant speed

B–C = deceleration

C–D = no motion

D–E = acceleration

E–F = constant speed

12.1 (page 159)

(a) where the force is being applied (point of application)

(b) direction of the force

(c) size of the force

12.2 (page 163)

 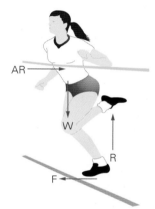 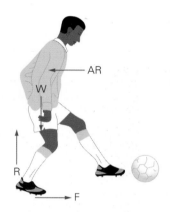

13.1 (page 167)

Activity	Optimum angle of release
A lofted football pass to the foot of a team-mate	45°
A lofted football pass to the head of a team-mate	more than 45°
High jump take-off	more than 45°
Tennis smash	less than 45°

14.1 (page 176)

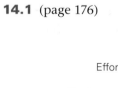 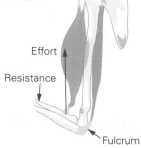

14.2 (page 178)

Any three sporting examples when a force is applied outside the centre of mass: free kick to curve the ball, top spin in tennis, spin bowling in cricket.

15.1 (page 187)

Activities that predominantly use the ATP-PC system are high intensity, lasting longer than 3 seconds but no more than 10 seconds. Examples include 100 m sprint, a short rally in tennis, full court press in basketball, short sprint for a through ball in football.

15.2 (page 191)

Name of game	ATP-PC system	Lactic acid system	Aerobic system
Football	A short sprint lasting longer than 3 seconds, e.g. to get free for the ball	A sprint lasting longer than 10 seconds, e.g. when on a break from the defensive half to the attacking half	Positional play when the intensity is low and the duration more than 3 minutes

16.1 (page 194)

Factor	Change
Temperature	Increases
ATP stores	Decrease
Phosphocreatine stores	Decrease
Glycogen stores	Decrease
Triglyceride stores	Decrease
Carbon dioxide levels	Increase
Oxygen/myoglobin stores	Decrease
Lactic acid levels	Increase

16.2 (page 196)

Examples of ways to delay a game by 30 seconds: a time-out, fake an injury, kick or hit the ball as far away as possible so someone has to go and get it. There are many sport-specific answers.

17.1 (page 205)

(a) VO_2 max is the maximum amount of oxygen that can be taken in and used in 1 minute/per unit of time. Factors that affect a performer's VO_2 max include:

- age
- gender
- physiological make-up, e.g. muscle fibre type
- training
- respiratory factors, e.g. lung capacity or similar
- cardiac factors, including stroke volume or maximum cardiac output
- vascular factors/blood, e.g. red blood cell count

(b) Factors you need to consider when planning your training programme:

- What is the aim of the training programme?
- What are the associated macro, meso and microcycles?
- Which energy systems need training?
- Which fitness components need improving? Test these first and then at the end you can re-test to see if there is any improvement.
- What are the main muscle groups used?
- What type of contractions are needed?
- Decide on the most suitable method(s) of training.
- Apply the principles of training — progression, overload, specificity, moderation, variance and reversibility.

17.2 (page 210)

(a) Adaptations to strength training.

Neural adaptations:

- More strength can be generated by the recruitment of more motor units.
- The inhibitory effect of the Golgi tendon organs is reduced.

Aerobic adaptations in slow oxidative fibres:

- hypertrophy of slow-twitch fibres
- increase in mitochondria and myoglobin
- increase in glycogen and triglyceride stores
- increase in capillaries

Anaerobic adaptations to fast twitch fibres:

- hypertrophy of fast oxidative glycolytic and fast glycolytic fibres
- hyperplasia, which refers to the splitting of muscle fibres leading to the creation of new ones
- increase in ATP and PC stores
- increase in glycogen stores
- greater tolerance of lactic acid

(b) Strength tests:

- maximum strength — hand grip dynamometer/1 rep max test
- strength endurance — NCF abdominal curl

17.3 (page 212)

Factors affecting flexibility:

- the elasticity of ligaments and tendons
- amount of stretch allowed by surrounding muscles
- the type of joint
- the structure of a joint, e.g. hip joint has a deeper joint cavity and tighter ligaments to keep it more stable but less mobile than the shoulder

- the temperature of surrounding muscle and connective tissue
- training
- age
- gender

17.4 (page 214)

Methods of measuring body composition.

Skin fold test

- The skin fold test involves taking all skin fold measurements from one side of the body.
- Callipers are placed over the skin fold and a measurement taken.
- All the measurements are added together and comparisons made with standardised tables.

Bioelectric impedence

- Small electrical current is passed through the body.
- The greater the impedance, the greater the percentage of body fat.

Hydrostatic weighing

- The body is submerged in water.
- Body mass is divided by the volume of water displaced when immersed.
- This calculates body density which can be used to predict the percentage of body fat.

Body mass index (BMI)

This test considers total body mass and is calculated as:

$$\frac{\text{weight (kg)}}{\text{height (m)} \times \text{height (m)}}$$

17.5 (page 215)

Energy requirements without exercise	1872 kcal day^{-1}
Energy requirements including exercise	2892 kcal day^{-1}
% carbohydrates	60–75%
% fats	20–25%
% proteins	10–15%

18.1 (page 218)

Answers will reflect students' own sport. General answers:

(a) Off season — rest and some light fitness work

(b) Pre-season — fitness work, gradual increase in intensity

(c) Competitive season — maintain fitness levels and skill/tactic work

Answers

18.2 (page 220)

Training aim	Details of training session
A session to improve lactate tolerance	This needs to be a session that works the lactic acid system, e.g. interval training. The athlete completes a work interval of 200m at 90% maximum heart rate followed by a 90-second rest interval. This should be repeated six times, followed by a 5-minute rest and then another set
A session to improve strength in the upper body	Weight training exercises, e.g. shoulder press, lateral pull-downs, lateral raises, biceps curls, triceps extensions

19.1 (page 224)

Pharmaceutical aids for the power athlete could include creatine, anabolic steroids and HGH.

Pharmaceutical aids for the endurance athlete could include gene doping, blood doping, EPO and HGH.

Practice makes perfect

Chapter 1

1 Characteristics of early pedestrianism. Any three for 3 marks:
- Footmen were hired by the gentry for their speed.
- Pedestrians competed against gentlemen — the latter 'proving' themselves.
- Pedestrian competitions enabled the gentry to wager on outcomes.
- Wagers were on the number of miles covered in a certain number of hours.
- Walking/running races developed over set distances on race courses and around the country.

2 Key features of recreational mob football. Any three for 3 marks.
- lower class/male participants
- occasional
- localised variations
- violent and cruel involving brute force
- few rules
- natural — with limited equipment and facilities
- played on 'holy days'
- rural

3 Importance of recreational bathing for the masses. Any two for 2 marks:
- health, therapeutic, cleanliness
- survival/safety for those working and/or living on the waterfront
- recreation — occasional 'dips' on hot days for fun and pleasure

4 Reasons to account for the exclusivity of real tennis. Any three for 3 marks:
- expensive to play (needed courts and equipment)

- required a lot of free time
- had a dress code/etiquette
- high literacy levels needed to understand complex written rules

Chapter 2

1 The AAA versus the amateur code. Any three for 3 marks:
- The AAA was the first governing body.
- The amateur code of the earlier AAC had excluded all professionals/pedestrians or men who earned their living through athletics.
- It had excluded tradesmen and artisans from participating in events.
- The AAA removed the exclusion clause.
- An amateur athlete became anyone who had not received money for running/ no prize money.

2 Reasons why public baths developed in urban industrial towns in the second half of the nineteenth century. Any four for 4 marks:
- Towns grew in size as a result of the Industrial Revolution, which led to river pollution and poor housing sanitation.
- This encouraged local councils to apply for grants to build public baths as a result of the Public Baths and Wash Houses Acts.
- Baths reflected a town's status. Different levels of facilities were available for the middle class.
- It was much safer to bathe/swim in baths than in urban rivers.
- Washing facilities were provided for the lower classes (e.g. for washing clothes).
- To clean the 'unwashed' and prevent disease.
- To avoid the loss of work through illness.
- Safety — learn to swim.
- Many baths had hot water/plunge baths for recreational swimming.

3 An explanation of the changes in football from the popular to the rational form. 2 marks are available for each section.

(a) Changes in working conditions:
- factory system — regular work times
- reduction in working week (e.g. Saturday half day)
- pro football a relatively good job
- workmen had enough money to pay to watch on a Saturday afternoon

(b) Urbanisation (urban expansion):
- loss of space
- specialist facilities developed
- potential business opportunities in running clubs
- large numbers of people in a small space needed entertaining

(c) Transport
- trains, trams, buses
- allowed for regular fixtures/competitions
- facilitated development of spectatorism
- required standardised rules

4 Amateurism and professionalism during the second half of the nineteenth century. A maximum of 3 marks are available for each section up to a maximum of 5 marks.
(a) Football:
- FA formed by ex-public school boys (amateurs)
- amateurs were middle and upper class; professionals were working class
- professionals needed payment as they would lose money if they missed work to play — broken time payments to compensate for this loss of earnings
- professionalism was insecure (e.g. discarded if injured)
- violence in games increased due to increased competitiveness (livelihood at stake)
- 'amateur only' leagues, cups and internationals developed and were of a very good standard (e.g. Old Corinthians)

(b) Cricket:
- William Clarke XI — early professional touring side
- such touring sides and professionalism developed due to improved transport
- amateurs recognised the skills of professionals but wanted to keep them in their place
- amateurs had different travel and eating arrangements and different roles — an amateur was the captain, opening batsman, etc.
- later on, professionals coached in public schools as a means of employment/ earning an income

Chapter 3

1 Athleticism is the combination of physical endeavour with moral integrity. *(1 mark)*

2 Sports characteristics of public schools in 1870. Any four for 4 marks:
- Organised — planned programme of games activities
- Regular — games played most afternoons
- Fixtures — inter-school and inter-house
- Rules — structure in place, e.g. officials, pitch and kit
- Specialist support — coaches/'Blues' employed as masters to develop games prowess
- Physical endeavour — trying your best, healthy mind and healthy body via escape from academia
- Inherent values — fair play, teamwork, leadership, loyalty to house, bravery.

3 Reasons for the slower development of athleticism in girls' public schools (as compared with boys' public schools). Any four for 4 marks:

- Tradition — role of women in society
- Inferiority — women perceived as subservient to men and physically inferior/ unable to cope with exertion
- Social norms — games were 'manly', sweating was 'unladylike'
- Medical reasons — fear of medical harm if physically active (e.g. affecting women's fertility)
- Lack of leadership — no female equivalent to boys' headmasters who encouraged games
- Clothing/kit — concern over wearing 'revealing' clothes for games
- School curriculum — girls' schools already focused their attention on other things (e.g. music)

4 How late nineteenth-century English public schools promoted sports and games. Any four for 4 marks:

- lots of time available at boarding schools
- regular income (endowments and fees) to improve provision
- specialist facilities provided (e.g. pools, playing fields)
- employment of specialist coaches
- sixth formers as positive role models
- use of games for social control/discipline
- played regularly (e.g. inter-house, inter-school, in curriculum)
- athletics sports days
- highly organised games programmes

5 Reasons why participation/excellence in team games were encouraged by public school headmasters. Any four for 4 marks:

- social control/channelling energies
- improve prestige of school/impress parents
- rational sport promoted middle class values (e.g. fair play and teamwork)
- improve health and fitness
- Clarendon Report stressed the educational value of team games
- Christian values, i.e. Muscular Christianity
- reflected competitive nature of British society — to learn to win and lose with honour

Chapter 4

1 Main aims of military drill. Any two for 2 marks:

- to develop obedience
- to improve fitness for war
- weapon familiarity

Main characteristics of military drill. Any two for 2 marks:

- static/in unison/regimented
- command style teaching
- taught by NCOs

2 PE teaching in the 1950s (5 marks in total).

Objectives. Any three for up to 3 marks:

- to learn physical skills, body management, dance, games, gymnastics, swimming skills
- to learn social skills
- to learn cognitive skills
- enjoyment
- to get all pupils involved
- to give a varied programme of lessons

Teaching methods. Any three for up to 3 marks:

- child-centred approach
- problem solving/individual interpretation of tasks
- use of apparatus
- decentralised (teacher as 'educator' not 'instructor')

3 Comparison of 1902 Model Course, PT syllabuses and state PE in the 1950s.

(i) 1902 Model Course. Any three for 3 marks:

- objectives — preparation for war; weapons training; discipline; military training; fit to fight
- content — marching; drill exercises; staves as mock weapons
- delivery methods — command style; unison response; ranks; led by NCOs

(ii) 1904–33 PT syllabuses. Any three for 3 marks:

- objectives — holistic aims; systematic exercising; health-related fitness; posture development
- content — systematic tables; repetitive; some group work and skills work
- delivery methods — direct teaching by teachers (in the main); some play (so more enjoyable)

(iii) 1950s. Any three for 3 marks:

- objectives — more varied activities than previously; more physical, social, cognitive skill development; some decision making; self development
- content — movement programmes; gymnastics, dance etc.
- delivery methods — indirect teaching; child centred; creative; problem solving

Chapter 5

1 Different initiatives designed to increase participation in sport by school-aged children. Any three for 3 marks:

- Physical Education, School Sport and Club Links (PESSCL)/Physical Education, School Sport and Young People (PESSYP)
- Sports colleges
- School Sport Coordinators (SSCos)
- Sporting Champions
- School Sport Partnerships/Competition Managers
- National School Sport Week
- reference to NGB initiatives
- training of more coaches/sports leaders to take sessions
- awards for good practice, including extra curricular sports provision, e.g. Sportsmark

2 National institutes of sport and development of elite performers. Any three for 3 marks:
- Provision of a network of local/regional centres for elite performer development
- Free access for elite performers
- Nationally organised/regionally delivered for closer access to home
- High-class/top-level training facilities
- Top-level coaching
- General sport science/medical back-up
- Performance lifestyle advice provided to support/advise on education/career/personal issues
- Links to National Governing Bodies/talent ID programmes

3 Social status of amateurs v. professionals in nineteenth century Britain. Any two for 2 marks:
- Amateurism was a concept devised by the middle classes/upper classes (higher social classes)
- Emphasis on moral/physical qualities of sport more associated with upper classes
- Exclusion clauses led to membership restrictions for the working classes, limiting their participation in certain sports (e.g. rugby union)
- National Governing Bodies/universities/public schools were important in the development of sport and held amateur principles dear to their hearts

Chapter 6

1 Cultural factors influencing the development of professional sport in the USA. Any four for 4 marks:
- achievement of the American Dream
- capitalist society leads to high accumulation of wealth
- sport is big business/highly commercialised
- sport is highly competitive/Lombardianism
- society is becoming more equal

- hire and fire policy (dismiss coach if unsuccessful)
- sports mirror frontierism/reflection of toughness/endeavour/sport is 'last frontier'
- sports need to be high scoring/high action (no draws)

2 Comparison between extra-curriculum sport in the USA and the UK. Any four for 4 marks:

- UK traditionally decentralised, National Curriculum more centralised; USA decentralised at state level, centralised at local level
- Non-specialist teachers at primary school in both UK and USA
- Specialist teachers at secondary level in both countries with more of an objective emphasis in the USA (e.g. fitness testing/measuring)
- UK PE programme guided by National Curriculum but some teacher choice allowed; USA programme is drawn up by the local school board so there is less flexibility in teaching content
- UK PE compulsory and of higher status; USA gives more status to the competitive sports programme
- UK extra-curricular participation is voluntary/traditionally poor links between schools and clubs in UK; USA extra-curricular participation has a much higher profile, with sports coaches employed to develop talents to the full

3 How the nature of professional sport deters participation in the USA. Any five for 5 marks:

- win at all costs/competitive ethic puts people off
- aggressive/violent nature of games does not encourage mass participation
- the majority of the population cannot aspire/achieve the high standard of athleticism required in sport
- the majority of the population does not pursue the 'frontier image'
- the commercial approach encourages passive spectatorism not participation
- only the best can play (post-selection drop out)
- there is little opportunity to pursue the big four sports as an amateur
- the big four sports are male dominated/open to young, fit males only/lack equality
- the concepts of stacking/centrality still exist

4 Reasons for the increased achievement of ethnic minorities in sport in the USA. Any four for 4 marks:

- more opportunities to play/increased provision
- increase in cultural esteem among ethnic groups
- higher levels of representation/disproportionate representation in major sports (e.g. 'white flight' syndrome in basketball)
- media promotion of role models/ethnic group success

- increased tolerance in American society of 'ethnic culture' in the late twentieth/early twenty-first century (less discrimination in society)

Chapter 7

1 Influential factors in relation to development of sport in Australia (8 marks in total).

(a) Social factors. Any two for 2 marks:
- obsession with sport
- desire for healthy lifestyle
- sport is fashionable/popular
- an affluent population supports sport/has a strong inclination to participate with others in society

(b) Ideological factors. Any two for 2 marks:
- desire of a 'young culture' to prove itself/excel on the world stage
- drive to prove emergence from old 'bush culture'/lose old frontier image
- show success of nation by beating the motherland

(c) Traditions. Any two for 2 marks:
- tradition of sports excellence/expectation of success (e.g. Donald Bradman, Cathy Freeman, Ian Thorpe)
- historical development from British games
- traditions from other immigrant populations assimilated

(d) Geographical factors. Any two for 2 marks:
- favourable climate for outdoor activities
- urban development/population mainly around the coast fuels sports participation
- favourable transport/international communication systems promote sporting involvement

2 Talent development in Australian schools. Any four for 4 marks:
- primary school skill tests/fundamental skills programme
- each state has a department for school sport/full-time officers administer sport in each state
- schools are linked to appropriate senior sports governing bodies
- school sport linked to Active Australia
- state and federally run PE/sport programmes (e.g. PASE/SEPEP)
- all young people are screened for sports talent/Sports Search

3 Comparison of school sport between the UK and Australia. Any five for 5 marks:
- Australia school sport is compulsory; UK school sport is optional as after-school extra-curricular activity

- Australia, all children involved in school sport; UK school sport normally linked to the best few
- Australia has central policy and funding; UK traditionally down to individual school organisation/funding
- Australia school sport is part of teacher's paid contract; UK school sport involves voluntary teacher commitment
- Australia has a wide range of activities on offer; UK concentrates on a few major games
- Australia has a high time allocation (100 minutes per week); UK time varies, but tends to be less due to its optional nature
- Australia has a highly structured programme (e.g. basic skill development at early age); UK has a variable programme which is left to individual teachers
- Australia keeps statistical records of participation; UK has limited statistical development/data collection

4   Government participation initiatives in Australia. Any three for 3 marks:
- More Active Australia — ASC has set up this initiative
- educates the community about the importance of physical activity and health
- aims to increase the membership of sports clubs in Australia
- the ASC addresses issues of equality
- the ASC funds and administers sport on a national scale
- the Sport Performance and Development group in the ASC is the unit with responsibility to increase sports participation
- the ASC reviews initiatives/trends to continue raising participation levels among Australians

Chapter 8

1   Any three for 3 marks:

Trait theory states that characteristics of personality:
- are innate/we are born with them/inherited
- are stable/consistent behaviour/same in most situations
- are enduring/last a long time
- can be used to predict behaviour

2   Any four for 4 marks:

A negative attitude can be changed into a positive attitude by:
- using persuasion/persuasive communication
- persuasion is more effective if given by an expert
- cognitive dissonance/challenge beliefs
- showing positive role models of similar age and ability

- making activities fun/varied training
- pointing out health benefits

3   Any four for 4 marks:

Aggressive tendencies can be reduced by:

- using relaxation techniques
- using cognitive techniques, such as imagery or mental rehearsal
- using channelling to change the aggression into assertion
- walking away from the situation/calming down/counting to ten
- punishing aggressive acts/substituting the player
- reinforcing non-aggressive acts in training
- setting non-aggressive goals

Chapter 9

1   A group has interaction *(1 mark)*, a common goal *(1 mark)*, an identity *(1 mark)*.

2   Any five for 5 marks:

- A prescribed leader is from outside the group.
- An emergent leader is from within the group.

Leader characteristics include:

- charisma
- empathy
- motivation
- communication skills
- experience

3   **(a)** Potential productivity is the group's best possible performance *(1 mark)*.

   (b) Any three for 3 marks:

   Influences that produce faulty processes include:

- coordination problems/tactics/strategies
- social loafing
- lack of motivation
- Ringlemann effect

Chapter 10

1   Up to 3 marks for benefits of goal setting:

- improves confidence
- provides motivation
- lowers anxiety
- gives something to aim for/provides target

Up to 3 marks for SMARTER principle:

- specific
- measured
- agreed
- realistic
- timed
- exciting
- recorded

Goals should not just include winning; include performance/process goals as well

(6 marks in total)

2 1 mark for each form of anxiety:

- state anxiety — in a particular situation/temporary
- trait anxiety — innate/more permanent/consistent
- cognitive anxiety — psychological/worry/irrational thoughts
- somatic anxiety — physiological/tension/heart rate

(4 marks in total)

3 Effects of an audience. 1 mark for including mention of Zajonc theory.

1 mark for each of:

- increased arousal
- evaluation apprehension
- dominant response
- better performance or facilitation if task is well learned — dominant response likely to be correct
- worse performance or inhibition if task is new — dominant response likely to be incorrect
- facilitation if task is performed by an expert/inhibition if task is performed by a novice

(7 marks in total)

4 Any six for 6 marks:

Learned helplessness:

- is the sense that failure is inevitable
- is blaming internal and stable reasons for losing
- can be global
- or specific

Can be countered by:

- attributional retraining
- changing internal/stable reasons for failure to external/unstable ones
- giving positive feedback

- redefining failure
- setting easier goals

Chapter 11

1 Any four for 4 marks:

(a)

- acceleration $= \dfrac{\text{change in velocity (m s}^{-1})}{\text{time taken (s)}}$

- change in velocity = final velocity – initial velocity

- $\dfrac{0.58 - 0}{1.72} = \dfrac{0.58}{1.72}$

- $= 0.34 \, \text{m s}^{-2}$

(b)

- $\dfrac{9.8 - 0.58}{1.02} = \dfrac{9.22}{1.02}$

- $= 9.04 \, \text{m s}^{-2}$

2 Any six for 6 marks:

- First law of motion/law of inertia. A body remains in a constant state of motion unless acted upon by a force.
- The high jumper applies a force to change his/her state of motion from the run-up to the take-off.
- Second law of motion/law of acceleration. The magnitude/size of force governs acceleration at take-off/change of momentum.
- The direction of force controls the direction of acceleration.
- The more force that is applied, the more height results.
- Third law of motion/law of action and reaction. To every force there is an equal and opposite reaction force.
- The ground reaction force needs to generate a large vertical component for the high jump.

Chapter 12

1 Definition of impulse (up to 2 marks):

- impulse = force × time (Ft)
- and equates to change in momentum

Use of impulse (up to 2 marks):

- body has a constant mass
- impulse has direction (horizontal for sprinting, vertical for take-off)
- measured in a single footfall
- positive impulse is needed for acceleration at take-off

- negative impulse occurs when foot lands/braking action
- if the net impulse is positive, acceleration occurs

(4 marks in total)

2　Any two for 2 marks:
- force = mass × acceleration ($F = m \times a$)
- 75×6.9
- $= 517.5\,\text{N}$

3　One mark for each force labelled (up to 3 marks):

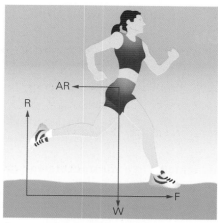

One mark for showing $F > AR$.

(4 marks in total)

Chapter 13

1　Forces affecting a projectile during flight. Any three for 3 marks:
- parabolic flight path/trajectory/parabola
- gravity reduces height achieved/brings projectile back to earth
- acts on the vertical component
- air resistance has no/negligible effect on the hockey and rugby ball
- horizontal component of most sports projectiles
- some projectiles affected by air resistance/shape, e.g. golf ball dimples

2　Identification of types of spin.
Diagram A = back spin *(1 mark)*
Diagram B = top spin *(1 mark)*

3　Factors affecting maximum horizontal distance of a kick. Any four for 4 marks:
- angle of release
- optimum angle for maximum horizontal distance is 45°
- velocity of release

- increase in velocity = increase in horizontal distance
- height of release
- greater height of release = greater horizontal distance

Chapter 14

1 How an ice skater changes speed of rotation. Any six for 6 marks:
- ice is a friction-free surface
- during rotation, angular momentum remains constant
- angular momentum = moment of inertia × angular velocity
- angular momentum = quantity of motion/rotation
- moment of inertia = spread/distribution of mass around axis/reluctance to rotate
- angular velocity = speed of rotation
- change in moment of inertia leads to change in angular velocity/speed/spin of rotation
- skater brings arms/legs closer to/further away from axis of rotation/body
- leads to increase/decrease in angular velocity/speed of rotation/spin

2 Angular motion diagram. One mark for each correctly labelled curve:

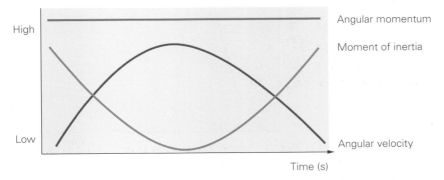

(3 marks in total)

3 Identify and sketch the lever in the arm as a dumb-bell is lowered.

This is a first-class lever. *(1 mark)*

Correct sketch of a first-class lever with fulcrum, load and effort labelled *(1 mark)* and in the correct position *(1 mark)*

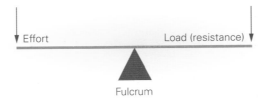

Chapter 15

1   The sprinter uses the ATP-PC system/phosphocreatine system/alactic system. *(1 mark)*
Any three for 3 marks:
- PC is the fuel/stored in the muscles
- produces 1 ATP
- controlling enzyme = creatine kinase
- ADP + Pi + energy = ATP
- takes place in the sarcoplasm
- anaerobic/no oxygen
- coupled reaction

2   Relationship between energy system and duration of exercise. One mark for each line for each energy system, one mark for the axes labelled and one mark for correct durations. 4 marks in total.

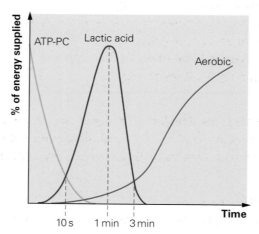

3   Aerobic system. One mark for each answer (up to 4 marks):

Site of reaction	Fuel used	Active enzyme	Molecules of ATP produced
Mitochondria/cristae/matrix	Carbohydrate/glycogen/glucose/fats	PFK	34–38

Chapter 16

1   Any six for 6 marks:
- A = alactacid component/fast component
- restoration of ATP and phosphocreatine stores and the resaturation of myoglobin with oxygen
- complete restoration of phosphocreatine takes up to 3 minutes/50% of stores can be replenished after only 30 seconds

- requires 3 litres of oxygen
- B = lactacid/slow component
- removal of lactic acid
- takes up to an hour
- uses 5–6 litres of oxygen

2 Explanation of removal of lactic acid. Any four for 4 marks:
- can be oxidised into carbon dioxide and water
- converted into glycogen
- converted into glucose
- in liver
- converted into protein

3 Function of myoglobin during recovery. Any three for 3 marks:
- myoglobin has a high affinity for oxygen
- stores oxygen in the muscle and transports it from the capillaries to the mitochondria for energy provision
- restoration takes up to 2 minutes
- using approximately 0.5 litres of oxygen

Chapter 17

1 **(a)** Training methods for developing aerobic capacity. One mark for each of the following up to 4 marks. Only the first two methods of training will be accepted with a maximum of 3 marks available for each training method.

Continuous
- exercise without rest intervals
- emphasis on distance not speed/30–45 min duration
- 60–75% max heart rate

Repetition running
- set distance is run a specific number of times
- complete rest between runs
- 70–80% max heart rate

Fartlek training
- varies the intensity
- more demanding/higher max heart rate target

Interval training
- periods of work are interspersed with recovery periods
- depends on the duration of the work interval
- the intensity or speed of the work interval

Answers

- the duration of the recovery period
- the number of work intervals and recovery periods

(b) Any four for 4 marks:
  - hypertrophy of the myocardium
  - increase in stroke volume/maximum cardiac output
  - lower *resting* heart rate/bradycardia
  - increased elasticity of the arterial walls
  - decreased blood viscosity
  - more red blood cells/haemoglobin
  - greater tolerance to lactic acid/buffering

2 Factors affecting strength. Any four for 4 marks:
- muscle fibre type
- fast twitch fibres contract more quickly and produce more power and maximum strength
- fast twitch fibres grow larger as a result of training
- genetically determined
- cross-sectional area of the muscle
- the greater the cross-sectional area, the greater the strength produced
- importance of the position of the muscle attachment
- muscles with the largest cross-sectional area tend to be found in the legs
- individuals can produce on average 4–8 kg of **force per cm² of muscle cross section**

3 **(a)** Any three for 3 marks:
  - PNF = proprioceptive neuromuscular facilitation
  - muscle is isometrically contracted
  - for a period of at least 10 seconds
  - it then relaxes and is stretched again

(b) Adaptations due to flexibility training. Any four for 4 marks:
  - a change in length of tendons/ligaments
  - a change in length of muscle tissue
  - more of a change to muscle tissue than to tendons or ligaments
  - a permanent change is known as a plastic change

4 **(a)** Definition of body composition. 1 mark for:
  Body composition is the physiological make-up of an individual in terms of the distribution of lean body mass and body fat.

(b) Health implications of obesity. Any three for 3 marks:
  - obesity carries an increased risk of heart disease/hypertension
  - high blood cholesterol, strokes and diabetes

OCR A2 Physical Education

- increased stress on joints
- limits flexibility
- psychological problems of dealing with being obese

Chapter 18

1 Explain periodisation. Any four for 4 marks:
- training is divided into sections/stages for a specific purpose
- macrocycle = a long-term goal
- mesocycle = a period of training lasting weeks/months on a particular aspect
- microcycle = a week of training sessions
- dividing the training year into competitive phases —peaking/tapering/playing
- pre-season training
- out of season recovery

2 Factors to take into account when planning an aerobic training programme. Any four for 4 marks:
- macro-, meso- and microcycles
- aerobic system
- test aerobic capacity first and retest at the end to see if there is any improvement
- multistage fitness test/Cooper's run/Douglas bag/Harvard step test/PWC160 test
- names of the main muscle groups used
- the type of contraction needed
- most suitable method of training, e.g. continuous, fartlek, repetition, aerobic interval
- progression, overload
- specificity/moderation
- variance/reversibility

Chapter 19

1 How do ice baths help performers. Any three for 3 marks:
- The performer should remain in the ice bath for 5 to 10 minutes.
- The cold water causes the blood vessels to tighten and drains the blood out of the legs.
- On leaving the bath, the legs fill up with new blood containing oxygen to help cells function better.
- The blood that leaves the legs takes away with it the lactic acid that has built up during the activity.

2 Illegal ergogenic aids. One mark for each of the following up to 6 marks. Only the first two aids listed will be accepted. A maximum of 4 marks is available for each aid.

HGH

Definition: artificially produced hormone

Advantages:

- increases muscle mass and causes a decrease in fats

Disadvantages:

- heart and nerve diseases
- glucose intolerance
- high levels of blood fats

Rh-EPO

Definition: artificially produced hormone

Advantages:

- increases haemoglobin levels
- increases the oxygen-carrying capacity of the blood

Disadvantages:

- can result in blood clotting
- can result in stroke/death

Gene doping

Definition: synthetic genes are taken to build muscle/increase red blood cells/example

Advantages:

- can improve oxygen uptake

Disadvantages:

- depends on the gene used but there have been reported problems with the heart and the liver

Blood doping

Definition: blood is removed and stored. The body compensates and makes more red blood cells. The stored blood is then injected back giving an even higher red blood cell count.

Advantages:

- improves aerobic capacity by increasing the oxygen-carrying capacity of the body

Disadvantages:

- increased viscosity of the blood could lead to clotting and a risk of death

3 Glycogen loading

Explanation (up to 2 marks):

- dietary restriction of carbohydrates
- days 4, 5 and 6 before competition — high-intensity work, low carbohydrate intake

- days 1, 2 and 3 before competition — low-intensity work/tapering
- increase carbohydrate intake
- allows more glycogen to be stored than normal

Advantages (up to 2 marks):
- increases glycogen synthesis
- increases glycogen stores in the muscle
- delays fatigue
- increases endurance capacity

Disadvantages (up to 2 marks):
- water retention, which results in bloating
- heavy legs
- affects digestion
- weight increase
- irritability during the depletion phase
- alters the training programme

(6 marks in total)

Index

Index

Index

Index